SOURCES OF UNOFFICIAL UK STATISTICS

Sources of Unofficial UK Statistics

Second edition

Compiled by David Mort

University of Warwick
Business Information Service

Gower

Published by
Gower Publishing Company Limited
Gower House
Croft Road
Aldershot
Hants GU11 3HR
England

Gower Publishing Company
Old Post Road
Brookfield
Vermont 05036
USA

Printed in Great Britain by
Billing & Sons Ltd, Worcester

British Library Cataloguing in Publication Data
Mort, D. (David)
    Sources of unofficial UK statistics.
    1. Great Britain. Statistics. Information sources –
    Lists
    I. Title
    314.1'07

ISBN 0–566–02795–X

Contents

Acknowledgements

We gratefully acknowledge the assistance of all the organizations and individuals who have provided information for the guide and those involved in business information who have offered their advice and comments.

Special thanks go to Steve Barber of the University of Warwick Library for his help in the preparation of the guide.

David Mort

The University of Warwick Business Information Service

The University of Warwick Business Information Service is a commercial information service based in the University Library. It was established over 10 years
ago and provides statistical, market and business information to companies and
other organizations. The service is based on a comprehensive international
collection of statistical and market research data.

In addition to the enquiry service, the Business Information Service organizes a
regular programme of seminars and is involved in a series of research projects. It
has published a number of reviews, directories and newsletters.

David Mort

David Mort was manager of the University of Warwick Business Information
Service from 1980–86. From 1986–88 he was Information Officer at the Centre for
Local Economic Strategies and now runs an information consultancy, Business
Information Associates.

Introduction

Statistical sources play an important role in the provision of information for business, industry and economic research. Economic analysis, corporate planning, financial planning, forecasting, market research and marketing are just some of the areas where statistics are important. In the United Kingdom, Central Government are the main suppliers of statistical information and these statistics are usually referred to as 'official statistics'. However, there are many other organizations involved in compiling and disseminating statistical information. They include trade associations, professional bodies, local authorities and development corporations, stockbrokers, banks, chambers of commerce, economic research and forecasting organizations, consultants, academic institutions, limited companies and commercial publishers. Many of these sources provide original, more detailed or simply different information which is not available elsewhere, but tracking them down can be a costly and time-consuming exercise.

This second edition of *Sources of Unofficial UK Statistics* (first edition – 1985) provides details of 1077 non-official UK statistical titles and services and is a unique source of information on an increasingly important area of business information.

Non-official Statistics

Central Government may be the major producer of statistics but, for various reasons, these statistics do not always provide sufficient detail for those in business and industry. Non-official sources can cover product areas and sectors excluded from Central Government data and also different types of data not usually included in official sources: for example, end-user statistics, local area statistics, salary surveys, opinion surveys, product price information and forecasts.

In some cases non-official sources simply repackage and comment on official data, but these commentaries often provide a useful analysis of the major trends in official statistics.

Pric :s of non-official sources vary considerably from a few pounds to thousands of pounds for detailed market research, but over 50 per cent of the titles are available free or for less than £30.

One disadvantage of non-official statistics is that, in many cases, the material is not available generally. Many trade associations, for example, only circulate material to member companies and some organizations limit access to clients, survey participants, etc. Another problem is that very few sources give any details on how the figures have been compiled and the reliability and accuracy of the data can vary considerably from one source to another.

As well as the traditional type of statistical publication consisting of tables and graphs a surprisingly large number of regular statistics appear in other non-statistical sources such as journals, yearbooks, annual reports, directories, press releases, newspapers, reports, monographs, conference proceedings, machine-readable databanks, etc.

Sources Included in the Guide

1077 statistical titles and services produced by over 600 organizations are included in the guide. The information on the sources was obtained between March and September 1988.

Statistics of interest to business and industry which are produced regularly are included. For a source to be considered as regular it must be produced at least once every six years; one-off surveys or market reports do not qualify.

Only sources issued in and concerning the United Kingdom are covered. Material with an international coverage has generally been excluded.

Sources are included even if they have a restricted circulation, but in some cases the publishers have asked to be excluded from the guide and we have agreed to this request.

As well as the standard time series statistics, forecasts, trend surveys and opinion polls are included but data dealing with only one corporate body, such as company annual reports, has generally been excluded. Most of the items included are clearly statistical publications, but non-statistical sources listed in the previous section are included if they contain a regular statistical series or feature.

The guide covers sources on the United Kingdom as a whole and those dealing with particular areas, such as local authority areas or local planning regions. However, some local authorities were concerned that they might not be able to cope with any demand generated by the inclusion of their publications and reluctantly asked us to omit their publications.

Finally, the sources listed cover a range of physical formats including the standard book form, those which are produced on one or two sheets of paper, such as press releases, through to machine readable data.

The Format of the Guide

The main part of the guide (Part I) comprises 1077 entries arranged alphabetically by publishing organization and numbered consecutively. The entries have been based on responses from the publishing bodies themselves supplemented, where possible, by a scanning of the source document. Usually if an organization publishes more than one title each has a separate entry. The exceptions are regularly produced market research surveys on various topics. As most of these surveys follow the same format they are included in one general entry rather than listed separately. Each entry contains the following information, where available:

Name of the publishing body
Address
Telephone; Telex; Fax
Title of source and frequency; date of first issue
General description of contents including details of subjects covered, currency, the source of the data and any samples used (i.e. own research, Central Government, other non-official source) and the proportion of text. The data sources and proportion of text are usually expressed as percentages.
Availability of source
Cost per annum and/or per issue
ISSN/ISBN
Other comments, including the availability of data in machine readable form.

The range of information noted above represents the 'ideal' entry. In various instances, however, some of the items are not applicable or it has been impossible to obtain every item of information.

Part II is an alphabetical listing by title of all the sources included in the guide. The name of the publishing body is included with each title.

Part III is an alphabetical subject index to the entries in Part I. Under each subject term will be found the relevant source number or numbers.

Whilst every effort has been made to ensure the accuracy of the contents, the compilers cannot accept any responsibility for any errors or omissions which may have occurred.

Part I

The statistics

1

Originator	ABACUS DATA SERVICES (UK) LTD
Title	UK IMPORT AND EXPORT STATISTICS, continuous
Coverage	Import and export data for any traded product with basic data available by value, volume, month or year to date, country of origin, country of destination, port of entry or departure, flag of carrier or container depot used. Abacus is an officially appointed agent of HM Customs and Excise.
Availability	General
Cost	Depends on information required.
Comments	Data available on tape, disc or microfiche; tailor-made packages and reports also available.
Address	Causeway House, 24 South Drive, Coulsdon, Surrey CR3 2BG
Telephone	01 936 9050; Telex: 266332

2

Originator	ABBEY NATIONAL BUILDING SOCIETY
Title	HOUSE PRICE STATISTICS, quarterly
Coverage	Comparative figures on average house prices across the country based on lending figures by the building society. A small amount of text accompanies the statistics.
Availability	General
Cost	Free
Address	Abbey House, Baker Street, London NW1 6XL
Telephone	01 486 5555; Telex: 266103; Fax: 01 486 4230

3

Originator	ABERDEEN PETROLEUM REPORT
Title	MOBILE RIG FLEET DRILLING, weekly in a weekly journal. 1981–
Coverage	Weekly drilling statistics for drilling areas in the North Sea. Data usually refers to the previous week's activities.
Availability	General
Cost	£295
Comments	ISSN 0263 5054. Also publishes the 'Scottish Petroleum Annual' with some statistics.
Address	Aberdeen Petroleum Publishing Ltd, 37 Huntly Street, Aberdeen AB1 1TJ
Telephone	0224 644725; Telex: 73315; Fax: 0224 644326

4

Originator	ABERDEEN PETROLEUM REPORT
Title	NORTH SEA OIL PRODUCTION, monthly in a weekly journal. 1981–
Coverage	Oil production figures in barrels per day by North Sea oil field. Statistics are usually 2 weeks old.
Availability	General
Cost	£295
Comments	ISSN 0263 5054. Also publishes the 'Scottish Petroleum Annual' with some statistics.
Address	Aberdeen Petroleum Publishing Ltd, 37 Huntly Street, Aberdeen AB1 1TJ
Telephone	0224 644725; Telex: 73315; Fax: 0224 644326

5

Originator	ABP COMPUTER SERVICES LTD
Title	OVERSEAS TRADE STATISTICS, continuous. 1987–
Coverage	Statistics on the imports and exports of any traded product by value and volume with additional data available on country of origin/destination, port of entry/departure etc. Appointed as an official agent by HM Customs and Excise.
Availability	General
Cost	On application, depending on services required
Comments	Available on disc, microfiche.
Address	Computer Centre, Hayes Road, Southall UB2 5NE
Telephone	01 573 5045; Telex: 9413625; Fax: 01 848 1945

6

Originator	ACCOUNTANCY PERSONNEL LTD
Title	SURVEY OF SALARIES IN ACCOUNTANCY, bi-annual
Coverage	Covers accountancy salaries and merchant and international banking salaries. Information based on surveys carried out in various regional centres in England and Wales. A general commentary accompanies the statistics.
Availability	General
Cost	£40
Address	41 London Wall, London EC2
Telephone	01 628 9015

7

Originator	ADMAP
Title	ADSTATS, approximately 3 times a year in a monthly journal
Coverage	Statistics on various aspects of advertising including total expenditure, expenditure by media, expenditure in selected product categories etc. Most of the data is compiled from Advertising Association surveys.
Availability	General
Cost	£110
Address	ADMAP Publications, 44 Earlham Street, London WC2H 9LA
Telephone	01 379 6576; Telex: 265906; Fax: 01 836 1310

8

Originator	ADSEARCH
Title	NEW PRODUCT NEWS: ALCOHOLIC AND SOFT DRINK, 10 issues per year. July 1986–
Coverage	Mainly data on specific new products launched but includes an index of new product activity by type of product and an index of product and pack innovation and change by product type. Data in numbers and as a % for the latest month and comparisons with earlier dates. Based on the company's continuous survey of new product launches.
Availability	General
Cost	£275
Address	47 Kew Road, Richmond-upon-Thames TW9 2NQ
Telephone	01 948 6488; Fax: 01 948 9239

9

Originator	ADVERTISING ASSOCIATION
Title	ADVERTISING FORECAST, quarterly
Coverage	Forecasts for the main media categories – TV, radio, newspapers, colour supplements, magazines, classified advertising, display advertising and posters. In addition there are forecasts of expenditure in the main product sectors – retail, industrial, financial, government, services, durables and consumables. Historical data is also given.
Availability	General
Cost	£360
Address	NTC Publications, 22/24 Bell Street, Henley on Thames RG9 2BG
Telephone	0491 574671

10

Originator	ADVERTISING ASSOCIATION
Title	ADVERTISING STATISTICS YEARBOOK, annual. 1983–
Coverage	General trends in advertising and the annual AA survey. Statistics by type of advertising, e.g. cinema, direct mail, poster, newspapers, magazines, directories, radio, TV etc. Plus statistics on prices, expenditure by product sector, top advertisers, agencies, complaints, attitudes and international trends. Data for earlier years and based on various sources.
Availability	General
Cost	£26
Address	NTC Publications, 22/24 Bell Street, Henley on Thames RG9 2BG
Telephone	0491 574671

11

Originator	ADVERTISING ASSOCIATION
Title	QUARTERLY SURVEY OF ADVERTISING EXPENDI-TURE, quarterly
Coverage	Summary tables on advertising trends by main media followed by specific sections on the total press, national newspapers, regional newspapers, consumer magazines, business and professional magazines and all magazines. A final section looks at trends in specific industry sectors.
Availability	General
Cost	£150
Address	NTC Publications, 22/24 Bell Street, Henley on Thames RG9 2BG
Telephone	0491 574671

12

Originator	ADVERTISING STANDARDS AUTHORITY
Title	ASA ANNUAL REPORT, annual
Coverage	Gives a summary of complaints received by media and by type. Also statistics on the number of publications monitored. Based on complaints received by the ASA. The report is mainly text (90%).
Availability	General
Cost	£2.75
Address	Brook House, 2/16 Torrington Place, London WC1E 7HN
Telephone	01 580 5555; Telex: 27950

13

Originator   AGB

Title   CONSUMER PANELS, continuous
Coverage   Various continuous surveys of consumer spending and purchases of
             goods, particularly groceries and foods. Based on various sample
             surveys of households and individuals.

Availability General
Cost   On application
Comments   Various other services and analyses available.
Address   Research Centre, West Gate, London W5 1UA
Telephone   01 997 8484; Telex: 262251

14

Originator   AGRICULTURAL ENGINEERS ASSOCIATION

Title   SELECTED ECONOMIC INDICATORS, bi-monthly. 1980–
Coverage   General statistics on the agricultural economy based on a variety of
             sources: 20% own research, 40% from Central Government sour-
             ces and 40% from other non-official sources. Some supporting text
             (33%).

Availability Members
Cost   Free
Address   Paxton House, Orton Centre, Peterborough PE2 0LT
Telephone   0733 371381; Telex: 32901; Fax: 0733 370664

15

Originator   AGRICULTURAL ENGINEERS ASSOCIATION

Title   TRADE ANALYSIS, quarterly. 1983–
Coverage   Import and export data for agricultural products and machinery
             based on data from HM Customs and Excise.

Availability Members
Cost   Varies according to range of statistics required
Address   Paxton House, Orton Centre, Peterborough PE2 0LT
Telephone   0733 371381; Telex: 32901; Fax: 0733 370664

16

Originator   AGRICULTURAL ENGINEERS ASSOCIATION

Title   UK TRACTOR REGISTRATION ANALYSIS, monthly. 1984–
Coverage   Data on tractor registrations in the UK by power group and region.
             Based on Central Government statistics.

Availability	Members
Cost	Free
Address	Paxton House, Orton Centre, Peterborough PE2 0LT
Telephone	0733 371381; Telex: 329201; Fax: 0733 370664

17

Originator	AGRICULTURAL SUPPLY INDUSTRY
Title	ANALYSIS OF FEED INGREDIENTS, bi-annual in a weekly journal. 1977–
Coverage	Analysis of supplies of the main raw material ingredients in manufactured feeds for cattle, pigs and poultry. One table based entirely on Central Government statistics.
Availability	General
Cost	£60 or £1.15 for a single issue
Comments	ISSN 0140 4822
Address	Royal Works, Royal Parade, Chislehurst, Kent BR7 6NR
Telephone	01 467 2660; Telex: 28439; Fax: 01 467 1091

18

Originator	AGRICULTURAL SUPPLY INDUSTRY
Title	HARVEST REVIEW, annual supplement in a weekly journal
Coverage	Yield details for varieties of wheat, barley, oilseed rape plus details of the tonnages sold. Based largely (85%) on the journal's own research and other non-official sources. Some supporting text and published 2 months after the data has been collected.
Availability	General
Cost	£60 or £1.25 for a single issue
Comments	ISSN 0140 4822
Address	Royal Works, Royal Parade, Chislehurst, Kent BR7 6NR
Telephone	01 467 2660; Telex: 28439; Fax: 01 467 1091

19

Originator	AGRICULTURAL SUPPLY INDUSTRY
Title	THIS WEEK'S MARKETS, weekly in a weekly journal. 1971–
Coverage	Prices of various materials used for animal feed. Based on a survey by the journal and supplemented by other non-official sources. Published within 2 days of collecting the data.
Availability	General
Cost	£60 or £1.25 for a single issue
Comments	ISSN 0140 4822
Address	Royal Works, Royal Parade, Chislehurst, Kent BR7 6NR
Telephone	01 467 2660; Telex: 28439; Fax: 01 467 1091

20

Originator ALUMINIUM FEDERATION LTD

Title ALUMINIUM STATISTICS PRESS RELEASE, monthly
Coverage Production, imports and despatches of primary aluminium, secondary aluminium and wrought and cast products. Based mainly on a survey of members. Usually published 4–6 weeks after the date to which the statistics refer.

Availability General
Cost Free
Comments More detailed statistics available to members who complete returns.
Address Broadway House, Calthorpe Road, Five Ways, Birmingham B15 1TN
Telephone 021 456 1103; Telex: 333349

21

Originator ANGLIA TELEVISION

Title ANGLIA MARKETING GUIDE, regular
Coverage General data on the Anglia TV region including sections on the geography, communications, population, employment, industry, finance, living standards, sport, leisure and retailing. Based on various sources.

Availability General
Address Brook House, 113 Park Lane, London W1Y 4DX
Telephone 01 408 2288

22

Originator ARCHITECTS JOURNAL

Title COST FORECAST, quarterly in a weekly journal. 1976–
Coverage Trends and short-term forecasts for building costs and tender prices. Data relates to the previous quarter.

Availability General
Cost £45, or £1 for a single issue
Comments ISSN 0003 8466
Address Architectural Press, 9 Queen Anne's Gate, London SW1H 9BY
Telephone 01 222 4333; Telex: 8953505; Fax: 01 222 5196

23

Originator   ASKHAM BRYAN COLLEGE OF AGRICULTURE AND HORTICULTURE

Title   FARMING IN YORKSHIRE, annual. 1976–
Coverage   Financial and physical data, together with commentary (30%) on different farming systems in 3 counties of Yorkshire, North Humberside and Cleveland. Based largely on the College's survey of a random sample of farmers in Yorkshire (90%).

Availability   General
Cost   £3
Comments   ISSN 0309 6114. Data collected for the Ministry of Agriculture.
Address   Askham Bryan, York YO2 3PR
Telephone   0904 702121

24

Originator   ASSOCIATION FOR PAYMENT CLEARING SERVICES (APACS)

Title   ANNUAL SUMMARY OF CLEARING STATISTICS, annual. January 1921–
Coverage   Statistics on the turnover of inter-bank clearings through the clearing house, automated clearings through BACS (from 1976), inter-branch clearings (from 1985), Scottish clearings (from 1985) and London currency clearings (from 1986). Based on figures collected by APACS from all members.

Availability   General
Cost   Free
Address   Mercury House, Triton Court, 14 Finsbury Square, London EC2A 1BR
Telephone   01 628 7080; Telex: 268885; Fax: 01 256 5527

25

Originator   ASSOCIATION FOR PAYMENT CLEARING SERVICES (APACS)

Title   CLEARING STATISTICS, monthly. 1950–
Coverage   Statistics on the turnover of inter-bank clearings through the clearing house and automated clearings through BACS (from 1976). Based on figures collected by APACS from all members.

Availability   General
Cost   Free
Address   Mercury House, Triton Court, 14 Finsbury Square, London EC2A 1BR
Telephone   01 628 7080; Telex: 268885; Fax: 01 256 5527

26

Originator	ASSOCIATION OF BRITISH CHAMBERS OF COMMERCE
Title	CHAMBERS REGIONAL BUSINESS SURVEY, quarterly. 1985–
Coverage	A survey of business conditions covering home orders, exports, employment, investment, business factors and confidence. Brings together the results of 13 Chamber of Commerce surveys around the country covering a sample of about 2,881 companies (4th quarter 1987 survey). Includes data on services as well as manufacturing. A detailed commentary by area (50%).
Availability	General
Cost	£25
Address	Sovereign House, 212A Shaftesbury Avenue, London WC2H 8EW
Telephone	01 240 5831; Telex: 265871; Fax: 01 379 6331

27

Originator	ASSOCIATION OF BRITISH INSURERS
Title	GENERAL BUSINESS STATISTICS, annual. 1987–
Coverage	Statistics on premiums, revenue account by class of business and underwriting results. Based on the Association's own records with some supporting text (20%).
Availability	General
Cost	Free
Address	Aldermary House, Queen Street, London EC4N 1TT
Telephone	01 248 4477; Telex: 937035; Fax: 01 489 1120

28

Originator	ASSOCIATION OF BRITISH INSURERS
Title	INSURANCE STATISTICS, annual. 1986–
Coverage	Statistics on general insurance and life insurance. In the former category sections on premiums, underwriting results, investments, overseas earnings, family expenditure. The other section covers revenue account, new business and business in force. Based largely on the Association's own records (90%) plus Central Government data (10%). Some text (20%).
Availability	General
Cost	Free
Comments	ISSN 0950 3668. Brings together material previously published by the British Insurance Association/Life Offices Association.
Address	Aldermary House, Queen Street, London EC4N 1TT
Telephone	01 248 4477; Telex: 937035; Fax: 01 489 1120

29

Originator	ASSOCIATION OF BRITISH INSURERS
Title	LONG-TERM BUSINESS STATISTICS, annual. 1986–
Coverage	Statistics on new business, business in force, revenue account and sources of business. Based on the Association's own records with a small amount of supporting text (10%).
Availability	General
Cost	Free
Address	Aldermary House, Queen Street, London EC4N 1TT
Telephone	01 248 4477; Telex: 937035; Fax: 01 489 1120

30

Originator	ASSOCIATION OF BRITISH INSURERS
Title	NEW LIFE BUSINESS, bi-annual
Coverage	New life business in February and progress statement on the home service life assurance business in June. Based on the Association's records with some supporting text (50%).
Availability	General
Cost	Free
Comments	Issued as a press release. Previously produced by the Industrial Life Offices Association.
Address	Aldermary House, Queen Street, London EC4N 1TT
Telephone	01 248 4477; Telex: 937035; Fax: 01 489 1120

31

Originator	ASSOCIATION OF BRITISH INSURERS
Title	QUARTERLY NEW INDIVIDUAL BUSINESS FIGURES, quarterly. 1978–
Coverage	New business for ordinary life assurances based on the Association's own records. Some supporting text (30%).
Availability	General
Cost	Free
Comments	Issued as a press release. Previously published by the Life Offices Association.
Address	Aldermary House, Queen Street, London EC4N 1TT
Telephone	01 248 4477; Telex: 937035; Fax: 01 489 1120

32

Originator	ASSOCIATION OF BRITISH INSURERS
Title	UK MARKET STATISTICS, annual. 1982–

Coverage   Estimate of the size of the UK insurance market based on 'net retention', i.e. gross premiums received plus reinsurance accepted less reinsurance ceded and retrocessions. Based on the Association's own records with a large amount of text (60%).

Availability   General
Cost   Free
Comments   Previously published by the British Insurance Association.
Address   Aldermary House, Queen Street, London EC4N 1TT
Telephone   01 248 4477; Telex: 937035; Fax: 01 489 1120

33

Originator   ASSOCIATION OF CONTACT LENS MANUFACTURERS

Title   CLASS ANNUAL STATISTICS, annual
Coverage   Annual statistics relating to the sales of contact lenses and contact lens solutions. Based on a survey of members' sales by the Association.

Availability   General
Comments   Published in the Association's journal 'CLASS' circulated with the journal 'Optician'. Statistics appear in April/May.
Address   PO Box 83, Bracknell RG12 5BY
Telephone   0344 481800

34

Originator   ASSOCIATION OF MANUFACTURERS OF DOMESTIC ELECTRICAL APPLIANCES (AMDEA)

Title   AMDEA QUARTERLY STATISTICS, quarterly
Coverage   Deliveries and imports of various electrical appliances covering over 25 product headings. Similar data to that contained in the AMDEA Yearbook (see below) with statistics for the latest quarter and summary data for the earlier quarter. Mainly based on AMDEA data (80%) with some Central Government data (20%).

Availability   General
Cost   £400, with the AMDEA Statistical Yearbook. Free to members
Address   8 Leicester Street, London WC2H 7BN
Telephone   01 437 0678; Telex: 263536; Fax: 01 437 4901

35

Originator   ASSOCIATION OF MANUFACTURERS OF DOMESTIC ELECTRICAL APPLIANCES (AMDEA)

Title   AMDEA STATISTICAL YEARBOOK, annual
Coverage   Deliveries by UK manufacturers and imports by country of origin for various appliances including refrigerators, freezers, dryers,

washing machines, cookers, vacuum cleaners, heaters, electric
blankets etc. Some statistics on prices, employment etc. Based
mainly on AMDEA data (75%) plus data from Central Government sources (25%). Some text with the data (10%).

Availability	General
Cost	£100, free to AMDEA members
Comments	A combined subscription of £400 also includes the quarterly statistics (see above)
Address	8 Leicester Street, London WC2H 7BN
Telephone	01 437 0678; Telex: 263536; Fax: 01 437 4901

36

Originator	ASSOCIATION OF MARKET SURVEY ORGANISATIONS (AMSO)
Title	RESEARCH INDUSTRY ANNUAL TURNOVER DATA, annual. About 1970–
Coverage	Total turnover of AMSO members analysed by client type, data collection type and research technique. Based on a survey of members with a large amount of supporting text (60%).
Availability	General
Cost	Free
Comments	Issued as a press release in March of each year.
Address	c/o Ince House, 60 Kenilworth Road, Leamington Spa CV32 6JY
Telephone	0926 36425; Telex: 312378; Fax: 0926 833600

37

Originator	ATTWOOD STATISTICS LTD
Title	HOUSEHOLD OMNIBUS PANEL/INDIVIDUALS OMNIBUS PANEL, continuous
Coverage	Regular surveys of about 4,000 households and 10,000 individuals looking at purchasing trends for foods and other goods.
Availability	General
Cost	On application
Comments	Various other services available on request.
Address	Northbridge Road, Berkhamsted HP4 1EH
Telephone	04427 3311; Telex: 825939

38

Originator	AUDIENCE SELECTION
Title	KEY DIRECTORS OMNIBUS, quarterly

Coverage	Data on new purchasing trends, brand awareness, advertising awareness, readership trends etc. amongst company directors. Based on a sample of 600 directors from the top 10% of companies in 'Key British Enterprises'.
Availability	General
Cost	Varies according to amount and nature of data required
Comments	Other packages and special analysis available.
Address	10/14 Macklin Street, London WC2B 5NF
Telephone	01 404 5015; Telex: 893753; Fax: 01 405 3793

39

Originator	AUDIT BUREAU OF CIRCULATIONS LTD (ABC)
Title	ABC CIRCULATION REVIEW, bi-annual. 1932–
Coverage	Audited certified average net sales, circulation and distribution data for over 2000 publications. Covers journals, magazines and newspapers. Based on an ABC survey.
Availability	Members
Cost	Free
Comments	The data is computerized. The British Library has a microfilm of the results. Access to students by appointment.
Address	13 Wimpole Street, London W1M 7AB
Telephone	01 631 1343; Telex: 252476; Fax: 01 940 12104

40

Originator	BANK OF ENGLAND
Title	BANK OF ENGLAND QUARTERLY BULLETIN, quarterly. December 1960–
Coverage	Articles, comment and a statistical annex covering UK and international banking, money stock, official market operations, government finance, reserves and official borrowing, exchange rates, interest rates and national financial accounts. Mainly the bank's own figures (80%) and a significant amount of text (66%).
Availability	General
Cost	£27, or £7.50 for a single issue
Comments	ISSN 0005 5166. Some statistics first published in a press release. Most tables available on magnetic tape.
Address	Threadneedle Street, London EC2R 8AH
Telephone	01 601 4030; Telex: 885001; Fax: 01 601 4771

41

Originator	BANKING INFORMATION SERVICE
Title	PRESS INFORMATION, regular

Coverage	Text and statistics usually giving details of advances, balances etc. Based on data from the Committee of London and Scottish Bankers (see other entries).
Availability	General
Cost	Free
Comments	Issued as a press release.
Address	10 Lombard Street, London EC3V 9AR
Telephone	01 626 8486

42

Originator	BAR ASSOCIATION FOR COMMERCE, FINANCE AND INDUSTRY
Title	REMUNERATION SURVEY, every 2 or 3 years
Coverage	A survey of members' salaries in all sectors of industry divided into 5 legal categories. Analysis by age and job and information on fringe benefits.
Availability	General
Cost	£25
Comments	Prepared by Inbucon Management Consultants Ltd at the address below.
Address	Park House, Wick Road, Egham TW2D 0HW
Telephone	0784 34411

43

Originator	BARCLAYS BANK
Title	BARCLAYS REVIEW, quarterly
Coverage	A general commentary on the UK and international economy and a statistical appendix with data on exchange rates, interest rates, money market etc. Text covers 50% of the report.
Availability	General
Cost	Free
Comments	ISSN 0269 7009
Address	Economics Department, 54 Lombard Street, London EC3P 3AH
Telephone	01 283 8989; Telex: 894076; Fax: 01 621 0386

44

Originator	BARCLAYS DE ZOETE WEDD SECURITIES LTD
Title	BZW EQUITY-GILT STUDY. INVESTMENT IN THE LONDON MARKET SINCE 1918. annual. 1956–

Coverage   Comparison of returns on equity and fixed interest investment, adjusted for inflation, for any period since 1918. Also investment history since 1918 and the impact of taxation on investment returns. Based mainly on BZW's own data (80%). A large amount of text (70%).

Availability Primarily clients but available to others if stocks available
Cost   £15
Address   4th Floor, Ebbgate House, 2 Swan Lane, London EC4B 3TS
Telephone   01 623 2323; Telex: 8812124; Fax: 01 626 1753

45

Originator   BARNSLEY METROPOLITAN BOROUGH COUNCIL

Title   BARNSLEY ECONOMIC REVIEW, quarterly
Coverage   Mainly commentary on national and local economic trends and company news but includes some statistics on unemployment, redundancies etc.

Availability General
Address   Barnsley Enterprise Centre, Pontefract Road, Barnsley ST1 1AJ
Telephone   0226 733291; Telex: 547376; Fax: 0226 248711

46

Originator   BARTON PUBLISHERS LTD

Title   GRIFFITHS BUILDING PRICE BOOK, annual. 1953–
Coverage   Price guide for pricing medium to smaller building contracts, i.e. new to about £150,000 and alterations and repairs to £25,000. Based on various non-official surveys.

Availability General
Cost   £34.95
Comments   ISSN 0142 713X. Edited by Geoffrey Smith & Partners, Chartered Quantity Surveyors.
Address   North Street, Stoke sub Hamdon, Somerset TA14 6QZ
Telephone   0935 822542

47

Originator   BEAMA LTD

Title   BEAMA CONTRACT PRICE ADJUSTMENT CLAUSE AND FORMULAE, monthly. 1969–
Coverage   Labour cost indices and producer price index numbers for electrical and mechanical equipment. Based on a regular survey of members.

Availability General, although some restrictions on sales to public libraries
Cost   £95

Comments	Also offers an Exchange Rate Fluctuation Service covering 5 countries.
Address	Leicester House, 8 Leicester Street, London WC2H 7BN
Telephone	01 437 0678; Telex: 263536

48

Originator	BEAUFORT RESEARCH LTD
Title	WELSH OMNIBUS SURVEY, quarterly. 1986–
Coverage	A regular survey of a representative quota sample of a minimum of 1000 adults aged 15 and over resident in Wales spread over 60 locations. Data on opinions and attitudes, advertising and product awareness and recall, purchasing and usage, image perception and social issues. Breakdowns by sex, age, class and region.
Availability	General
Cost	£85 entry fee plus additional fees for questions
Comments	Data available on disc.
Address	18 Park Grove, Cardiff CF1 3PP
Telephone	0222 378565; Fax: 0222 382872

49

Originator	BEDFORDSHIRE COUNTY COUNCIL
Title	BEDFORDSHIRE POPULATION CHANGE, annual. 1977–
Coverage	Estimates and projections for the county population up to 5 years ahead. Covers composition of the population, number and type of households, economic activity, births, deaths, migration etc. Based on a combination of local government and Central Government data. A small amount of supporting text (10%).
Availability	General
Cost	On application
Address	County Hall, Bedford MK42 9AP
Telephone	0234 63222; Telex: 82244; Fax: 0234 228619

50

Originator	BENCHMARK RESEARCH LTD
Title	COMPUTERS IN THE PROCESS INDUSTRIES SURVEY, annual. 1988–
Coverage	Statistics on the uptake of computers for manufacturing purposes in the process industries. Detailed hardware and applications information plus unit and value estimates for future purchases and acquisitions. Based on the company's own survey with some supporting text (50%).

19

Availability	General
Cost	£95
Comments	Cost above is for the summary report.
Address	Franks Hall, Franks Lane, Horton Kirby DA4 9LL
Telephone	0322 77755; Telex: 8954447; Fax: 0322 76903

51

Originator BENCHMARK RESEARCH LTD

Title ENERGY SURVEY, biennial. 1987–
Coverage Statistics on various aspects of energy use in UK manufacturing. Data on fuel use and heat recovery, heating systems, boilers, lighting, energy retention and energy management. Based on the company's own survey with some supporting text (50%).

Availability	General
Cost	£95
Comments	Cost above is for the summary report.
Address	Franks Hall, Franks Lane, Horton Kirby DA4 9LL
Telephone	0322 77755; Telex: 8954447; Fax: 0322 76903

52

Originator BENCHMARK RESEARCH LTD

Title ENGINEERING COMPUTERS SURVEY, annual. 1983–
Coverage Data on the uptake of computers for engineering and manufacturing purposes. Detailed hardware and applications information plus unit and value estimates for future purchases and acquisitions. Based on a survey by the company with some supporting text (50%).

Availability	General
Cost	£95
Comments	Cost above is for the summary report.
Address	Franks Hall, Franks Lane, Horton Kirby DA4 9LL
Telephone	0322 77755; Telex: 8954447; Fax: 0322 76903

53

Originator BENCHMARK RESEARCH LTD

Title HANDLING AND STORAGE SURVEY, annual. 1987–
Coverage Statistics on the use of materials handling and storage equipment in UK manufacturing. Sections cover forklift trucks, AGVs, conveyors, cranes and storage equipment. Based on the company's own survey and some supporting text (50%).

Availability General

Cost	£95
Comments	Cost above is for the summary report.
Address	Franks Hall, Franks Lane, Horton Kirby DA4 9LL
Telephone	0322 77755; Telex: 8954447; Fax: 0322 76903

54

Originator	BERKSHIRE COUNTY COUNCIL
Title	FUTURE POPULATION OF THE ROYAL COUNTY OF BERKSHIRE, annual
Coverage	Projections of population down to parish level with the latest figures covering 1986 to 1996. Population of local government districts given by age and sex. Based on the Council's own data with some supporting text (30%).
Availability	General
Cost	£4
Address	Shire Hall, Shinfield Park, Reading RG2 9XD
Telephone	0734 873521, x3027; Fax: 0734 873521

55

Originator	BERKSHIRE COUNTY COUNCIL
Title	POPULATION ESTIMATES, annual
Coverage	Population down to parish level by age, sex, components of population change, households, dwellings and economic activity. Based on the Council's own data with some supporting text (30%).
Availability	General
Cost	£4
Address	Shire Hall, Shinfield Park, Reading RG2 9XD
Telephone	0734 875444,x3027; Fax: 0734 873521

56

Originator	BICYCLE ASSOCIATION OF GREAT BRITAIN LTD
Title	BICYCLE STATISTICS, annual
Coverage	Production, exports, imports and home market deliveries of bicycles with data for a number of years. Based on data collected by the Association.
Availability	General
Cost	Free
Address	Starley House, Eaton Road, Coventry CV1 2FH
Telephone	0203 553838

57

Originator	BIG FARM WEEKLY
Title	COMMODITIES/MARKET PRICES, weekly in a weekly journal
Coverage	Prices of agricultural commodities and supplies, e.g. cereals, livestock, foods, hay, straw etc.
Availability	Controlled circulation but available to others on request
Cost	On application
Address	International Thomson Publishing, 100 Avenue Road, London NW3 3TB
Telephone	01 935 6611; Telex: 299973; Fax: 01 586 4649

58

Originator	BIRDS EYE WALL'S LTD
Title	BIRDS EYE REVIEW, annual
Coverage	A review of the marketing and consumer trends affecting the consumption of frozen foods. Based mainly on the company's own survey (80%), with some Central Government statistics (20%). A significant amount of supporting text – about 60%. Usually published 2-3 months after the company surveys.
Availability	General
Cost	Free
Address	Station Avenue, Walton-on-Thames, Surrey KT12 1NT
Telephone	0932 228888; Fax: 0932 244109

59

Originator	BIRDS EYE WALL'S LTD
Title	POCKET MONEY MONITOR, annual. 1975–
Coverage	A survey by Gallup of pocket money given to 5-16 year olds in the UK. Covers average weekly pocket money by age, region and sex plus earnings from Saturday jobs and gifts from friends and relatives. Based on a sample of 1200 respondents and usually published 2 months after the survey.
Availability	General
Cost	Free
Address	Station Avenue, Walton-on-Thames, Surrey KT12 1NT
Telephone	0932 228888; Fax: 0932 244109

60

Originator	BIRDS EYE WALL'S LTD
Title	WALLS REPORT, annual

Coverage	A review of marketing and consumer trends over the past year affecting the consumption and sales of ice cream. Based entirely on the company's own survey.
Availability	General
Cost	Free
Address	Station Avenue, Walton-on-Thames, Surrey KT12 1NT
Telephone	0932 228888; Fax: 0932 244109

61

Originator	BIRMINGHAM CHAMBER OF INDUSTRY AND COMMERCE
Title	QUARTERLY ECONOMIC SURVEY, quarterly
Coverage	A survey of member companies covering deliveries and orders, production, stocks, cashflow, labour, investment, confidence and business factors. Usually published about 3 weeks after the survey.
Availability	General
Cost	Free
Comments	There is no mailing list for regular copies to non-members – specific issues can be supplied on request.
Address	PO Box 360, 75 Harborne Road, Birmingham B15 3DH
Telephone	021 454 6171; Telex: 338024; Fax: 021 455 8670

62

Originator	BIRMINGHAM CITY COUNCIL
Title	BIRMINGHAM ECONOMIC BULLETIN, quarterly
Coverage	Mainly news items on the local economy and local initiatives but includes statistics on the local labour market, unemployment etc. Based largely on Central Government data. Text covers 70%.
Availability	General
Cost	Free
Comments	Other statistical surveys produced.
Address	Development, Baskerville House, Broad Street, Birmingham B1 2NA
Telephone	021 235 3157

63

Originator	BISCUIT, CAKE, CHOCOLATE AND CONFECTIONERY ALLIANCE (BCCCA)
Title	BCCCA FOUR-WEEKLY SUMMARIES: BISCUITS, 13 issues a year. 1987–

Coverage   Statistics on the deliveries of various types of biscuits to the UK and export markets. Based on four-weekly returns from Alliance members covering their finished products.

Availability General
Cost   £150
Comments   BCCCA was formed in 1987 by a merger of the Cake and Biscuit Alliance and the Cocoa, Chocolate and Confectionery Alliance.
Address   11 Green Street, London W1Y 3RF
Telephone   01 629 8971; Telex: 24738; Fax: 01 493 4885

64

Originator   BISCUIT, CAKE, CHOCOLATE AND CONFECTIONERY ALLIANCE (BCCCA)

Title   BCCCA FOUR-WEEKLY SUMMARIES: CEREAL/MUESLI BARS, 13 issues a year. 1988–
Coverage   Statistics on the deliveries of cereal and muesli bars to the UK and export markets. Based on four-weekly returns from Alliance members covering their finished products.

Availability General
Cost   £150
Comments   BCCCA was formed in 1987 by a merger of the Cake and Biscuit Alliance and the Cocoa, Chocolate and Confectionery Alliance.
Address   11 Green Street, London W1Y 3RF
Telephone   01 629 8971; Telex: 24738; Fax: 01 493 4885

65

Originator   BISCUIT, CAKE, CHOCOLATE AND CONFECTIONERY ALLIANCE (BCCCA)

Title   BCCCA FOUR-WEEKLY SUMMARIES: CHOCOLATE CONFECTIONERY, 13 issues a year. 1987–
Coverage   Statistics on the deliveries of various types of chocolate confectionery to the UK and export markets. Based on four-weekly returns from Alliance members covering their finished products.

Availability General
Cost   £150
Comments   BCCCA was formed in 1987 by a merger of the Cake and Biscuit Alliance and the Cocoa, Chocolate and Confectionery Alliance.
Address   11 Green Street, London W1Y 3RF
Telephone   01 629 8971; Telex: 24738; Fax: 01 493 4885

66

Originator	BISCUIT, CAKE, CHOCOLATE AND CONFECTIONERY ALLIANCE (BCCCA)
Title	BCCCA FOUR-WEEKLY SUMMARIES: SUGAR CONFEC-TIONERY, 13 issues a year. 1987–
Coverage	Statistics on the deliveries of sugar confectionery to the UK and export markets. Based on four-weekly returns from the Alliance's members covering their finished products.
Availability	General
Cost	£150
Comments	BCCCA was formed in 1987 by a merger of the Cake and Biscuit Alliance and the Cocoa, Chocolate and Confectionery Alliance.
Address	11 Green Street, London W1Y 3RF
Telephone	01 629 8971; Telex: 24738; Fax: 01 493 4885

67

Originator	BISCUIT, CAKE, CHOCOLATE AND CONFECTIONERY ALLIANCE (BCCCA)
Title	STATISTICAL YEARBOOK, annual. 1987–
Coverage	Statistics on the deliveries to the home and export markets of biscuits and sugar and chocolate confectionery. Biscuits data goes back to 1969 and confectionery data to 1954. Over 50 tables are included with data on specific product areas. Based on returns from members.
Availability	General
Cost	£150
Comments	BCCCA was formed in 1987 by a merger of the Cake and Biscuit Alliance and the Cocoa, Chocolate and Confectionery Alliance.
Address	11 Green Street, London W1Y 3RF
Telephone	01 629 8971; Telex: 24738; Fax: 01 493 4885

68

Originator	BOOKSELLER
Title	AVERAGE BOOK PRICES, bi-annual in a weekly journal. 1949–
Coverage	Prices of books in total for the latest half year and the previous 3 half years. Also prices by category for the latest half year and the previous half year. Based on the journal's own survey.
Availability	General
Cost	£61, or £1.05 for a single issue
Comments	ISSN 0006 7539. Other statistics on the stock market performance of publishers also produced.
Address	J Whitaker & Sons Ltd, 12 Dyott Street, London WC1A 1DF
Telephone	01 836 8911; Telex: 987117; Fax: 01 836 2909

69

Originator	BOOKSELLER
Title	PUBLIC LIBRARIES, annual in a weekly journal
Coverage	Annual feature article with some statistics on the estimated expenditure on books by public libraries. Gives % change in expenditure over the previous year.
Availability	General
Cost	£61, or £1.05 for a single issue
Comments	ISSN 0006 7539. Other statistics on the stock market performance of publishers and books recorded also published.
Address	J Whitaker & Sons Ltd, 12 Dyott Street, London WC1A 1DF
Telephone	01 836 8911; Telex: 987117; Fax: 01 836 2909

70

Originator	BOOKSELLER
Title	PUBLISHERS OUTPUT, bi-annual in a weekly journal. 1949–
Coverage	Mainly details of output by individual publisher but statistics covering total output, number of titles and average price per book are also given. Based on the journal's own survey.
Availability	General
Cost	£61, or £1.05 for a single issue
Comments	ISSN 0006 7539. Other statistics on the stock market performance of publishers and books recorded also published.
Address	J Whitaker & Sons Ltd, 12 Dyott Street, London WC1A 1DF
Telephone	01 836 8911; Telex: 987117; Fax: 01 836 2909

71

Originator	BOOKSELLER
Title	UNIVERSITY LIBRARIES, annual in a weekly journal
Coverage	Annual feature article on university library book funds based on data from Blackwells, the University Grants Committee and the LISU academic book price index. Gives a 5-year run of data on expenditure in total and by major category.
Availability	General
Cost	£61, or £1.05 for a single issue
Comments	ISSN 0006 7539. Other statistics on the stock market performance of publishers and books recorded also published.
Address	J Whitaker & Sons Ltd, 12 Dyott Street, London WC1A 1DF
Telephone	01 836 8911; Telex: 987117; Fax: 01 836 2909

72

Originator	BOOKSELLERS ASSOCIATION OF GREAT BRITAIN AND IRELAND
Title	CHARTER GROUP ECONOMIC SURVEY, annual. 1964–
Coverage	Analysis of the economic performance and profitability of the book trade based on leading bookshops and carried out by Manchester Business School. Sales, profits and performance by specialization. Some supporting text (20%).
Availability	Book trade and general
Cost	£25
Address	154 Buckingham Palace Road, London SW1W 9TZ
Telephone	01 730 8214

73

Originator	BORDER TELEVISION
Title	MARKETING FACTS, biennial
Coverage	General data on the Borders region of Scotland including population, households, income and expenditure, retailing, services, agriculture etc. Based on various sources – Central Government data (40%), non-official sources (60%). A commentary supports the data (50%).
Availability	General
Cost	Free
Address	33 Margaret Street, London W1N 7LA
Telephone	01 637 4363

74

Originator	BRADFORD CITY COUNCIL
Title	BRADFORD IN FIGURES, annual
Coverage	Compendium of data on the area including population, economy, housing, land use etc. Based mainly on Central Government statistics (75%) with some local authority data (25%).
Availability	General
Cost	£2.50
Address	Policy Coordinator, City Hall, Bradford BD1 1HY
Telephone	0274 752014; Fax: 0274 752065

75

Originator	BRADFORD CITY COUNCIL
Title	DISTRICT TRENDS, annual

Coverage   Trends and issues currently facing Bradford, e.g. economy, politics, equal opportunities, environment, health and new technology.

Availability General
Address   Policy Coordinator, City Hall, Bradford BD1 1HY
Telephone   0274 752014; Fax: 0274 752065

76

Originator BRADWELL, JOHN ASSOCIATES

Title   BEER: SMALL CONTAINERS IMPORTS ANALYSIS SERVICE, quarterly. 1983–
Coverage   Analysis and interpretation of recorded imports of packaged beer and lager (in containers not exceeding 10 litres) with a particular emphasis on the implications for the UK market. Based on a combination of sources – Bradwell's own research (40%), Central Government statistics (40%), other sources (20%). Some supporting text (33%).

Availability General
Cost   £70
Address   21 Great Spilmans, London SE22 8SZ
Telephone   01 693 5692

77

Originator BRADWELL, JOHN ASSOCIATES

Title   SOFT DRINKS IMPORT ANALYSIS SERVICE, quarterly. 1982–
Coverage   Analysis and interpretation of recorded imports of bottled drinking water and their share of the UK market. Summary data on the imports of concentrated cordials and fruit squashes. Based on various sources – Bradwell's own research (40%), Central Government statistics (40%), other sources (20%). Supporting text covers 50%.

Availability General
Cost   £88
Address   21 Great Spilmans, London SE22 8SZ
Telephone   01 693 5692

78

Originator BREWERS SOCIETY

Title   BREWING REVIEW, regular

Coverage	Mainly articles and news items on developments in the brewing industry but includes a 'Statistical Review' with data over a number of years on beer production, imports, exports, lager production, wine consumption, spirit consumption, consumers expenditure, prices etc. Data from various sources
Availability	General
Cost	On application
Comments	Publication dates are not particularly systematic. At the time of writing the latest issue was July 1987.
Address	42 Portman Square, London W1H 0BB
Telephone	01 486 4831; Telex: 261946

79

Originator	BREWERS SOCIETY
Title	UK STATISTICAL HANDBOOK, annual
Coverage	Production and consumption of beer, brewing materials, prices, inter-drink comparisons, incomes, duties, licensing data, drunkenness and structure of the industry. Based largely on Central Government statistics (80%) with some data from the Society (10%) and other sources (10%). A small amount of supporting text (10%).
Availability	General
Cost	£18
Comments	ISSN 0306 6002. Publishes an information card summarizing the data.
Address	42 Portman Square, London W1H 0BB
Telephone	01 486 4831; Telex: 261946

80

Originator	BRICK DEVELOPMENT ASSOCIATION
Title	DATA ON BRICK USAGE AND DELIVERIES, quarterly. 1969–
Coverage	Analysis of brick deliveries by member firms into the various construction sectors. Based on a survey of the Association's large members covering about 57% of the industry.
Availability	Members
Cost	Free
Address	Woodside House, Winkfield, Windsor SL4 2DX
Telephone	0344 885651; Telex: 847840; Fax: 0344 885651

81

Originator	BRISTOL AND WEST BUILDING SOCIETY
Title	FACTUAL BACKGROUND, quarterly. 1969–
Coverage	General data and articles on building societies, personal savings, personal credit (including mortgages), housing and general economic and financial data. Mainly based on Central Government statistics (80%) with some supporting text (20%).
Availability	General
Cost	Free
Address	PO Box 27, Broad Quay, Bristol BS99 7AX
Telephone	0272 294271; Telex: 44741; Fax: 0272 293787

82

Originator	BRISTOL AND WEST BUILDING SOCIETY
Title	PROPERTY PROSPECTS, quarterly. Spring 1988–
Coverage	A review of the property market in the West and South West of England including data on house prices. Based on the Society's own data with a large amount of supporting commentary (80%).
Availability	General
Cost	Free
Address	PO Box 27, Broad Quay, Bristol BS99 7AX
Telephone	0272 294271; Telex: 44741; Fax: 0272 293787

83

Originator	BRITISH ADHESIVES AND SEALANTS ASSOCIATION
Title	SALES OF SEALANTS – ALL APPLICATIONS AND SALES HOME AND EXPORT – CERTAIN TYPES, bi-annual
Coverage	Sales in value terms for all types of sealants and sales value and volume for products split by chemical type. Based on a survey of members.
Availability	Members
Address	2A High Street, Hythe, Southampton SO4 6YW
Telephone	0703 842765

84

Originator	BRITISH AEROSOL MANUFACTURERS ASSOCIATION
Title	BAMA ANNUAL REPORT. annual
Coverage	Gives details of aerosol filling statistics by various product categories. Based on a survey of members

Availability	General
Cost	Free
Address	Kings Building, Smith Square, London SW1P 3JJ
Telephone	01 828 5111; Telex: 916672; Fax: 01 834 4469

85

Originator	BRITISH AGGREGATE CONSTRUCTION MATERIALS INDUSTRIES (BACMI)
Title	BACMI STATISTICAL YEARBOOK, annual. 1985–
Coverage	Statistics on the number and location of quarries, pits and plants with additional data on the use of various types of construction materials. Based mainly on returns from members.
Availability	General
Cost	£10
Comments	More detailed and more regular statistics available to members.
Address	156 Buckingham Palace Road, London SW1 9TR
Telephone	01 730 8194

86

Originator	BRITISH AGROCHEMICALS ASSOCIATION
Title	BAA ANNUAL REPORT, annual
Coverage	Contains a section on agrochemicals industry sales and employment and pesticide use. Based on a combination of sources and mainly text (80%).
Availability	General
Cost	Free
Address	4 Lincoln Court, Lincoln Road, Peterborough PE1 2RP
Telephone	0733 49225; Telex: 329176

87

Originator	BRITISH BATTERY MAKERS SOCIETY
Title	UK BATTERY MARKET STATISTICS, monthly and annual
Coverage	General statistics on the UK battery market.
Availability	Members
Cost	Free
Address	J. Hallows, c/o Lucas Batteries, Formans Road, Birmingham B11 3DA
Telephone	021 777 3292

88

Originator	BRITISH CARPET MANUFACTURERS ASSOCIATION
Title	ANNUAL REPORT, annual
Coverage	A statistical appendix gives carpet sales by type of construction, trade and fibres used in carpet surface yarns. General market data on carpets is given for the last 5 years. Based on Central Government data with a large amount of text in the main part of the report (60%).
Availability	General
Cost	Free
Address	Royalty House, 4th Floor, 72 Dean Street, London W1V 5HB
Telephone	01 734 9853

89

Originator	BRITISH CEMENT ASSOCIATION
Title	CEMENT STATISTICS, regular
Coverage	The Association collects statistics and is likely to publish these on a regular basis in the near future. In the mean time it can provide statistics on request. Up to 1987 it published cement channel of sale data on a monthly and quarterly basis.
Availability	General
Cost	On application
Comments	Previously called the Cement and Concrete Association; name change in 1987.
Address	Wexham Springs, Slough SL3 6PL
Telephone	02816 2727; Telex: 848352; Fax: 02816 2251

90

Originator	BRITISH CERAMIC MANUFACTURERS FEDERATION
Title	IMPORTS AND EXPORTS OF CERAMIC GOODS, monthly
Coverage	Cumulative import and export data in value and volume with comparative data for the previous 2 years. Analysed by sector and major countries only. Based on Central Government data.
Availability	Members
Cost	Free
Address	Federation House, Station Road, Stoke-on-Trent ST4 2SA
Telephone	0782 744631; Telex: 367446; Fax: 0782 744102

91

Originator	BRITISH CERAMIC MANUFACTURERS FEDERATION
Title	IMPORTS AND EXPORTS OF CERAMIC GOODS, quarterly
Coverage	Cumulative import and export data for ceramic goods by value and volume with comparative data for the previous 2 years. A more detailed analysis than the monthly reports (see above). Based on Central Government data.
Availability	Members
Cost	Free
Address	Federation House, Station Road, Stoke-on-Trent ST4 2SA
Telephone	0782 744631; Telex: 367446; Fax: 0782 744102

92

Originator	BRITISH CERAMIC MANUFACTURERS FEDERATION
Title	SALES OF CERAMIC PRODUCTS BY UK MANUFAC-TURERS, quarterly
Coverage	Total, home market and export sales of ceramic products plus imports analysed by sector and given in value and quantity. Comparative figures for the previous 2 years. Based on Central Government data.
Availability	Members
Cost	Free
Address	Federation House, Station Road, Stoke-on-Trent ST4 2SA
Telephone	0782 744631; Telex: 367446; Fax: 0782 744102

93

Originator	BRITISH CERAMIC REVIEW
Title	UK POTTERY EXPORTS, monthly in a monthly journal
Coverage	Value figures for exports of various types of pottery over the previous 2 months. A % change figure is also given. The British Ceramic Manufacturers Federation is given as the source of the data (see above).
Availability	General
Cost	On application
Comments	ISSN 0306 7076
Address	PO Box 378, Stoke-on-Trent ST3 4LT
Telephone	0782 320869

94

Originator	BRITISH CLOTHING INDUSTRY ASSOCIATION
Title	STATISTICAL REPORT ON THE BRITISH CLOTHING INDUSTRY, annual
Coverage	Clothing production trends plus data on imports and exports, prices, employment, earnings and consumer spending on clothes. Based largely on Central Government data (90%). Usually published 6 months after the latest year to which it relates and figures for earlier years in most tables.
Availability	General
Address	7 Swallow Place, London W1
Telephone	01 408 0020

95

Originator	BRITISH COAL
Title	BRITISH COAL REPORT AND ACCOUNTS, annual. 1947–
Coverage	A report of the year's activities with supporting statistics on output, production, manpower etc. Figures for the 2 latest years are given.
Availability	General
Cost	£3.25
Address	Coal House, Doncaster DN1 3HD
Telephone	0302 66611

96

Originator	BRITISH DIRECT MARKETING ASSOCIATION
Title	DIRECT MARKETING STATISTICS, annual. 1986–
Coverage	A compilation of statistics on direct marketing from a variety of non-official sources.
Availability	General
Cost	Free
Address	Grosvenor Gardens House, Grosvenor Gardens, London SW1W 0BS
Telephone	01 630 7322; Fax: 01 836 1122

97

Originator	BRITISH DISPOSABLE PRODUCTS ASSOCIATION
Title	DISPOSABLE PRODUCTS SALES, quarterly

Coverage	Sales figures for various types of disposable products including paperboard and fibre plates, paper cups, plastic cutlery, paper napkins and place mats. Based on returns from the Association's 20 member companies.
Availability	Members and selected data to others
Comments	General data from the survey is published in a press release by Edelman Public Relations, 536 Kings Road, London SW10 0TE.
Address	Leicester House, 8 Leicester Street, London WC2H 7BN
Telephone	01 437 0678; Telex: 263536; Fax: 01 437 4901

98

Originator	BRITISH EDUCATIONAL EQUIPMENT ASSOCIATION
Title	EXPENDITURE ON TEACHING MATERIALS: SCHOOL BOOKS/ EQUIPMENT/ STATIONERY, annual
Coverage	Expenditure in England and Wales by counties, districts and metropolitan boroughs with historical data over a 10-year period. Based on a combination of Central Government and non-official sources. Some supporting text (10%).
Availability	General
Cost	Free
Comments	Sponsored by the Publishers Association.
Address	Sunley House, 10 Gunthorpe Street, London E1 7RW
Telephone	01 247 9320; Fax: 01 247 5367

99

Originator	BRITISH EFFLUENT AND WATER ASSOCIATION
Title	ANNUAL REPORT, annual. 1969–
Coverage	Municipal and industrial water and effluent orders booked by members. Home and export markets. Based on a survey of members.
Availability	Members and some others
Cost	Free
Comments	Collects but does not publish sales data.
Address	5 Castle Street, High Wycombe HP13 6RZ
Telephone	0494 444544

100

Originator	BRITISH FIBREBOARD PACKAGING ASSOCIATION
Title	ANNUAL PRODUCTION STATISTICS, annual
Coverage	Production by weight and area and the sales invoice value of solid and corrugated fibreboard produced in the UK by BFPA members. Based on a survey of members.

Availability	Members
Comments	One table of figures is produced annually.
Address	Sutherland House, 5/6 Argyll Street, London W1V 1AD
Telephone	01 434 3851; Telex: 8953808; Fax: 01 439 0781

101

Originator	BRITISH FOOD INFORMATION SERVICE OF FOOD FROM BRITAIN
Title	PRODFACT, annual. March 1982–
Coverage	British agricultural and horticultural production, consumption, imports, expenditure etc. for over 80 product areas. Based on various sources.
Availability	General
Cost	£9.50 + £1.25 p+p
Comments	Compiled by Daphne MacCarthy to whom any queries should be referred.
Address	542/544 Market Towers, Nine Elms Lane, London SW8 5NQ
Telephone	01 720 7551

102

Originator	BRITISH FOOD MANUFACTURING INDUSTRIES RE-SEARCH ASSOCIATION (LEATHERHEAD FOOD R.A.)
Title	UK FOOD AND DRINK MARKET SIZE DATA SHEETS, regular
Coverage	Statistics on specific product areas with data on markets, production, consumption, trade etc. Based on various sources.
Availability	General
Cost	£60 per issue
Comments	Usually published every 6 months. Also publishes an international edition.
Address	Randalls Road, Leatherhead KT22 7RY
Telephone	0372 376761; Telex: 929846; Fax: 0372 386228

103

Originator	BRITISH FOOD MANUFACTURING INDUSTRIES RE-SEARCH ASSOCIATION (LEATHERHEAD FOOD R.A.)
Title	UK NEW PRODUCTS ANALYSIS, annual
Coverage	Mainly information on specific new product launches but includes statistics on general trends, areas of new product activity and market trends.
Availability	General

Cost	£150
Address	Randalls Road, Leatherhead KT22 7RY
Telephone	0372 376761; Telex: 929846; Fax: 0372 386228

104

Originator	BRITISH FOOTWEAR MANUFACTURERS FEDERATION
Title	FOOTWEAR INDUSTRY STATISTICAL REVIEW, annual. 1969–
Coverage	Statistics on the industry structure, materials, production, profitability, employment and earnings, wholesale and retail prices, supplies to the home market, expenditure, retail distribution and imports and exports. Some comparative EEC data. Based mainly on Central Government sources (90%). Usually published 9 months after the year to which it relates.
Availability	General
Cost	£26
Address	Royalty House, 72 Dean Street, London W1V 5HB
Telephone	01 437 5573; Fax: 01 494 1300

105

Originator	BRITISH FOOTWEAR MANUFACTURERS FEDERATION
Title	MONTHLY STATISTICS, monthly
Coverage	Short-term economic indicators for the industry with a brief commentary. Data covers deliveries, employment, prices, retail sales and trade.
Availability	General
Cost	£35 with other titles
Comments	The subscription covers the above plus 'Quarterly Review' and 'Quarterly Statistical Supplement' – see below.
Address	Royalty House, 72 Dean Street, London W1V 5HB
Telephone	01 437 5573; Fax: 01 494 1300

106

Originator	BRITISH FOOTWEAR MANUFACTURERS FEDERATION
Title	QUARTERLY REVIEW, quarterly
Coverage	Economic indicators for the industry in more detail than the 'Monthly Statistics' (see above). Data on deliveries, production, consumption in total and by individual sectors, prices, trade etc.
Availability	General
Cost	£35 with other titles
Comments	The subscription covers the above plus 'Monthly Statistics' and 'Quarterly Statistical Supplement'.

37 107–109

Address	Royalty House, 72 Dean Street, London W1V 5HB
Telephone	01 437 5573; Fax: 01 494 1300

107

Originator	BRITISH FOOTWEAR MANUFACTURERS FEDERATION
Title	QUARTERLY STATISTICAL SUPPLEMENT, quarterly
Coverage	Detailed production, import/export and consumption statistics for specific sectors of the footwear industry. Based on Central Government data.
Availability	General
Cost	£35 with other titles
Comments	The subscription covers the above title plus 'Monthly Statistics' and 'Quarterly Review'.
Address	Royalty House, 72 Dean Street, London W1V 5HB
Telephone	01 437 5573; Fax: 01 494 1300

108

Originator	BRITISH FORGING INDUSTRY ASSOCIATION
Title	BFIA ANNUAL REPORT, annual
Coverage	Contains some statistics on the general economic performance of the forging sector.
Availability	Requests considered from non-members
Cost	Free
Comments	The Association previously published a regular 'Economic Review'.
Address	245 Grove Lane, Handsworth, Birmingham B20 2HB
Telephone	021 554 3311; Fax: 021 523 0761

109

Originator	BRITISH FORGING INDUSTRY ASSOCIATION
Title	STATISTICAL BULLETIN, annual
Coverage	Current statistical information on the forging industry including market developments, prices, deliveries and a European output summary. Based on the Association's own surveys.
Availability	General
Cost	£20
Address	Grove Hill House, 245 Grove Lane, Birmingham B20 2HB
Telephone	021 554 3311; Fax: 021 523 0761

110

Originator BRITISH FROZEN FOOD FEDERATION

Title BRITISH FROZEN FOOD YEARBOOK, annual
Coverage A section on frozen food statistics covering consumption and expenditure, freezer ownership, markets for ice cream, vegetables, fish and meat, gateaux and retail and catering trends. Some data on other countries. Based on Central Government data (40%) and data from the Federation and other non-official sources (60%).

Availability General
Cost £24
Address Honeypot Lane, Colsterworth, Grantham NG33 5LX
Telephone 0476 860914

111

Originator BRITISH GAS PLC

Title KEY STATISTICS, annual. 1987–
Coverage General information on the gas industry plus operating figures for British Gas and figures on its share of the fuel market. Based on the company's own data.

Availability General
Cost Free
Comments Produced in the form of a pocket card. Annual Report and 'Financial & Operating Statistics' also available.
Address Public Relations, 152 Grosvenor Road, London SW1V 3JL
Telephone 01 821 1444; Telex: 938529; Fax: 01 724 1317

112

Originator BRITISH HARDWARE FEDERATION

Title TODAY'S TRADING TRENDS, quarterly. 1981–
Coverage Performance trends in the key hardware sectors covering profits, sales, stocks, wages etc. Based on returns from member companies.

Availability Members
Cost Free
Comments Summary data published in the journal 'Hardware Today' – see other entry.
Address 20 Harborne Road, Edgbaston, Birmingham B15 3AB
Telephone 021 454 4385; Telex: 338024; Fax: 021 455 8670

113

Originator   BRITISH HARDWARE AND HOUSEWARES MANUFAC-
                TURERS ASSOCIATION

Title   STATISTICS SUPPLEMENT, quarterly. 1983–
Coverage   Industry trends, trade, consumers' expenditure, unemployment
                and a tax and price index. Based largely on Central Government
                statistics (80%) with some original data (10%) and other non-
                official data (10%). Some supporting text (25%).

Availability Members
Cost   Free
Address   35 Billing Road, Northampton NN1 5DD
Telephone   0604 22023

114

Originator   BRITISH HOLIDAY & HOME PARKS ASSOCIATION

Title   STATISTICS, regular
Coverage   The association compiles statistics on holiday parks and sites for its
                members, for tourist boards and ministerial use.

Availability Members
Address   Chichester House, 31 Park Road, Gloucester GL1 1LH
Telephone   0452 26911; Fax: 0452 307226

115

Originator   BRITISH INVISIBLE EXPORTS COUNCIL

Title   ANNUAL REPORT, annual
Coverage   Britain's share of world invisible trade, invisibles in Britain's cur-
                rent account and what the City of London earns abroad. Based on a
                combination of the Council's own survey (70%) and Central
                Government statistics (30%). A large amount of supporting text
                (80%).

Availability General
Cost   Free
Comments   Issues 'World Invisible Trade' annually.
Address   6th Floor, Windsor House, 39 King Street, London EC2V 8DQ
Telephone   01 600 1198; Telex: 9413342; Fax: 01 606 4248

116

Originator   BRITISH INVISIBLE EXPORTS COUNCIL

Title   INFORMATION CARD, bi-annual

Coverage	UK invisible earnings, invisibles in the UK's current account, what the City of London earns overseas and employment. Based on a combination of the Council's own survey (30%) and Central Government statistics (70%). Some supporting text (50%).
Availability	General
Cost	40p
Comments	Issues 'World Invisible Trade' annually.
Address	6th Floor, Windsor House, 39 King Street, London EC2V 8DQ
Telephone	01 600 1198; Telex: 9413342; Fax: 01 606 4248

117

Originator	BRITISH JEWELLER
Title	MARKET REPORTS, monthly in a monthly journal
Coverage	Mainly news and features on the jewellery trade but it includes a monthly market reports section with data on precious metal prices for the previous month and fine gold prices over the last 12 months.
Availability	General
Cost	£26, or £2.60 for a single issue
Comments	Published by the British Jewellery & Giftware Federation at the address below.
Address	27 Frederick Street, Birmingham B1 3HJ
Telephone	021 236 2657; Telex: 340033; Fax: 021 236 3921

118

Originator	BRITISH MAN-MADE FIBRES FEDERATION
Title	BETTER LIVING WITH MAN-MADE FIBRES, annual. 1987–
Coverage	A descriptive booklet with a statistical summery giving UK and world production and consumption data for fibres. Based on various sources with a large amount of text (85%).
Availability	General
Cost	Free
Address	24 Buckingham Gate, London SW1 6LB
Telephone	01 828 0744

119

Originator	BRITISH MARINE INDUSTRIES FEDERATION
Title	BMIF INDUSTRY STATISTICS, annual
Coverage	Data on the production, sales, imports and exports of boats, inflatables, sailboards and marine equipment.
Availability	On application
Address	Boating Industry House, Vale Road, Weybridge KT13 9NS
Telephone	0932 854511; Telex: 885471; Fax: 0932 852874

120

Originator   BRITISH MARKET RESEARCH BUREAU LTD

Title   TARGET GROUP INDEX (TGI), annual. October 1968–
Coverage   A national product and media survey based on information from 24,000 adults. Breakdowns by social grades, attitudes and household income. Consists of 34 volumes on different sectors.

Availability Advertisers and media owners
Cost   £2,050 (1 volume), £350 (1 field), £50 (1 brand)
Comments   Available on-line from Holborn Research Services, IMS UK Ltd, Telmar Communications Ltd and CACI.
Address   Saunders House, 53 The Mall, Ealing, London W5 3TE
Telephone   01 579 0417; Telex: 935526; Fax: 01 840 1655

121

Originator   BRITISH PAPER AND BOARD INDUSTRY FEDERATION (BPBIF)

Title   BPBIF GREEN BOOK, monthly
Coverage   Statistics on the production, sales, stocks and consumption of various grades and groups of grades of paper, pulp and board. Data on waste paper is also included. Based on a combination of official and non-official sources.

Availability General
Cost   On application
Address   Papermakers Hse, Rivenhall Road, Swindon SN5 7BE
Telephone   0793 886086; Telex: 445759; Fax: 0793 886182

122

Originator   BRITISH PAPER AND BOARD INDUSTRY FEDERATION (BPBIF)

Title   BPBIF GREY BOOK, monthly
Coverage   Statistics on the production, stocks, sales, imports, exports and consumption of different grades of paper, pulp and board. Based on a combination of official and non-official sources.

Availability General
Cost   On application
Address   Papermakers Hse, Rivenhall Road, Swindon SN5 7BE
Telephone   0793 886086; Telex: 445759; Fax: 0793 886182

123

Originator	BRITISH PAPER AND BOARD INDUSTRY FEDERATION (BPBIF)
Title	BPBIF REFERENCE TABLES, annual
Coverage	Statistics over a 10-year period covering production, stocks, sales, consumption, imports, exports of paper, pulp and board. Also includes some industry financial data and employment figures. Based on a combination of official and non-official sources.
Availability	General
Cost	£75
Address	Papermakers Hse, Rivenhall Road, Swindon SN5 7BE
Telephone	0793 886086; Telex: 445759; Fax: 0793 886182

124

Originator	BRITISH PAPER AND BOARD INDUSTRY FEDERATION
Title	BRITISH PAPER AND BOARD INDUSTRY FACTS, annual
Coverage	Various statistics on the industry including details of consumption, production, trade, capacity, raw materials, energy consumption, water usage, manpower, expenditure etc. Based on a combination of official (30%) and non-official sources (70%).
Availability	General
Cost	£7 for 10 brochures, free to members
Address	Papermakers Hse, Rivenhall Road, Swindon SN5 7BE
Telephone	0793 886086; Telex: 445759; Fax: 0793 886182

125

Originator	BRITISH PHONOGRAPHIC INDUSTRY LTD
Title	BPI YEARBOOK, annual
Coverage	Includes statistics on the production of records and tapes plus imports and exports, deliveries, sales, prices, advertising expenditure, hardware ownership, video trends and piracy and leisure market trends.
Availability	General
Cost	£7.50. Free to members
Comments	Although usually an annual publication there were no issues published for 1980 and 1981.
Address	Roxburghe House, 273/287 Regent Street, London W1R 7PB
Telephone	01 629 8642

126

Originator	BRITISH PLASTICS FEDERATION
Title	BPF BUSINESS TRENDS SURVEY, annual. 1975–
Coverage	A survey of companies in 3 areas: materials supplies (33 firms responded in 1986); processing (117 firms responded); and machinery manufacturers (15 firms responded). Data on sales, orders, exports, stocks, investment, profits, prices and capacity utilization. Usually published in September/October and refers to previous year and forthcoming year.
Availability	General
Cost	£25, free to contributing members, £20 to other members
Address	5 Belgrave Square, London SW1X 8PH
Telephone	01 235 9483; Telex: 8951528; Fax: 01 235 8045

127

Originator	BRITISH PLASTICS FEDERATION
Title	BPF STATISTICS HANDBOOK, annual. 1986–
Coverage	Statistics on the UK consumption of plastics materials, material consumption by major end-use, imports, exports and plastics in packaging, building and the automotive sectors. 40% of the data is collected by BPF and a supporting text covers 30%.
Availability	General
Cost	£75
Address	5 Belgrave Square, London SW1X 8PH
Telephone	01 235 9483; Telex: 8951528; Fax: 01 235 8045

128

Originator	BRITISH PORTS FEDERATION
Title	MANPOWER OF THE UK PORTS INDUSTRY, annual. 1983–
Coverage	Statistics of employment in the UK ports industry based on a survey of all port employers by the Federation. Some supporting text (50%).
Availability	General
Cost	£15
Comments	First published in 1983 but no further issues until 1986 when it became an annual publication.
Address	Commonwealth House, 1/19 New Oxford Street, London WC1A 1DZ
Telephone	01 242 1200; Telex: 295741; Fax: 01 405 1069

129

Originator	BRITISH PORTS FEDERATION
Title	PORT STATISTICS, annual. 1980–
Coverage	Statistics of the UK ports industry by port plus various port-related trade statistics. Based on information collected by the Department of Transport and published jointly with the Department. A small amount of text (10%).
Availability	General
Cost	£25
Address	Commonwealth House, 1/19 New Oxford Street, London WC1A 1DZ
Telephone	01 242 1200; Telex: 295741; Fax: 01 405 1069

130

Originator	BRITISH PORTS FEDERATION
Title	UK TRADE DATA, quarterly. March 1987–
Coverage	UK trade figures by port and key commodity groups, by volume and value. Based entirely on Central Government import and export data.
Availability	General
Cost	£40, or £10 per issue
Address	Commonwealth House, 1/19 New Oxford Street, London WC1A 1DZ
Telephone	01 242 1200; Telex: 295741; Fax: 01 405 1069

131

Originator	BRITISH PRINTING INDUSTRIES FEDERATION
Title	BPIF LABOUR FORCE INQUIRY, annual
Coverage	Manpower data in the printing industry based on a survey of members.
Availability	Members
Cost	Free
Comments	Various other surveys available to members.
Address	11 Bedford Row, London WC1R 4DX
Telephone	01 242 6904; Fax: 01 405 7784

132

Originator	BRITISH PRINTING INDUSTRIES FEDERATION
Title	BPIF SALARY SURVEY, annual

Coverage	Data on the salaries of white collar staff in the printing industry based on a survey of members.

Availability	Members
Cost	£40
Comments	Various other surveys available to members.
Address	11 Bedford Row, London WC1R 4DX
Telephone	01 242 6904; Fax: 01 405 7784

133

Originator	BRITISH PRINTING INDUSTRIES FEDERATION

Title	BPIF WAGES SURVEY, annual
Coverage	Details of wages of production workers in the printing industry based on a survey of members. A regional analysis is also included.

Availability	Members
Cost	Free
Comments	Various other surveys available to members.
Address	11 Bedford Row, London WC1R 4DX
Telephone	01 242 6904; Fax: 01 405 7784

134

Originator	BRITISH PRINTING INDUSTRIES FEDERATION

Title	ECONOMIC TRENDS, 10 issues per year
Coverage	Economic trends generally and in the printing industry; 4 issues per year contain the results of an opinion survey of Federation members. Based on a combination of Central Government data (50%) and the Federation's own survey (50%).

Availability	General
Cost	£5
Comments	Various other surveys available to members.
Address	11 Bedford Row, London WC1R 4DX
Telephone	01 242 6904; Fax: 01 405 7784

135

Originator	BRITISH PRINTING INDUSTRIES FEDERATION

Title	PRINTERS YEARBOOK, annual
Coverage	A commentary with a statistical section on general trends in the printing industry. Based on a combination of Central Government data and the Federation's surveys.

Availability	General
Cost	£40
Comments	Various other surveys available to members.

Address	11 Bedford Row, London WC1R 4DX
Telephone	01 242 6904; Fax: 01 405 7784

136

Originator	BRITISH RADIO AND ELECTRONIC EQUIPMENT MANU-FACTURERS ASSOCIATION (BREEMA)
Title	DELIVERIES OF SELECTED AUDIO AND VIDEO PRODUCTS TO THE UK MARKET, quarterly
Coverage	Deliveries to the trade of televisions, videography, music centres and compact disc players. Based on a survey of members and supported by a commentary on the figures (40%).
Availability	General
Cost	Free
Address	Landseer House, 19 Charing Cross Road, London WC2H 0ES
Telephone	01 930 3206; Telex: 296215; Fax: 01 839 4613

137

Originator	BRITISH RADIO AND ELECTRONIC EQUIPMENT MANU-FACTURERS ASSOCIATION (BREEMA)
Title	UK MARKET FOR DOMESTIC AUDIO EQUIPMENT, annual
Coverage	Detailed analysis and statistics on the UK market for audio equipment covering total UK production, imports, exports, trade deliveries, consumer offtake and manufacturers' and distributors' stocks. Published in 2 volumes. The first volume gives data for the latest year and the second volume gives historical statistics for the last 50+ years.
Availability	General
Cost	£35 Volume 1, £100 Volume 2
Comments	If both volumes are purchased a discount of £50 is available.
Address	Landseer House, 19 Charing Cross Road, London WC2H 0ES
Telephone	01 930 3206; Telex: 296215; Fax: 01 839 4613

138

Originator	BRITISH RADIO AND ELECTRONIC EQUIPMENT MANU-FACTURERS ASSOCIATION (BREEMA)
Title	UK MARKET FOR DOMESTIC TELEVISION SETS, annual
Coverage	Detailed analysis and statistics on the UK market for televisions with data on total UK production, imports, exports, trade deliveries, consumer offtake and manufacturers' and distributors' stocks. Published in 2 volumes. The first volume gives detailed statistics and analysis for the latest year and the second volume gives historical data over a 40 year period.

Availability	General
Cost	£45 Volume 1, £200 Volume 2
Comments	If both volumes are purchased a discount of £50 is available.
Address	Landseer House, 19 Charing Cross Road, London WC2H 0ES
Telephone	01 930 3206; Telex: 296215; Fax: 01 839 4613

139

Originator	BRITISH RADIO AND ELECTRONIC EQUIPMENT MANU-FACTURERS ASSOCIATION (BREEMA)
Title	UK MARKET FOR VIDEOGRAPHY, annual
Coverage	Detailed analysis and statistics on the UK market for video recorders and camcorders with statistics on total UK production, imports, exports, trade deliveries, consumer offtake and manufacturers' and distributors' stocks. Published in 2 volumes. The first volume gives data for the latest year and the second volume gives historical data over 10 years.
Availability	General
Cost	£20 Volume 1, £100 Volume 2
Comments	If both volumes are purchased a discount of £50 is available.
Address	Landseer House, 19 Charing Cross Road, London WC2H 0ES
Telephone	01 930 3206; Telex: 296215; Fax: 01 839 4613

140

Originator	BRITISH RAILWAYS BOARD
Title	ANNUAL REPORT AND ACCOUNTS, annual
Coverage	Largely financial statistics on the accounts and business performance but includes statistics on performance indicators in the passenger, freight and parcels sectors. Based on surveys by the Board.
Availability	General
Cost	£4
Comments	ISSN 0305 1420
Address	Euston House, 24 Eversholt Street, Box 100, London NW1 1DZ
Telephone	01 928 5151; Telex: 299431; Fax: 01 922 6994

141

Originator	BRITISH ROAD FEDERATION
Title	BASIC ROAD STATISTICS, annual. 1934–
Coverage	Roads and road transport including data on traffic, energy, taxation, public expenditure, accidents and some international comparisons. Mainly taken from Central Government sources (95%).

Availability	General
Cost	£15
Comments	ISSN 0309 3638
Address	Cowdray House, 6 Portugal Street, London WC2A 2HG
Telephone	01 242 1285; Fax: 01 831 1898

142

Originator BRITISH ROBOT ASSOCIATION

Title ROBOT FACTS, annual
Coverage Statistics on robot use by industry sector with additional data on the country of origin of the robots installed. Some statistics on world trends in the robot population. Data over a number of years is given. Based on the Association's survey.

Availability	General
Cost	£17
Comments	The journal 'Industrial Robot' has summary data from the Association.
Address	Aston Science Park, Love Lane, Birmingham B7 4BJ
Telephone	021 359 0981

143

Originator BRITISH SCRAP FEDERATION

Title BRITISH SCRAP FEDERATION ANNUAL REPORT, annual
Coverage Includes statistics on scrap consumption, scrap stocks, exports, imports and average annual scrap prices. A number of tables give trends over a 10-year period. Based on the Federation's own data (50%) and other sources, mainly Central Government (50%). The statistics form the main part of the report.

Availability	General
Cost	Free
Address	16 High Street, Brampton, Huntingdon PE18 8TU
Telephone	0480 55249; Telex: 32546; Fax: 0480 53680

144

Originator BRITISH SECONDARY METALS ASSOCIATION

Title BSMA MEMBER SURVEY, regular
Coverage A survey of member companies by employment size, number of sites, investment, turnover etc.

Availability	Requests from non-members considered
Cost	Free
Comments	Latest survey published – 1985.

Address   25 Park Road, Runcorn WA7 4SS
Telephone   09285 72400; Telex: 629034

145

Originator   BRITISH SOFT DRINKS ASSOCIATION LTD

Title   FACTSHEETS, annual. 1984–
Coverage   Information sheets containing statistics on various aspects of the
              industry, e.g. sales, consumption, packaging etc. Each factsheet
              contains a large amount of text (80%) supported by statistics mainly
              collected by the Association.

Availability General
Cost   Free
Address   6 Catherine Street, London WC2B 5UA
Telephone   01 379 5737; Telex: 299388

146

Originator   BRITISH STEEL CORPORATION/BRITISH INDEPENDENT
              STEEL PRODUCERS ASSOCIATION

Title   STEEL INDUSTRY STATISTICS, monthly
Coverage   Data on steel output by month with data over a number of recent
              years. Production trends are also broken down by standard regions.
              Based on surveys by the 2 publishing bodies. The latest month's
              publication usually has data up to the previous month.

Availability General
Comments   Produced in the form of a press release.
Address   BSC, 9 Albert Embankment, London SE1
Telephone   01 735 7654; Telex: 916061

147

Originator   BRITISH TEXTILE CONFEDERATION

Title   ANNUAL REPORT AND REVIEW, annual. 1973–
Coverage   A profile of the textile industry covering the value of the industry,
              employment, production, capital expenditure, final consumption
              and trade. Based mainly on Central Government data (75%) with
              supporting data from the Confederation (25%). A large amount of
              supporting commentary (90%). Usually published 3-4 months after
              the year to which it relates.

Availability General
Cost   Free
Address   24 Buckingham Gate, London SW1E 6LB
Telephone   01 828 5222; Telex: 8814217; Fax: 01 828 6237

148

Originator	BRITISH TEXTILE CONFEDERATION
Title	TRENDS IN TEXTILE AND CLOTHING TRADE, quarterly. 1977–
Coverage	Textiles and clothing imports by products or product groups and exports by product groups. Based on Central Government data (100%).
Availability	General
Cost	£75, or £25 for a single issue
Address	24 Buckingham Gate, London SW1E 6LB
Telephone	01 828 5222; Telex: 8814217; Fax: 01 828 6237

149

Originator	BRITISH TOURIST AUTHORITY
Title	ANNUAL REPORT, annual
Coverage	Includes summary statistics on tourism in the United Kingdom with a general review of the short term outlook for tourism. Also includes information on the work and organization of the authority.
Availability	General
Cost	£5
Comments	Various 'one-off' reports also produced.
Address	Finance, Thames Tower, Black's Road, London W6 9EL
Telephone	01 846 9000; Telex: 21231

150

Originator	BRITISH TOURIST AUTHORITY
Title	CONFERENCE AND EXHIBITION MARKET SURVEY, quarterly
Coverage	Data on the number, size, length and earnings of conferences and exhibitions in the UK and on the proportion of attendees who come from overseas. Based on surveys among panels of different types of conference and exhibition venues carried out by the Authority.
Availability	General
Cost	£80
Comments	Various 'one-off' reports also produced.
Address	Market Research, Thames Tower, Black's Road, London W6 9EL
Telephone	01 846 9000; Telex: 21231

151

Originator	BRITISH TOURIST AUTHORITY
Title	DIGEST OF TOURIST STATISTICS, every 3 or 4 years
Coverage	Includes extracts from various travel surveys including the DTIs International Passenger Survey which measures tourist flows into and out of the UK. Also summary results from the Authority's survey.
Availability	General
Cost	£10
Comments	Last published in 1983, 11th edition. Various 'one-off' reports also produced.
Address	Finance, Thames Tower, Black's Road, London W6 9EL
Telephone	01 846 9000; Telex: 21231

152

Originator	BRITISH TOURIST AUTHORITY
Title	OVERSEAS VISITOR SURVEY, annual. 1987–
Coverage	A survey of overseas visitors to the UK with data on their behavioural patterns and opinions. Based on a regular annual survey by the Authority although the results were published widely for the first time in 1987.
Availability	General
Cost	£22
Comments	Various 'one-off' reports also produced.
Address	Finance, Thames Tower, Black's Road, London W6 9EL
Telephone	01 846 9000; Telex: 21231

153

Originator	BRITISH TOURIST AUTHORITY
Title	SURVEY AMONG OVERSEAS VISITORS TO LONDON, annual. 1973–
Coverage	A picture of the types of overseas visitors to London, details of their stay, their activities and reactions to the city. Comparisons are made with previous years.
Availability	General
Cost	£22
Comments	From 1986 edition onwards copies are available from London Tourist Board. Various 'one-off' reports also produced.
Address	Finance, Thames Tower, Black's Road, London W6 9EL
Telephone	01 846 9000; Telex: 21231

154

Originator	BRITISH TOURIST AUTHORITY
Title	TOURISM INTELLIGENCE QUARTERLY, quarterly
Coverage	Collates and interprets current statistical data and forecasts relating to tourism in the UK. Includes details of overseas visitors, hotel occupancy, UK residents travelling abroad and within Britain, UK travel account and traffic at UK air and seaports. Based mainly on data collected by the Authority.
Availability	General
Cost	On application
Comments	Various 'one-off' reports also produced.
Address	Finance, Thames Tower, Black's Road, London W6 9EL
Telephone	01 846 9000; Telex: 21231

155

Originator	BRITISH TOURIST AUTHORITY
Title	VISITS TO TOURIST ATTRACTIONS, annual
Coverage	Statistics on visitor numbers for 4 categories of attraction: historic properties and gardens; museums and galleries; wildlife attractions; 'other' such as theme parks, steam railways etc. Also includes a list of the top 20 attractions in each group plus data on charges, openings, ownership etc. Data for the last 2 years based on the Authority's survey.
Availability	General
Cost	£5.50
Comments	Various 'one-off' reports also produced.
Address	Finance, Thames Tower, Black's Road, London W6 9EL
Telephone	01 846 9000; Telex: 21231

156

Originator	BRITISH TOY AND HOBBY MANUFACTURERS ASSOCIATION
Title	TOY AND HOBBY STATISTICS, annual
Coverage	Statistics on the sales and imports/exports of specific types of toys and hobbies. Sales figures for the latest 3 years and trade data for the latest 2 years.
Availability	General
Cost	Free
Comments	Statistics can be supplied to non-members on request – there is no mailing list. A BTHMA Factbook is being updated.
Address	80 Camberwell Road, London SE5 0EG
Telephone	01 701 7271

157

Originator   BRITISH VEHICLE RENTAL AND LEASING ASSOCI-
              ATION

Title   BVRLA ANNUAL STATISTICAL SURVEY, annual. 1977–
Coverage   Data on the size of the chauffeur drive/private hire, rental and
              leasing fleets operated by members of the BVRLA. 1,283 members
              were circulated in 1986 and 1047 responded. Usually published 6-8
              months after completion of the survey. A large amount of commen-
              tary (70%) supports the statistics.

Availability General
Cost   £25, free to members
Address   13 St Johns Street, Chichester PO19 1UU
Telephone   0243 786782; Telex: 86402; Fax: 0243 786930

158

Originator   BRITISH VENTURE CAPITAL ASSOCIATION

Title   REPORT ON INVESTMENT ACTIVITY, annual. 1984–
Coverage   Investment trends and activity of member companies over the
              previous year. Commentary and statistics based on the Associ-
              ation's survey.

Availability General
Cost   £15
Address   1 Surrey Street, London WC2R 2PS
Telephone   01 836 5702

159

Originator   BRITISH WATERWAYS BOARD

Title   ANNUAL REPORT AND ACCOUNTS, annual. 1963–
Coverage   Largely concerned with the Board's activities and finances but
              contains some general statistics, e.g. engineering, traffic,
              employment etc. Based on the Board's own data. Usually produced
              6 months after the year to which it relates.

Availability General
Cost   £5
Address   Melbury House, Melbury Terrace, London NW1 6JX
Telephone   01 725 8000; Telex: 263605; Fax: 01 403 0168

160

Originator	BRITISH WOODPULP ASSOCIATION
Title	ANNUAL REPORT, annual
Coverage	Includes a statistical section with data on imports of pulp by grade and country of origin, production and consumption of paper and board.
Availability	Members and some others on request
Cost	£2, free to members
Comments	The registered office is at 25/35 City Road, London EC1Y 1AR but publication details from the address below.
Address	75 Billington Road, Leighton Buzzard LU7 8TG
Telephone	0525 379038

161

Originator	BRITISH WOODPULP ASSOCIATION
Title	DIGEST OF WOODPULP IMPORT STATISTICS, monthly
Coverage	Tonnage imports of wood pulp for paper making and other purposes. Based on data supplied by HM Customs and Excise.
Availability	Members and some others on request
Cost	£10, or £2 per issue. Free to members
Comments	The registered office is at 25/35 City Road, London EC1Y 1AR but publication details from the address below.
Address	75 Billington Road, Leighton Buzzard LU7 8TG
Telephone	0525 379038

162

Originator	BRITISH WOOL MARKETING BOARD
Title	ANNUAL REPORT AND ACCOUNTS, annual
Coverage	Mainly details of the Board and its finances but also contains statistics on wool production by type of wool produced. Based on the Board's own figures.
Availability	Primarily members/wool producers, but other requests considered
Cost	Free
Address	Oak Mills, Station Road, Bradford, West Yorkshire BD14 6JD
Telephone	0274 882091; Telex: 51406; Fax: 0274 818277

163

Originator	BRITISH WOOL MARKETING BOARD
Title	ANNUAL STATISTICS, annual

Coverage   Data on wool production, average clip size, weight of wool taken up and the number of registered producers by UK region. Based on the Board's own survey and produced 1–2 months after the survey. Text (30%) supports the statistics.

Availability   Primarily members/wool producers, but other requests considered
Cost   Free
Address   Oak Mills, Station Road, Bradford, West Yorkshire BD14 6JD
Telephone   0274 882091; Telex: 51406; Fax: 0274 818277

164

Originator   BRITISH WOOL MARKETING BOARD

Title   BASIC DATA, annual
Coverage   Summary information on the sheep population, wool production, prices, registered producers and the production of mutton and lamb. Based on a Board survey and produced on one sheet of paper.

Availability   Primarily members/wool producers, but other requests considered.
Cost   Free
Address   Oak Mills, Station Road, Bradford, West Yorkshire BD14 6JD
Telephone   0274 882091; Telex: 51406; Fax: 0274 818277

165

Originator   BUCKINGHAMSHIRE COUNTY COUNCIL

Title   BUCKINGHAMSHIRE COUNTY COUNCIL MONITORING REPORT: KEY STATISTICS, annual. December 1978–
Coverage   Statistics on housing, employment, unemployment by district and sub-district, retailing and planning permissions and completions. Based largely on the Council's own surveys (95%).

Availability   General
Cost   £2.50
Address   County Hall, Aylesbury HP20 1UX
Telephone   0296 395000; Telex: 83101; Fax: 0296 382830

166

Originator   BUILDERS MERCHANTS FEDERATION

Title   BMF SALES INDEX SURVEY, monthly
Coverage   Indexed comparison of turnovers of builders merchants by region and commodity classification. Both adjusted and unadjusted figures are produced. Based largely on BMF's own survey (95%).

Availability   General
Cost   £84, free to members
Address   15 Soho Square, London W1V 5FB
Telephone   01 439 1753; Fax: 01 734 2766

167

Originator	BUILDING
Title	BUILDING INDICATORS, monthly in a weekly journal
Coverage	Graphs and a short commentary on general trends in the building industry covering housing, industry, repairs, maintenance, output workload etc. based largely on Central Government data (60%) plus various non-official sources (30%) and the journal's own data (10%).
Availability	General
Cost	£40
Comments	ISSN 0007 3318
Address	Building (Publishers) Ltd, 1/3 Pemberton Row, London EC4P 4HL
Telephone	01 353 2300; Telex: 25212; Fax: 01 353 8311

168

Originator	BUILDING
Title	COST FILE, monthly in a weekly journal
Coverage	Prices and costs of specific building materials and products plus wage rates. Based on returns from builders merchants and some research by the journal.
Availability	General
Cost	£40
Comments	ISSN 0007 3318
Address	Building (Publishers) Ltd, 1/3 Pemberton Row, London EC4P 4HL
Telephone	01 353 2300; Telex: 25212; Fax: 01 353 8311

169

Originator	BUILDING
Title	HEATING AND ELECTRICAL SUPPLEMENT, quarterly in a weekly journal
Coverage	Prices for heating and electrical materials and work done on medium- to large-scale projects.
Availability	General
Cost	£40
Comments	ISSN 0007 3318.
Address	Building (Publishers) Ltd, 1/3 Pemberton Row, London EC4P 4HL
Telephone	01 353 2300; Telex: 25212; Fax: 01 353 8311

170

Originator	BUILDING
Title	HOUSING COST INDEX, monthly in a weekly journal
Coverage	The % change in housing costs by month over a 12 month period with specific data on materials, building, labour etc. Based on data collected by the journal.
Availability	General
Cost	£40
Comments	ISSN 0007 3318
Address	Building (Publishers) Ltd, 1/3 Pemberton Row, London EC4P 4HL
Telephone	01 353 2300; Telex: 25212; Fax: 01 353 8311

171

Originator	BUILDING
Title	MEASURED RATES SUPPLIES, quarterly in a weekly journal
Coverage	Rates for materials and work done on medium sized projects over £200,000. Covers material costs, plant hire and wages for specific types of project.
Availability	General
Cost	£40
Comments	ISSN 0007 3318
Address	Building (Publishers) Ltd, 1/3 Pemberton Row, London EC4P 4HL
Telephone	01 353 2300; Telex: 25212; Fax: 01 353 8311

172

Originator	BUILDING
Title	THIS WEEK'S INDICES, weekly in a weekly journal
Coverage	Changes over the previous week in the FT indices covering building and building materials and the 'Building 50 Index'. Also gives all-time high and all-time low figures.
Availability	General
Cost	£40
Comments	ISSN 0007 3318
Address	Building (Publishers) Ltd, 1/3 Pemberton Row, London EC4P 4HL
Telephone	01 353 2300; Telex: 25212; Fax: 01 353 8311

173

Originator	BUILDING EMPLOYERS CONFEDERATION
Title	BEC QUARTERLY CONSTRUCTION REVIEW, quarterly

Coverage	Summary results from the BEC and HBF State of Trade Enquiries (see below), and general statistics on new orders, housebuilding, construction forecasts etc. Based on a combination of official and non-official figures with a supporting text (50%).
Availability	General
Cost	Free
Address	82 New Cavendish Street, London W1M 8AD
Telephone	01 580 5588; Telex: 265763; Fax: 01 631 3872

174

Originator	BUILDING EMPLOYERS CONFEDERATION
Title	BEC STATE OF TRADE ENQUIRY REPORT, quarterly
Coverage	Prospects for the building workload, capacity of operations, tender prices and the availability of labour and materials. Based on a survey of 600 member firms weighted by region and size. Text accounts for 20%.
Availability	General
Cost	£25
Address	82 New Cavendish Street, London W1M 8AD
Telephone	01 580 5588; Telex: 265763; Fax: 01 631 3872

175

Originator	BUILDING SERVICES RESEARCH AND INFORMATION ASSOCIATION (BSRIA)
Title	BSRIA STATISTICS BULLETIN, quarterly. 1976–
Coverage	Market review of heating, ventilating, air conditioning, electrical and plumbing services plus forecasts up to 18 months ahead of sales of heating equipment. Also a general review of housebuilding and a special profile each quarter on a specific product. Based on Central Government sources (45%), BSRIA's own data (35%) and other sources (20%). Some text (20%).
Availability	General
Cost	£85
Comments	ISSN 0308 6224. Has also published a report on the domestic boiler market (1984) which may be updated.
Address	Old Bracknell Lane West, Bracknell RG12 4AH
Telephone	0344 426511; Telex: 848288; Fax: 0344 487575

176

Originator	BUILDING SOCIETIES ASSOCIATION
Title	HOUSING BULLETIN, quarterly

Coverage   Data on loans by societies, assets, advances, new commitments,
              mortgages, house prices etc.

Availability General
Cost   £15
Comments   ISSN 0261 6394. Various other reports also produced.
Address   3 Savile Row, London W1X 1AF
Telephone   01 437 0655; Telex: 24538; Fax: 01 734 6416

177

Originator   BUILDING SOCIETIES ASSOCIATION

Title   BUILDING SOCIETY FACTBOOK, annual
Coverage   Annual report on the activities of societies with data on loans,
              assets, mortgages, commitments etc.

Availability General
Cost   £5
Comments   ISSN 0266 4828. Various other reports also produced.
Address   3 Savile Row, London W1X 1AF
Telephone   01 437 0655; Telex: 24538; Fax: 01 734 6416

178

Originator   BURTON UPON TRENT AND DISTRICT CHAMBER OF
              COMMERCE AND INDUSTRY

Title   ECONOMIC SURVEY, quarterly
Coverage   General statistics on the local trends in manufacturing, labour,
              cashflow and investment. Based on a survey of a cross-section of
              Chamber members.

Availability General
Cost   £3 per copy plus p+p
Address   158 Derby Street, Burton upon Trent, Staffordshire DE14 2NZ
Telephone   0283 63761; Fax: 0283 510753

179

Originator   BUSINESS AND TRADE STATISTICS LTD

Title   BETTING AND GAMING BULLETIN, monthly. January 1987–
Coverage   Receipts from betting and gaming duties by type of betting and
              gaming. Based entirely on Central Government data.

Availability General
Cost   £12
Comments   Also available on tape, discs.
Address   Lancaster House, More Lane, Esher KT10 8AP
Telephone   0372 63121; Telex: 8951417; Fax: 0372 66365

180

Originator	BUSINESS AND TRADE STATISTICS LTD
Title	INDUSTRIAL ECONOMIC INDICATORS, monthly. January 1988–
Coverage	Data on up to 300 industrial sectors with information on 60 variables. Based entirely on Central Government data.
Availability	General
Cost	From £100 depending on the number of industries, variables etc.
Comments	Also available on tape, discs.
Address	Lancaster House, More Lane, Esher KT10 8AP
Telephone	0372 63121; Telex: 8951417; Fax: 0372 66365

181

Originator	BUSINESS AND TRADE STATISTICS LTD
Title	SPIRITS BULLETIN, monthly. January 1987–
Coverage	Home production, imports and total clearances from bond of whisky, rum, cognac and gin. Based entirely on Central Government data.
Availability	General
Cost	£18
Comments	Also available on tape, discs.
Address	Lancaster House, More Lane, Esher KT10 8AP
Telephone	0372 63121; Telex: 8951417; Fax: 0372 66365

182

Originator	BUSINESS AND TRADE STATISTICS LTD
Title	UK IMPORTS AND EXPORTS, monthly. January 1987–
Coverage	Trade data on over 11,000 products, 250 trading partner countries and 100 ports of entry and exit. Based on Central Government data and appointed as an official agent of HM Customs and Excise.
Availability	General
Cost	From £6 per month depending on the amount and type of data
Comments	Also available on tapes, disc.
Address	Lancaster House, More Lane, Esher KT10 8AP
Telephone	0372 63121; Telex: 8951417; Fax: 0372 66365

183

Originator	BUSINESS AND TRADE STATISTICS LTD
Title	UK MARKET SIZE, annual. 1976–

Coverage   Output data for approximately 4000 separate products covering all
                  manufacturing industry. 3 years figures by value and volume where
                  available. Based almost entirely on Central Government data.

Availability General
Cost   £120
Comments   Data also available on tape, discs.
Address   Lancaster House, More Lane, Esher KT10 8AP
Telephone   0372 63121; Telex: 8951417; Fax: 0372 66365

184

Originator   BUSINESS AND TRADE STATISTICS LTD

Title   WINE BULLETIN, monthly. January 1987–
Coverage   The quantities released from bond of various types of wine. Based
                  entirely on Central Government data.

Availability General
Cost   £18
Comments   Also available on tape, discs.
Address   Lancaster House, More Lane, Esher KT10 8AP
Telephone   0372 63121; Telex: 8951417; Fax: 0372 66365

185

Originator   BUSINESS EQUIPMENT AND INFORMATION TECH-
                  NOLOGY ASSOCIATION

Title   ANNUAL REVIEW, annual
Coverage   An annual review of the sector including statistics on sales,
                  turnover, employment etc. Based on a survey of member and
                  non-member companies.

Availability General
Cost   Free
Address   8 Southampton Place, London WC1A 2EF
Telephone   01 405 6233; Telex: 297083

186

Originator   CABINET MAKER AND RETAIL FURNISHER

Title   BUSINESS AT A GLANCE, monthly in a weekly journal
Coverage   Furniture retail prices, retail sales, producer prices, orders and
                  deliveries, carpet output and soft furnishings sales. Most of the
                  statistics originate from Central Government sources and usually
                  cover the previous month.

Availability General
Cost   £50 and £1.30 plus p+p for a single issue

Comments	ISSN 007 9278
Address	Benn Publications, Sovereign Way, Tonbridge, Kent TN9 1RW
Telephone	0732 364422; Telex: 95162; Fax: 0732 361534

187

Originator	CABINET MAKER AND RETAIL FURNISHER
Title	IMPORT/EXPORT TRENDS IN FURNITURE, quarterly in a weekly journal
Coverage	Imports and exports of furniture by major geographical regions with a commentary. Based entirely on Central Government statistics.
Availability	General
Cost	£50 or £1.30 plus p+p for a single issue
Comments	ISSN 0007 9278
Address	Benn Publications, Sovereign Way, Tonbridge, Kent TN9 1RW
Telephone	0732 364422; Telex: 95162; Fax: 0732 361534

188

Originator	CACI
Title	ACORN PROFILES/MONICA CLASSIFICATION/ SHOPPING CENTRES PLANNER, continuous
Coverage	Various demographic profiles and models for different geographical areas based on the company's own research and Central Government population data. Has also produced an update for 1986 of the 1981 Census Small Area Statistics (SAS).
Availability	General
Cost	Depends on the range and nature of the data required
Comments	Various statistics available in machine readable form including SAS data, JUVOS unemployment data, electoral roll, market sizes.
Address	59/62 High Holborn, London WC1V 6DX
Telephone	01 404 0834; Telex: 295446; Fax: 01 831 8820

189

Originator	CADBURY LTD
Title	CADBURY CONFECTIONERY MARKET REVIEW, annual
Coverage	Figures for recent years on the confectionery market with data on specific sectors, e.g. chocolate, sugar, seasonal etc. Also data on key brands, trade sector performance, advertising, the consumer and market innovations. A general commentary is accompanied by various graphs and tables but no sources are acknowledged.
Availability	General

63   **190–192**

Cost	£1.50
Address	PO Box 12, Bournville, Birmingham B30 2LU
Telephone	021 458 2000; Telex: 338011; Fax: 021 458 2660

190

Originator	CAMBRIDGE ECONOMETRICS (1985) LTD
Title	UK LONG TERM FORECASTING SERVICE, continuous
Coverage	Forecasts up to 15 years ahead for the economy and for 41 sectors with information on employment, output, prices, investment etc. Also forecasts for 49 types of consumer expenditure, 10 investment categories and by region.
Availability	Members
Cost	£3,750
Comments	Data available on disc.
Address	PO Box 114, St Andrew's Street, Cambridge CB2 3AX
Telephone	0223 460760; Telex: 265871; Fax: 0223 66274

191

Originator	CAMBRIDGESHIRE COUNTY COUNCIL
Title	CAMBRIDGESHIRE COMPUTER REGISTER, annual. 1982
Coverage	A list of all firms in the area engaged in the computer business. An accompanying statistical analysis covers the annual change in the sector by district, type of business and employment. The directory currently covers 445 businesses. The accompanying report has a detailed commentary (60%).
Availability	General
Cost	Free (statistical analysis), £5 plus p+p for the register
Address	Research Group, Shire Hall, Castle Hill, Cambridge CB3 0AP
Telephone	0223 317204; Fax: 0223 317201

192

Originator	CAMBRIDGESHIRE COUNTY COUNCIL
Title	CAMBRIDGESHIRE POPULATION ESTIMATES, annual. 1975–
Coverage	Parish and district population estimates produced each Spring/Summer for Cambridgeshire. Based on a Council survey (75%) plus data from the local health authority (25%).
Availability	General
Cost	£2.50
Address	Research Group, Shire Hall, Castle Hill, Cambridge CB3 0AP
Telephone	0223 317204; Fax: 0223 317201

193

Originator	CAMBRIDGESHIRE COUNTY COUNCIL
Title	HOUSE PRICES IN CAMBRIDGESHIRE, annual. 1983–
Coverage	House prices, based on advertisements in the local press, with data by districts, rural areas, urban areas, property type, age and size. The survey excludes new property. Some supporting text (50%).
Availability	General
Cost	£2.50
Comments	Produced in December each year.
Address	Research Group, Shire Hall, Castle Hill, Cambridge CB3 0AP
Telephone	0223 317204; Fax: 0223 317201

194

Originator	CAMBRIDGESHIRE COUNTY COUNCIL
Title	INDUSTRIAL NEWS IN CAMBRIDGESHIRE, monthly. 1982–
Coverage	Identifies new, expanding and contracting business sectors in Cambridgeshire primarily using information from local press sources. Analysed by SIC and the CODOT occupation classifications with a geographical split based on employment service areas.
Availability	General
Cost	£18, or £1.50 for a single issue
Address	Research Group, Shire Hall, Castle Hill, Cambridge CB3 0AP
Telephone	0223 317204; Fax: 0223 317201

195

Originator	CAMBRIDGESHIRE COUNTY COUNCIL
Title	MANUFACTURING EMPLOYMENT IN CAMBRIDGESHIRE, biennial. 1985–
Coverage	Analysis of employment by sector of manufacturing in Cambridgeshire and recent changes. Based on a 100% telephone survey of companies taken from the 'Directory of Commerce and Industry in Cambridgeshire' published by the Council. Some supporting text (50%).
Availability	General
Cost	Free
Address	Research Group, Shire Hall, Castle Hill, Cambridge CB3 0AP
Telephone	0223 317204; Fax: 0223 317201

65

196

Originator	CAMBRIDGESHIRE COUNTY COUNCIL
Title	UNEMPLOYMENT IN CAMBRIDGESHIRE, quarterly
Coverage	Provides ward-based unemployment figures and rate for Cambridgeshire. Includes age and duration statistics and recent time series. Based on Central Government data.
Availability	General
Cost	Free
Address	Research Group, Shire Hall, Castle Hill, Cambridge CB3 0AP
Telephone	0223 317204; Fax: 0223 317201

197

Originator	CAMPBELL NEILL & CO. LTD
Title	SCOTCH WHISKY INDUSTRY REVIEW, annual. 1976–
Coverage	Details of consumption, brand sales for 130 brands in the UK and overseas, production, costs, stocks, prices, and profit margins. Also includes a list of distillers. A combination of the company's own data (50%), Central Government statistics (30%) and other sources (20%). A supporting commentary (50%).
Availability	General
Cost	£175
Address	Stock Exchange House, 7 Nelson Mandela Place, Glasgow G2 1JN
Telephone	041 248 6271; Fax: 041 221 5962

198

Originator	CAN MAKERS INFORMATION SERVICE
Title	CAN MAKERS REPORT, biennial. 1981–
Coverage	Data on the beer and soft drinks markets plus other sections on consumer and retailer attitudes to packaging and resource management and recycling. Mainly based on the Service's own research (70%) with some data from other non-official sources (30%). About half the report is text.
Availability	General
Cost	Free
Comments	The service also produces regular press releases with statistics.
Address	36 Grosvenor Gardens, London SW1W 0ED
Telephone	01 629 9621; Telex: 886827; Fax: 01 730 9364

199

Originator	CAPEL, JAMES AND CO.
Title	MONTHLY ECONOMIC SIGNALS, monthly
Coverage	Data for the latest month, where available, and for the previous 12 months. Topics covered include inflation, PSBR, trade, earnings, banking etc.
Availability	Researchers and clients
Cost	Free
Comments	Various international publications also produced. Screen services on Reuters, Telerate and Topic.
Address	6 Bevis Marks, London EC3A 7JQ
Telephone	01 621 0011; Telex: 888866; Fax: 01 621 0496

200

Originator	CAPEL, JAMES AND CO.
Title	UK ECONOMIC ASSESSMENT, monthly
Coverage	Forecasts for inflation, PSBR, monetary aggregates, interest rates, balance of payments, sterling, corporate profits, consumer spending, capital investment and unemployment. Forecasts 1-2 years ahead. Also includes feature articles, a world summary and summary data for the last 10 years. Text covers 40%.
Availability	Researchers and clients
Cost	Free
Comments	Various international publications also produced. Screen services on Reuters, Telerate and Topic.
Address	6 Bevis Marks, London EC3A 7JQ
Telephone	01 621 0011; Telex: 888866; Fax: 01 621 0496

201

Originator	CAPEL, JAMES AND CO.
Title	WEEKLY GILT EDGED DATA SHEET, weekly
Coverage	Interest rates, prices and yields for a variety of stocks, mainly Government stocks. Also includes exchange rates, treasury bills, current rates on deposit to local authorities, trade data etc. Gives international comparisons.
Availability	Researchers and clients
Cost	Free
Comments	International publications also available. Screen services on Reuters, Telerate and Topic.
Address	6 Bevis Marks, London EC3A 7JQ
Telephone	01 621 0011; Telex: 88866; Fax: 01 621 0496

202

Originator   CAPITAL RADIO

Title   CAPITAL AUDIENCE, bi-annual. 1984–
Coverage   Statistics covering listener profiles, i.e. numbers, characteristics etc. for Capital programmes and listener behaviour. Based on non-official sources with a large amount of supporting text (80%).

Availability General
Cost   Free
Address   356 Euston Road, London NW1 3BW
Telephone   01 388 6801; Telex: 21365; Fax: 01 380 6150

203

Originator   CAPITAL RADIO

Title   CAPITAL MARKETING, bi-annual. 1983–
Coverage   General statistics on population trends, households, consumer expenditure and retailing in the London area. Based largely on a variety of non-official sources (80%) with some Central Government data (20%). A small amount of supporting commentary (20%).

Availability General
Cost   Free
Address   356 Euston Road, London NW1 3BW
Telephone   01 388 6801; Telex: 21365; Fax: 01 380 6150

204

Originator   CARPET AND FLOORCOVERINGS REVIEW

Title   CARPET IMPORT STATISTICS, every 6 weeks in a bi-monthly journal
Coverage   Statistics on the imports of tufted carpets by country into the UK. Based on data from HM Customs and Excise. Usually published 2 months after the month to which the data refers.

Availability General
Cost   £36
Comments   ISSN 0263 4236. Also publish regular surveys on wholesaling and retailing trends for carpets.
Address   Benn Publications, Sovereign Way, Tonbridge TN9 1RW
Telephone   0732 364422; Telex: 95162; Fax: 0732 361534

205

Originator	CARRICK JAMES MARKET RESEARCH
Title	CHILDRENS AND YOUTH OMNIBUS SURVEY, monthly
Coverage	Continuous survey of children and teenagers based on a sample of 2000 per month. Various syndicated and subscriber questions asked on behaviour, opinions, spending etc.
Availability	General
Cost	Varies according to the range of questions/information required
Address	11 Great Marlborough Street, London W1V 1DE
Telephone	01 734 7171; Telex: 21879

206

Originator	CATERER AND HOTELKEEPER
Title	CATERER AND HOTELKEEPER/GALLUP SURVEY OF MENUS, biennial in a weekly journal
Coverage	A sample survey of visitors to restaurants at lunchtime and in the evening with data on the most popular starters, main courses and sweets, changes from the previous survey and general trends in eating out.
Availability	General
Cost	£58, or £1 for a single issue
Comments	ISSN 0008 7777. The latest survey was published in the issue for 22 October 1987.
Address	Reed Publishing, Quadrant House, The Quadrant, Sutton SM2 5AS
Telephone	01 661 3500; Telex: 892084; Fax: 01 661 8973

207

Originator	CATERER AND HOTELKEEPER
Title	FOOD PRICES, weekly in a weekly journal
Coverage	Wholesale prices of vegetables, fruit, meat, poultry and fish based on data collected by the journal. A small amount of text accompanies the statistics (10%).
Availability	General
Cost	£58, or £1 for a single issue
Comments	ISSN 0008 7777
Address	Reed Publishing, Quadrant House, The Quadrant, Sutton SM2 5AS
Telephone	01 661 3500; Telex: 892084; Fax: 01 661 8973

208

Originator	CCN SYSTEMS LTD
Title	MOSAIC, continuous
Coverage	Statistical packages covering population and related data with specific local areas and target groups. Based on Central Government data.
Availability	General
Cost	Depends on the range of data required
Address	Talbot House, Talbot Street, Nottingham NG1 5HS
Telephone	0602 410888

209

Originator	CEMENT ADMIXTURES ASSOCIATION
Title	STATISTICAL RETURN, bi-annual
Coverage	Sales by weight and value for a variety of admixtures based on a survey of members.
Availability	Members
Cost	Free
Address	2A High Street, Hythe, Southampton SO4 6YW
Telephone	0703 842765

210

Originator	CENTRAL ELECTRICITY GENERATING BOARD
Title	CEGB ANNUAL REPORT, annual. 1958–
Coverage	Includes statistics on the generation and transmission of electricity. Based on the Board's own data and including a large amount of text (80%).
Availability	General
Cost	£2
Address	Sudbury House, 15 Newgate Street, London EC1A 7AU
Telephone	01 634 5111; Telex: 883141; Fax: 01 634 6628

211

Originator	CENTRAL ELECTRICITY GENERATING BOARD
Title	CEGB STATISTICAL YEARBOOK, annual. 1964–
Coverage	Includes data on financial results, operations, plant, power stations and transmission. Based on the Board's own data with a small amount of supporting text (10%). Usually produced 4-5 months after the year to which it relates.

Availability	General
Cost	Free
Address	Sudbury House, 15 Newgate Street, London EC1A 7AY
Telephone	01 634 5111; Telex: 883141; Fax: 01 634 6628

212

Originator	CENTRAL INDEPENDENT TELEVISION
Title	CENTRAL MARKETING MANUAL, regular
Coverage	Various figures on population trends, living standards, leisure, communications, retailing, finance, agriculture, motoring, holidays etc. Mainly based on non-official sources (80%) with some Central Government data (20%).
Availability	General
Cost	Free
Address	35/38 Portman Square, London W1A 2HZ
Telephone	01 486 6688; Telex: 24337

213

Originator	CENTRAL REGIONAL COUNCIL
Title	INFORMATION NOTE, quarterly
Coverage	Mainly regular unemployment statistics but often includes features and statistics on local population characteristics and the local economy.
Availability	General
Cost	Free
Address	Planning, Viewforth, Stirling FK8 2ET
Telephone	0786 73111; Fax: 0786 50802

214

Originator	CENTRAL SERVICES UNIT
Title	COLLEGES AND INSTITUTES OF HIGHER EDUCATION FIRST DEGREE AND HIGHER DIPLOMA STUDENTS, annual. June 1985–
Coverage	Details of employment and first destinations of college graduates by type of work, employer and fields of study. Based on data supplied by various institutions with some supporting text (33%).
Availability	General
Cost	£1.95
Address	Crawford House, Precinct Centre, Manchester M13 9EP
Telephone	061 273 4233; Telex: 666635; Fax: 061 273 6657

215

Originator	CENTRAL SERVICES UNIT
Title	CSU STATISTICAL QUARTERLY, quarterly
Coverage	Graduate vacancies by type of employer, type of work, degree discipline and salaries associated with these groups. Data taken from samples based on CSU's 'Current Vacancies' lists. Some supporting commentary (30%).
Availability	General
Cost	£20
Address	Crawford House, Precinct Centre, Manchester M13 9EP
Telephone	061 273 4233; Telex: 666635; Fax: 061 273 6657

216

Originator	CENTRAL SERVICES UNIT
Title	OUTPUT OF COLLEGES BY INSTITUTION AND DISCIPLINE, annual
Coverage	Data on all disciplines divided according to domicile and sex with figures for individual colleges. Based on data supplied by the various institutions.
Availability	General
Cost	£6.60
Address	Crawford House, Precinct Centre, Manchester M13 9EP
Telephone	061 273 4233; Telex: 666635; Fax: 061 273 6657

217

Originator	CENTRAL SERVICES UNIT
Title	OUTPUT OF POLYTECHNICS BY INSTITUTION AND DISCIPLINE, annual
Coverage	Data on all disciplines divided according to domicile and sex with data for individual polytechnics. Based on data supplied by the various institutions.
Availability	General
Cost	£6.60
Address	Crawford House, Precinct Centre, Manchester M13 9EP
Telephone	061 273 4233; Telex: 666635; Fax: 061 273 6657

218

Originator	CENTRAL SERVICES UNIT
Title	OUTPUT OF UK UNIVERSITIES BY INSTITUTION AND DISCIPLINE, annual

Coverage	Data on all disciplines divided according to domicile and sex with figures for individual universities. Based on data supplied by the various institutions.
Availability	General
Cost	£6.60
Address	Crawford House, Precinct Centre, Manchester M13 9EP
Telephone	061 273 4233; Telex: 666635; Fax: 061 273 6657

219

Originator	CENTRAL SERVICES UNIT
Title	POLYTECHNIC FIRST DEGREE AND HIGHER DIPLOMA STUDENTS, annual
Coverage	Details of destinations and employment of polytechnic graduates by type of work, employer and fields of study. Comparative figures for preceding years and longer trends. Based on data supplied by various institutions and some supporting text (33%)
Availability	General
Cost	£1.95
Address	Crawford House, Precinct Centre, Manchester M13 9EP
Telephone	061 273 4233; Telex: 666635; Fax: 061 273 6657

220

Originator	CENTRAL SERVICES UNIT
Title	SUPPLY OF POLYTECHNIC GRADUATES: TRENDS AND PREDICTIONS, annual. November 1986–
Coverage	Output of polytechnic first degree graduates over a 6-year period and the output of specific disciplines within 3 main interest groups: engineering, science and administration and business trends. Supply of polytechnic graduates available for employment. Based on a combination of CSU data (50%) and Central Government data (50%). Some supporting text (40%).
Availability	General
Cost	£6.60
Address	Crawford House, Precinct Centre, Manchester M13 9EP
Telephone	061 273 4233; Telex: 666635; Fax: 061 273 6657

221

Originator	CENTRAL SERVICES UNIT
Title	SUPPLY OF UNIVERSITY GRADUATES: TRENDS AND PREDICTIONS, annual

Coverage   Output of university first degree graduates over a 6-year period and the output of specific disciplines within 3 main interest groups: engineering, science and administration and business trends. Supply of university graduates available for employment. Based on CSU data (50%) and Central Government statistics (50%). Some supporting text (40%).

Availability General
Cost   £6.60
Address   Crawford House, Precinct Centre, Manchester M13 9EP
Telephone   061 273 4233; Telex: 666635; Fax: 061 273 6657

222

Originator CENTRAL SERVICES UNIT

Title   UNIVERSITY GRADUATES: SUMMARY OF FIRST DESTI-NATION AND EMPLOYMENT, annual
Coverage   Supply of graduates and those entering employment by employer, type of work and fields of study. Comparative figures for preceding year and longer trends. Based on data supplied by various institutions and some supporting text (33%).

Availability General
Cost   £1.95
Comments   Produced in conjunction with the Association of Graduates Careers Advisory Services (AGCAS).
Address   Crawford House, Precinct Centre, Manchester M13 9EP
Telephone   061 273 4233; Telex: 666635; Fax: 061 273 6657

223

Originator CENTRE FOR CONSTRUCTION MARKET INFORMATION (CCMI)

Title   BUILDING CENTRE READERSHIP SURVEY, biennial. 1983–
Coverage   Magazine, newspaper and product card readership among architects, quantity surveyors, building surveyors and construction industry managers. Also data on the use of new technology. Data by sex, age, function, job description, project size etc. Latest survey based on 1,726 analysed responses, a 44% response rate.

Availability General
Cost   £175
Address   26 Store Street, London WC1E 7BT
Telephone   01 580 4949; Fax: 01 580 9641

224

Originator	CENTRE FOR CONSTRUCTION MARKET INFORMATION (CCMI)
Title	BUILDING CENTRE TRENDS OF TRADE SURVEY, bi-annual. 1988–
Coverage	Deliveries, factors, prices, costs, cost movements, sectors and value of sales for 61 types of building materials and components in 5 main supply categories. Gives data for the last 6 months and estimates for the next 6 months. Based on CCMI's own survey with a small amount of supporting text (10%).
Availability	General
Cost	£65
Comments	First published in Spring 1988 with a second issue in Autumn 1988. Sponsored by the Building Centre Group.
Address	26 Store Street, London WC1E 7BT
Telephone	01 580 4949; Fax: 01 580 9641

225

Originator	CENTRE FOR CONSTRUCTION MARKET INFORMATION (CCMI)
Title	OFFICE CONSTRUCTION IN CENTRAL LONDON, biennial. November 1986–
Coverage	Data on the total Central London property market with specific information on total floorspace, development type, projects under construction and planned and projections up to 10 years ahead for all listed projects. Report also contains data on individual projects and an A-Z of companies. Data from various sources (80%) and some original data (20%). Some text (40%).
Availability	General
Cost	£95
Comments	Latest issue – 1988. Also publishes a 'Developer Directory' as a companion to this report at £50.
Address	26 Store Street, London WC1E 7BT
Telephone	01 580 4949; Fax: 01 580 9641

226

Originator	CHARITIES AID FOUNDATION
Title	CHARITY TRENDS, annual
Coverage	Commentary and statistics on the 'givers' and 'receivers'. A number of tables give figures for earlier years. Based largely on the Foundation's own data with a detailed supporting text.
Availability	General

Comments   Previously titled 'Charity Statistics' and just contained statistics
                with no commentary.
Address   48 Pembury Road, Tonbridge TN9 2JD
Telephone   0732 771333; Fax: 0732 350570

227

Originator   CHART ANALYSIS LTD

Title   COMMODITIES, weekly and monthly. 1972–
Coverage   Trends and prices in UK and USA futures markets. Covers over 33
                 different commodities in the food, grain, livestock/meat, industrial
                 softs, metals and money sectors. Based on the company's data.

Availability General
Cost   £570 weekly, £250 monthly
Comments   Also publish reports on European and international stock markets
                 plus currency and interest rate trends and futures.
Address   7 Swallow Street, London W1R 7HD
Telephone   01 439 4961; Telex: 269884; Fax: 01 439 4966

228

Originator   CHART ANALYSIS LTD

Title   UK POINT AND FIGURE LIBRARY, weekly and monthly.
                 1972–
Coverage   Comprehensive coverage of the UK Stock Market by market
                 sector. Tables cover industry group performance, FT Actuaries
                 Share Indices, British funds, money rates and indicators. Based on
                 the company's own data.

Availability General
Cost   £935 weekly, £405 monthly
Comments   Also publishes European and International versions and currency
                 and interest rate trends and futures.
Address   7 Swallow Street, London W12 7HD
Telephone   01 439 4961; Telex: 269884; Fax: 01 439 4966

229

Originator   CHARTERED INSTITUTE OF PUBLIC FINANCE AND
                 ACCOUNTANCY (CIPFA)

Title   ADMINISTRATION OF JUSTICE – ACTUALS, annual
Coverage   Expenditure and income figures for both magistrates' and coroners'
                 courts per thousand population. Based on data collected by CIPFA.

Availability General
Cost   £15. Total subscription to all publications also available.

Comments	'Estimates' publication on this topic is also produced – £15. Data also available on disc. Statistical inquiries dealt with.
Address	3 Robert Street, London WC2N 6BH
Telephone	01 930 3456

230

Originator	CHARTERED INSTITUTE OF PUBLIC FINANCE AND ACCOUNTANCY (CIPFA)
Title	AIRPORTS STATISTICS – ACTUALS, annual
Coverage	An analysis of the revenue accounts and balance sheets of local authority airports plus a range of non-financial information. Based on data collected from the local authorities by CIPFA.
Availability	General
Cost	£33. Total subscription to all publications is also available.
Comments	Data also available on disc. Statistical inquiries dealt with.
Address	3 Robert Street, London WC2N 6BH
Telephone	01 930 3456

231

Originator	CHARTERED INSTITUTE OF PUBLIC FINANCE AND ACCOUNTANCY (CIPFA)
Title	ARCHIVES – ESTIMATES, annual
Coverage	Statistics on the organization and financing of archives based on returns from local authorities collected by CIPFA.
Availability	General
Cost	£15. Total subscription to all publications is also available.
Comments	Data also available on disc. Statistical inquiries dealt with.
Address	3 Robert Street, London WC2N 6BH
Telephone	01 930 3456

232

Originator	CHARTERED INSTITUTE OF PUBLIC FINANCE AND ACCOUNTANCY (CIPFA)
Title	BLOCK GRANT STATISTICS – ESTIMATES, annual
Coverage	Total estimated expenditure for each local authority and the parameters necessary to calculate Block Grant in the current financial year and calculated entitlements to such grants. Based on data collected and calculations by CIPFA.
Availability	General
Cost	£25. Total subscription to all publications also available.
Comments	Data also available on disc. Statistical inquiries dealt with.

Address   3 Robert Street, London WC2N 6BH
Telephone   01 930 3456

233

Originator   CHARTERED INSTITUTE OF PUBLIC FINANCE AND ACCOUNTANCY (CIPFA)

Title   CAPITAL EXPENDITURE AND DEBT FINANCING STATISTICS – ACTUALS, annual
Coverage   Analysis of capital expenditure, capital receipts and debt statistics for individual local authorities in England, Wales, Scotland and Northern Ireland. Based on data collected by CIPFA.

Availability General
Cost   £33. Total subscription to all publications also available.
Comments   Data also available on disc. Statistical inquiries dealt with.
Address   3 Robert Street, London WC2N 6BH
Telephone   01 930 3456

234

Originator   CHARTERED INSTITUTE OF PUBLIC FINANCE AND ACCOUNTANCY (CIPFA)

Title   CEMETRIES AND CREMATORIA – ACTUALS, annual
Coverage   Expenditure, income, fees and non-financial data on cemetries and crematoria around the country. Based on data collected by CIPFA.

Availability General
Cost   £25. Total subscription to all publications also available.
Comments   Data also available on disc. Statistical inquiries dealt with.
Address   3 Robert Street, London WC2N 6BH
Telephone   01 930 3456

235

Originator   CHARTERED INSTITUTE OF PUBLIC FINANCE AND ACCOUNTANCY (CIPFA)

Title   DIRECT LABOUR ORGANISATIONS – ACTUALS, annual
Coverage   Financial, organizational and related data on direct labour organizations (DLOs) in specific local authorities. Based on data collected by CIPFA.

Availability General
Cost   £33. Total subscription to all publications also available.
Comments   Data also available on disc. Statistical inquiries dealt with.
Address   3 Robert Street, London WC2N 6BH
Telephone   01 930 3456

236

Originator	CHARTERED INSTITUTE OF PUBLIC FINANCE AND ACCOUNTANCY (CIPFA)
Title	EDUCATION: SCHOOL MEALS – ACTUALS, annual
Coverage	Financial and other data on the provision of school meals by local authority area. Based on data collected by CIPFA.
Availability	General
Cost	£15. Total subscription to all publications also available.
Comments	Data also available on disc. Statistical inquiries dealt with.
Address	3 Robert Street, London WC2N 6BH
Telephone	01 930 3456

237

Originator	CHARTERED INSTITUTE OF PUBLIC FINANCE AND ACCOUNTANCY (CIPFA)
Title	EDUCATION STATISTICS – ACTUALS, annual. 1970–
Coverage	Non-financial data on pupil, school and teacher numbers and financial data split by type of school and local authority area. Unit costs per pupil and totals for schools, teachers and pupils are also given. Based on Central Government data.
Availability	General
Cost	£25. Total subscription to all publications also available.
Comments	'Estimates' publication also produced – £33. Data also available on disc. Statistical inquiries dealt with.
Address	3 Robert Street, London WC2N 6BH
Telephone	01 930 3456

238

Originator	CHARTERED INSTITUTE OF PUBLIC FINANCE AND ACCOUNTANCY (CIPFA)
Title	EDUCATION UNIT COSTS – ACTUALS, annual
Coverage	Institutional costs, pupil and student support, capital costs, salary costs, pupil teacher ratios, recurrent expenditure and university costs. Based on Central Government data.
Availability	General
Cost	£15. Total subscription to all publications also available.
Comments	Data also available on disc. Statistical inquiries dealt with.
Address	3 Robert Street, London WC2N 6BH
Telephone	01 930 3456

239

Originator	CHARTERED INSTITUTE OF PUBLIC FINANCE AND ACCOUNTANCY (CIPFA)
Title	ENVIRONMENTAL HEALTH – ACTUALS, annual
Coverage	Financial and other data relating to environmental health in specific local authority areas. Based on data collected by CIPFA.
Availability	General
Cost	£25. Total subscription to all publications also available.
Comments	Data also available on disc. Statistical inquiries dealt with.
Address	3 Robert Street, London WC2N 6BH
Telephone	01 930 3456

240

Originator	CHARTERED INSTITUTE OF PUBLIC FINANCE AND ACCOUNTANCY (CIPFA)
Title	FINANCE AND GENERAL STATISTICS – ESTIMATES, annual. 1976–
Coverage	Summary information on local authority income and expenditure and data for each local authority in England and Wales. Based on estimated figures collected by CIPFA with additional data on estimated income and expenditure per head of the population.
Availability	General
Cost	£50. Total subscription to all publications also available.
Comments	Data also available on disc. Statistical inquiries dealt with.
Address	3 Robert Street, London WC2N 6BH
Telephone	01 930 3456

241

Originator	CHARTERED INSTITUTE OF PUBLIC FINANCE AND ACCOUNTANCY (CIPFA)
Title	FIRE STATISTICS – ACTUALS, annual
Coverage	Summary data on fire service income and expenditure and similar figures for each local authority and per thousand population. Figures are also given for fire stations, training, applications, return of calls, inspections and manpower. Based on data collected by CIPFA.
Availability	General
Cost	£20. Total subscription to all publications also available.
Comments	'Estimates' publication also available – £20. Data also available on disc. Statistical inquiries dealt with.
Address	3 Robert Street, London WC2N 6BH
Telephone	01 930 3456

242

Originator	CHARTERED INSTITUTE OF PUBLIC FINANCE AND ACCOUNTANCY (CIPFA)
Title	HIGHWAYS AND TRANSPORTATION STATISTICS – ACTUALS, annual
Coverage	The final outturn figures are shown for highways and transportation expenditure by county councils in England and Wales. Based on data collected by CIPFA.
Availability	General
Cost	£25. Total subscription to all publications also available.
Comments	'Estimates' publication also available – £25. Data also available on disc.
Address	3 Robert Street, London WC2N 6BH
Telephone	01 930 3456

243

Originator	CHARTERED INSTITUTE OF PUBLIC FINANCE AND ACCOUNTANCY (CIPFA)
Title	HOMELESSNESS STATISTICS – ACTUALS, annual
Coverage	A financial survey of the operations of the Housing (Homeless Persons) Act with data for individual local authorities. Based on data collected by CIPFA.
Availability	General
Cost	£25. Total subscription to all publications also available.
Comments	Data also available on disc. Statistical inquiries dealt with.
Address	3 Robert Street, London WC2N 6BH
Telephone	01 930 3456

244

Originator	CHARTERED INSTITUTE OF PUBLIC FINANCE AND ACCOUNTANCY (CIPFA)
Title	HOUSING RENTS – ACTUALS, annual
Coverage	An analysis of the housing stock by age and type, average weekly net unrebated rents and rebates and allowances for housing authorities in England and Wales. Summary tables give data by economic planning regions. Based on data collected by CIPFA.
Availability	General
Cost	£33. Total subscription to all publications also available.
Comments	Data also available on disc. Statistical inquiries dealt with.
Address	3 Robert Street, London WC2N 6BH
Telephone	01 930 3456

245

Originator	CHARTERED INSTITUTE OF PUBLIC FINANCE AND ACCOUNTANCY (CIPFA)
Title	HOUSING REVENUE ACCOUNT STATISTICS – ACTUALS, annual. 1950–
Coverage	The final outturn figures of Housing Revenue Account income and expenditure are shown in total and for each housing authority in England and Wales. Details are also given of rents, arrears, number of dwellings, average rates of loan interest and council house sales. Based on a combination of CIPFA data and Central Government statistics.
Availability	General
Cost	£33. Total subscription to all publications also available.
Comments	'Estimates' publication also produced – £25. Data also available on disc. Statistical inquiries dealt with.
Address	3 Robert Street, London WC2N 6BH
Telephone	01 930 3456

246

Originator	CHARTERED INSTITUTE OF PUBLIC FINANCE AND ACCOUNTANCY (CIPFA)
Title	LEISURE AND RECREATION STATISTICS – ESTIMATES, annual
Coverage	Estimated expenditure and income on sports and recreation, cultural and other facilities by local authority area. Based on data collected by CIPFA.
Availability	General
Cost	£33. Total subscription to all publications also available.
Comments	Data also available on disc. Statistical inquiries dealt with.
Address	3 Robert Street, London WC2N 6BH
Telephone	01 930 3456

247

Originator	CHARTERED INSTITUTE OF PUBLIC FINANCE AND ACCOUNTANCY (CIPFA)
Title	LEISURE CHARGES – ACTUALS, annual
Coverage	Sample survey of charges for leisure centre facilities, swimming pools and outdoor sports. Based on a sample of 150 local authorities.
Availability	General
Cost	£25. Total subscription to all publications also available.
Comments	Data also available on disc. Statistical inquiries dealt with.

Address	3 Robert Street, London WC2N 6BH
Telephone	01 930 3456

248

Originator	CHARTERED INSTITUTE OF PUBLIC FINANCE AND ACCOUNTANCY (CIPFA)
Title	LEISURE USAGE – ACTUALS, annual
Coverage	A sample survey of the use made of leisure centre facilities, swimming pools and outdoor sports based on a sample of 150 local authorities.
Availability	General
Cost	£20. Total subscription to all publications also available.
Comments	Data also available on disc. Statistical inquiries dealt with.
Address	3 Robert Street, London WC2N 6BH
Telephone	01 930 3456

249

Originator	CHARTERED INSTITUTE OF PUBLIC FINANCE AND ACCOUNTANCY (CIPFA)
Title	LOCAL GOVERNMENT COMPARATIVE STATISTICS, annual
Coverage	Statistical indicators covering the range of local authority services. Based on a combination of CIPFA data and other non-official sources.
Availability	General
Cost	£33. Total subscription to all publications also available.
Comments	Data also available on disc. Statistical inquiries dealt with.
Address	3 Robert Street, London WC2N 6BH
Telephone	01 930 3456

250

Originator	CHARTERED INSTITUTE OF PUBLIC FINANCE AND ACCOUNTANCY (CIPFA)
Title	LOCAL GOVERNMENT TRENDS, annual. 1973–
Coverage	General data for all local authorities in aggregate on various sectors such as education, health, housing, leisure, social services, transport and industrial development. Also summary data on population, employment, earnings, politics and total expenditure. Based on various sources but mainly Central Government (70%). Supporting text (12%).
Availability	General

Cost	£33. Total subscription to all publications also available.
Comments	Data also available on disc. Statistical inquiries dealt with.
Address	3 Robert Street, London WC2N 6BH
Telephone	01 930 3456

251

Originator	CHARTERED INSTITUTE OF PUBLIC FINANCE AND ACCOUNTANCY (CIPFA)
Title	PERSONAL SOCIAL SERVICES STATISTICS – ACTUALS, annual
Coverage	Analysis of residential, day and community care provision giving gross and net expenditure and the number of clients by local authority area. Expenditure on field work, administration and joint financing is also shown plus a breakdown of the total population by age group. Based on data collected by CIPFA.
Availability	General
Cost	£33. Total subscription to all publications also available.
Comments	'Estimates' publication also produced – £33. Data also available on disc. Statistical inquiries dealt with.
Address	3 Robert Street, London WC2N 6BH
Telephone	01 930 3456

252

Originator	CHARTERED INSTITUTE OF PUBLIC FINANCE AND ACCOUNTANCY (CIPFA)
Title	PLANNING AND DEVELOPMENT – ACTUALS, annual
Coverage	Capital and revenue expenditure on the planning and development functions in summary and by individual local authority. Based on data collected by CIPFA.
Availability	General
Cost	£25. Total subscription to all publications also available.
Comments	'Estimates' publication also available – £25. Data also available on disc. Statistical inquiries dealt with.
Address	3 Robert Street, London WC2N 6BH
Telephone	01 930 3456

253

Originator	CHARTERED INSTITUTE OF PUBLIC FINANCE AND ACCOUNTANCY (CIPFA)
Title	POLICE STATISTICS – ACTUALS, annual

Coverage	Final outturn figures are given for income, expenditure and manpower in total and by individual police force and regional crime squad. Based on data collected by CIPFA.
Availability	General
Cost	£25. Total subscription to all publications also available.
Comments	'Estimates' publication also produced – £25. Data also available on disc. Statistical inquiries dealt with.
Address	3 Robert Street, London WC2N 6BH
Telephone	01 930 3456

254

Originator	CHARTERED INSTITUTE OF PUBLIC FINANCE AND ACCOUNTANCY (CIPFA)
Title	PROBATION – ACTUALS, annual
Coverage	Expenditure and income in the probation service per thousand population aged 15-29 and manpower for the service in England and Wales. Based on data collected by CIPFA.
Availability	General
Cost	£25. Total subscription to all publications also available.
Comments	'Estimates' publication also produced – £25. Data also available on disc. Statistical inquiries dealt with.
Address	3 Robert Street, London WC2N 6BH
Telephone	01 930 3456

255

Originator	CHARTERED INSTITUTE OF PUBLIC FINANCE AND ACCOUNTANCY (CIPFA)
Title	PUBLIC LIBRARY STATISTICS – ACTUALS, annual. 1962–
Coverage	Final outturn figures for income and expenditure, manpower, agency services, books and other stocks and service points are given in total and for each library service in Great Britain and Northern Ireland. Summary tables are included for annual issues and interlibrary loans. Based on data collected by CIPFA.
Availability	General
Cost	£33. Total subscription to all publications also available.
Comments	'Estimates' publication also produced – £15. Data also available on disc. Statistical inquiries dealt with.
Address	3 Robert Street, London WC2N 6BH
Telephone	01 930 3456

256

Originator	CHARTERED INSTITUTE OF PUBLIC FINANCE AND ACCOUNTANCY (CIPFA)
Title	RATE COLLECTION STATISTICS – ACTUALS, annual. 1950–
Coverage	Data on rateable values and rate collection in total and by individual districts and boroughs in England and Wales. Includes details of rate income, arrears, costs and methods of collection, staff involved, number of hereditaments and rateable value by category. Based on data collected by CIPFA.
Availability	General
Cost	£25. Total subscription to all publications also available.
Comments	Data also available on disc. Statistical inquiries dealt with.
Address	3 Robert Street, London WC2N 6BH
Telephone	01 930 3456

257

Originator	CHARTERED INSTITUTE OF PUBLIC FINANCE AND ACCOUNTANCY (CIPFA)
Title	RATING REVIEW – (SCOTLAND) – ACTUALS, annual
Coverage	Statistics on rates and rateable values for the regions and districts in Scotland. Based on data collected by CIPFA.
Availability	General
Cost	£6. Total subscription to all publications also available.
Comments	'Estimates' publication also produced – £6. Data also available on disc. Statistical inquiries dealt with.
Address	3 Robert Street, London WC2N 6BH
Telephone	01 930 3456

258

Originator	CHARTERED INSTITUTE OF PUBLIC FINANCE AND ACCOUNTANCY (CIPFA)
Title	SMALLHOLDINGS – ACTUAL, annual
Coverage	Statistics on smallholdings in aggregate and by local authority area. Based on data collected by CIPFA.
Availability	General
Cost	£15. Total subscription to all publications also available.
Comments	Data also available on disc. Statistical inquiries dealt with.
Address	3 Robert Street, London WC2N 6BH
Telephone	01 930 3456

259

Originator CHARTERED INSTITUTE OF PUBLIC FINANCE AND ACCOUNTANCY (CIPFA)

Title TRADING STANDARDS – ACTUALS, annual
Coverage Financial and non-financial data on trading standards departments with data for individual local authorities. Based on data collected by CIPFA.

Availability General
Cost £15. Total subscription to all publications also available.
Comments 'Estimates' publication also available – £15. Data also available on disc. Statistical inquiries dealt with.
Address 3 Robert Street, London WC2N 6BH
Telephone 01 930 3456

260

Originator CHARTERED INSTITUTE OF PUBLIC FINANCE AND ACCOUNTANCY (CIPFA)

Title WASTE COLLECTION – ACTUALS, annual
Coverage Data on waste collection including income and expenditure, staff numbers, charges, quantities collected and methods and frequency of collection. Aggregate data and data by local authority area. Based on data collected by CIPFA.

Availability General
Cost £33. Total subscription to all publications also available.
Comments Data also available on disc. Statistical inquiries dealt with.
Address 3 Robert Street, London WC2N 6BH
Telephone 01 930 3456

261

Originator CHARTERED INSTITUTE OF PUBLIC FINANCE AND ACCOUNTANCY (CIPFA)

Title WASTE DISPOSAL – ACTUALS, annual
Coverage Data on revenue income and expenditure, capital expenditure and financing, treatment methods, waste arising and reclaimed waste by tonnage, vehicle disposals, manpower and unit costs in summary and by local authority area. Based on data collected by CIPFA.

Availability General
Cost £20. Total subscription to all publications also available.
Comments 'Estimates' publication also available – £20. Data also available on disc. Statistical inquiries dealt with.
Address 3 Robert Street, London WC2N 6BH
Telephone 01 930 3456

262

Originator	CHARTERED QUANTITY SURVEYOR
Title	QUARTERLY BUILDING PRICES AND BUILDING COSTS, quarterly in a monthly journal. January 1980–
Coverage	Includes the QSSD index of building tender prices, the PSA building costs index and the measured term contracts index. Data given for a number of years by quarter and month, where available. Based on a combination of official and non-official sources.
Availability	General
Cost	£28, or £2.80 for a single issue
Comments	ISSN 0142 5196. A publication of the Royal Institution of Chartered Surveyors (RICS).
Address	RICS, 12 Great George Street, London SW1P 3AD
Telephone	01 222 7000; Telex: 25212

263

Originator	CHARTERHOUSE PLC
Title	BUSINESS FORECAST, quarterly
Coverage	Economic forecasts up to 1 year ahead for the major economic variables plus a summary of forecasts from other organizations. Forecasts produced by the company (60%) with existing data from Central Government sources (40%). Supporting text takes up 55%.
Availability	General
Cost	Free
Address	1 Paternoster Row, London EC4M 7DH
Telephone	01 248 4000

264

Originator	CHEMICAL INDUSTRIES ASSOCIATION
Title	ECONOMICS BULLETIN, quarterly
Coverage	A general review of the economic situation in the UK chemicals industry usually covering the previous quarter. In one issue per year there is an Investment Intentions Survey.
Availability	General
Cost	£30
Comments	The Association has just started to publish international chemical industry statistics annually.
Address	Kings Building, Smith Square, London SW1P 3JJ
Telephone	01 834 3399; Telex: 916672; Fax: 01 834 4469

265

Originator	CHEMICAL INDUSTRIES ASSOCIATION
Title	UK CHEMICAL INDUSTRY FACTS, annual
Coverage	Includes statistics on industry sales, growth rate, output, capital investment, trade, costs, employees etc. Based largely on Central Government statistics (75%) plus some of the Association's own data (25%).
Availability	General
Cost	Free
Comments	The Association has just started to publish international chemical industry statistics annually.
Address	Kings Building, Smith Square, London SW1P 3JJ
Telephone	01 834 3399; Telex: 916672; Fax: 01 834 4469

266

Originator	CHEMIST AND DRUGGIST
Title	CHEMIST AND DRUGGIST MONTHLY PRICE LIST, monthly supplement to a weekly journal. 1960–
Coverage	Price data for various products sold by chemists. Based on the journal's own survey with prices usually 1 month old.
Availability	General
Cost	£70, part of the subscription to 'Chemist and Druggist'
Comments	A prices supplement is also included in the weekly journal.
Address	Benn Publications, Sovereign Way, Tonbridge TN9 1RW
Telephone	0732 364422; Telex: 95132; Fax: 0732 361534

267

Originator	CHESHIRE COUNTY COUNCIL
Title	CHESHIRE CURRENT FACTS AND FIGURES, monthly April 1977–
Coverage	General data on Cheshire including population trends, the economy, elections, education, social services, housing, transport, environment, countryside, recreation etc. Each monthly update covers a specific topic as new statistics become available. Based on various sources but mainly Central Government.
Availability	General
Cost	£8
Comments	Produced on loose-leaf sheets (binder provided). Also publishes population, unemployment data via Planning Dept.
Address	Research & Intelligence, County Hall, Chester CH1 1SG
Telephone	0244 603800

268

Originator	CIL SYSTEMS LTD
Title	ANNUAL REVIEW OF THE RETAIL MARKET, annual
Coverage	General trends and statistics on the non-food retailing sector with data on sales, industry structure, turnover etc. for the previous 12 months. Based on various sources.
Availability	General
Cost	£15
Address	Fonthill Road, London N4 3HN
Telephone	01 272 0222; Telex: 21610

269

Originator	CINEMA ADVERTISING ASSOCIATION LTD
Title	CAVIAR – CINEMA AND VIDEO INDUSTRY AUDIENCE RESEARCH, annual. November 1983–
Coverage	A national sample survey of over 2,900 people aged 7-64 sponsored by companies within the cinema and video sectors. Investigates cinema going habits and profiles of films seen, both in the cinema and on pre-recorded video cassettes. Survey carried out at 116 randomly selected sampling points in the UK.
Availability	General
Cost	Free to participants. Prices available to others on request
Comments	Survey carried out by Carrick James Market Research. On-line service available to members only.
Address	127 Wardour Street, London W1V 4AD
Telephone	01 439 9531; Fax: 01 439 2395

270

Originator	CINEMA ADVERTISING ASSOCIATION LTD
Title	COVERAGE AND FREQUENCY PROGRAM, annual
Coverage	In 2 parts: national information by age, sex, marital status and social grade; data relating to specific market areas such as ITV areas and counties. Average coverage and frequency for any number of weeks from 1 to 52. Statistics taken from the JICNARS National Readership Survey.
Availability	General
Cost	Free
Address	127 Wardour Street, London W1V 4AD
Telephone	01 439 9531; Fax: 01 439 2395

271

Originator	CINEMA ADVERTISING ASSOCIATION LTD
Title	MASTER LIST OF CINEMAS, annual
Coverage	A list of cinemas arranged alphabetically by county and their advertising rates. Number of screens by ITV area and rates for a week on all screens by county and countries. Based on the Association's own surveys.
Availability	General
Cost	Free
Comments	Although stated as an annual publication no issue has appeared since 1986.
Address	127 Wardour Street, London W1V 4AD
Telephone	01 439 9531; Fax: 01 439 2395

272

Originator	CITY DATA SERVICES LTD
Title	TRADE STATISTICS, continuous
Coverage	Import and export data for all UK traded products by value and volume. Breakdowns available include country of origin, country of destination, port of entry and exit. Appointed as an official agent for HM Customs and Excise Data.
Availability	General
Cost	Varies according to the information required
Comments	Data available on disc, tape and microfiche and an on-line service is being developed.
Address	30 Cursitor Street, London EC4A 1LT
Telephone	01 404 0104; Telex: 26150

273

Originator	CIVIL AVIATION AUTHORITY (CAA)
Title	ACCIDENTS TO AIRCRAFT ON THE BRITISH REGISTER, annual. 1949–
Coverage	Information on specific accidents and aggregate data on accidents by type, aircraft involved, service type, injuries, fatality rates, causes etc. Based on the CAA's own data.
Availability	General
Address	Greville House, 37 Gratton Road, Cheltenham GL50 2BN
Telephone	0242 35151; Fax: 0242 584139

274

Originator	CIVIL AVIATION AUTHORITY (CAA)
Title	UK AIRLINES, annual. 1983–
Coverage	Annual operating, traffic, personnel and financial statistics, based on the CAA's own data with some tables giving historical data over a number of years.
Availability	General
Cost	£9.50
Address	Greville House, 37 Grafton Road, Cheltenham GL50 2BN
Telephone	0242 35151; Fax: 0242 584139

275

Originator	CIVIL AVIATION AUTHORITY (CAA)
Title	UK AIRLINES, monthly. 1983–
Coverage	Operating and traffic statistics for UK airlines by domestic and international services and by types of operations, based on the CAA's own data. Statistics usually cover the previous month.
Availability	General
Cost	£31
Comments	ISSN 0265 0266. Up to 1983 published in 'CAA Monthly Statistics'.
Address	Greville House, 37 Gratton Road, Cheltenham GL50 2BN
Telephone	0242 35151; Fax: 0242 584139

276

Originator	CIVIL AVIATION AUTHORITY (CAA)
Title	UK AIRPORTS, annual. 1983–
Coverage	Annual statistics on UK airport movements, passengers and cargo trends, based on the CAA's own data with some tables containing historical data.
Availability	General
Cost	£9.50
Address	Greville House, 37 Gratton Road, Cheltenham GL50 2BN
Telephone	0242 35151; Fax: 0242 584139

277

Originator	CIVIL AVIATION AUTHORITY (CAA)
Title	UK AIRPORTS, monthly. 1983–
Coverage	Monthly statements of movements, passengers and cargo at UK airports, based on the CCA's own data. Statistics usually cover the previous month.

Availability	General
Cost	£31
Comments	ISSN 0265 0258. Up to 1983 published in 'CAA Monthly Statistics'.
Address	Greville House, 37 Gratton Road, Cheltenham GL50 2BN
Telephone	0242 35151; Fax: 0242 584139

278

Originator	CLEVELAND COUNTY COUNCIL
Title	CLEVELAND 19.. TO 19..: AN ECONOMIC DEMOGRAPHIC AND SOCIAL REVIEW, annual
Coverage	Commentary and statistics on local economic and social trends with data from Central Government and local authority sources. Also a discussion on the impact of new legislation and policy developments. Includes population projections.
Availability	General
Cost	On application
Comments	Various other statistical surveys and occasional reports published by the Council.
Address	Research & Intelligence, Melrose Street, Middlesborough TS1 2QH
Telephone	0642 248155; Fax: 0642 224558

279

Originator	CLEVELAND COUNTY COUNCIL
Title	CLEVELAND EMPLOYMENT REVIEW, quarterly
Coverage	General statistics on employment and unemployment trends in the county, based mainly on Central Government data.
Availability	General
Cost	On application
Comments	Various other statistical surveys and occasional reports published by the Council.
Address	Planning, Municipal Buildings, Middlesborough TS1 2QH
Telephone	0642 248155; Fax: 0642 224558

280

Originator	CLOTHING AND ALLIED PRODUCTS INDUSTRY TRAINING BOARD
Title	ANNUAL REPORT, annual
Coverage	A statistical section gives data on employment trends in the industry with a breakdown by area, company size, sector and sex. Also data on trainees and government grants.

Availability	General
Address	Tower House, Merrion Way, Leeds LS2 8NY
Telephone	0532 441331; Fax: 0532 431822

281

Originator	COMMERCIAL MOTOR
Title	TABLES OF OPERATING COSTS, annual in a supplement published separately from the journal
Coverage	Information on standing charges and running costs for various types of commercial vehicles. Also includes summaries of road tests.
Availability	General
Cost	£5
Comments	Compiled in association with Mercedes Benz.
Address	Reed Business Publishing Ltd, Quadrant House, The Quadrant, Sutton SM2 5AS
Telephone	01 661 3500; Telex: 892084; Fax: 01 661 8973

282

Originator	COMMITTEE OF DIRECTORS OF POLYTECHNICS
Title	FIRST DESTINATIONS OF POLYTECHNIC STUDENTS, annual. 1976–
Coverage	First destinations of those obtaining first degrees and higher diplomas by full-time and sandwich study, analysed by employer category and type of work.
Availability	General
Cost	£10.50
Address	Kirkman House, 12/14 Whitfield Street, London W1P 6AX
Telephone	01 637 9939; Fax: 01 436 4966

283

Originator	COMMITTEE OF DIRECTORS OF POLYTECHNICS
Title	POLYTECHNICS ENROLMENT SURVEY, annual. 1974–
Coverage	Enrolments to advanced courses at 30 polytechnics, analysed by level, subject and mode of study.
Availability	General
Cost	Free
Comments	Published as a press release.
Address	Kirkham House, 12/14 Whitfield Street, London W1P 6AX
Telephone	01 637 9939; Fax: 01 436 4966

284

Originator	COMMITTEE OF LONDON AND SCOTTISH BANKERS (CLSB)
Title	ABSTRACT OF BANKING STATISTICS, annual. 1984–
Coverage	Information covering the member banks of the CLSB. Includes balance sheet data, infrastructure, annual accounts, clearing and credit card statistics and miscellaneous financial statistics. The majority of the data is based on CLSB's own figures with some data from Central Government and other non- official sources. A small amount of text is included.
Availability	General
Cost	Free
Comments	Clearing statistics previously published by CLSB are now published by APACS – see entries 24 and 25.
Address	10 Lombard Street, London EC3V 9AP
Telephone	01 283 8866; Telex: 888364; Fax: 01 283 7037

285

Originator	COMMITTEE OF LONDON AND SCOTTISH BANKERS (CLSB)
Title	ANALYSIS OF LENDING TO UK RESIDENTS BY THE CLSB GROUPS, quarterly. 1974–
Coverage	Industrial sector analysis of lending in sterling and foreign currencies by offices of the CLSB groups. Data taken from figures collected by the CLSB.
Availability	General
Cost	Free
Comments	Clearing statistics previously published by CLSB are now published by APACS – see entries 24 and 25.
Address	10 Lombard Street, London EC3V 9AP
Telephone	01 283 8866, Telex:888364; Fax: 01 283 7037

286

Originator	COMMITTEE OF LONDON AND SCOTTISH BANKERS (CLSB)
Title	BALANCES OF THE CLSB GROUPS, monthly. 1973–
Coverage	Liabilities and assets of offices of the CLSB groups, based on figures collected by CLSB. A brief amount of text supports the data.
Availability	General
Cost	Free
Comments	Clearing statistics previously published by CLSB are now published by APACS – see entries 24 and 25.

Address	10 Lombard Street, London EC3V 9AP
Telephone	01 283 8866; Telex: 888364; Fax: 01 283 7037

287

Originator	COMMITTEE OF LONDON AND SCOTTISH BANKERS (CLSB)
Title	HOUSE PURCHASE FINANCE, quarterly. 1987–
Coverage	Analysis of lending by offices of the CLSB groups to UK residents for house purchase. Data is based on figures collected by CLSB and at present there is one table per issue with a few lines of text.
Availability	General
Cost	Free
Comments	Clearing statistics previously published by CLSB are now published by APACS – see entries 24 and 25.
Address	10 Lombard Street, London EC3V 9AP
Telephone	01 283 8866; Telex: 888364; Fax: 01 283 7037

288

Originator	COMPANY CAR
Title	DATABANK, monthly in a monthly journal
Coverage	Prices of new cars and the standing, running and operating costs of car fleets. Uses data prepared by Fleet Management Services Ltd.
Availability	General
Cost	£25, free to businesses with fleets
Address	Queensway House, 2 Queensway, Redhill RH1 1QS
Telephone	0737 768611; Telex: 948669; Fax: 0737 760564

289

Originator	COMPUTER ECONOMICS LTD
Title	COMPUTER STAFF SALARY SURVEY, bi-annual. 1968–
Coverage	A survey of 50 job descriptions analysed by location, age, experience, areas of responsibility, level of technology and fringe benefits. Survey carried out by Computer Economics. A small commentary (15%) accompanies the data.
Availability	Participants
Cost	£250–£575
Address	Survey House, 51 Portland Road, Kingston-upon-Thames KT1 2SH
Telephone	01 549 8726

290

Originator	COMPUTER WEEKLY
Title	ANNUAL SURVEY OF DATA PROCESSING USERS, annual in a weekly journal
Coverage	A random sample of 10,000 journal subscribers to gather information on systems used and their operation, such as principal applications, source of applications programs, type of industry, programming language used and future acquisition plans. Survey results appear in 2 or 3 issues at the beginning of the year.
Availability	Controlled circulation
Cost	Free
Comments	ISSN 0010 4787. Survey undertaken in association with Datapro. Datapro publish the detailed survey results separately.
Address	Quadrant House, The Quadrant, Sutton SM2 5AS
Telephone	01 661 3122; Telex: 892084; Fax: 01 661 3948

291

Originator	COMPUTER WEEKLY
Title	DATA PROCESSING JOB CHANGING SURVEY, annual in a weekly journal
Coverage	A survey examining the reasons why people in IT posts change jobs, what they are looking for and why and how they find and choose new jobs.
Availability	Controlled circulation
Cost	Free
Comments	ISSN 0010 4787. Produced in association with Computer People.
Address	Quadrant House, The Quadrant, Sutton SM2 5AS
Telephone	01 661 3122; Telex: 892084; Fax: 01 661 3948

292

Originator	COMPUTER WEEKLY
Title	DATA PROCESSING RECRUITMENT SURVEY, annual in a weekly journal
Coverage	A detailed study of recruitment advertisements in computer journals with data on the types of jobs and experience in demand, salary levels and the major trends and implications.
Availability	Controlled circulation
Cost	Free
Comments	ISSN 0010 4787. Produced in association with the Salary Survey Project.
Address	Quadrant House, The Quadrant, Sutton SM2 5AS
Telephone	01 661 3122; Telex: 892084; Fax: 01 661 3948

293

Originator	COMPUTER WEEKLY
Title	DATA PROCESSING SALARY SURVEY, annual
Coverage	A survey of over 700 computer installations in the UK with approximately 11,500 staff. It covers salaries, perks and job turnover in 8 job categories with a regional breakdown.
Availability	Controlled circulation
Cost	Free
Comments	ISSN 0010 4787. Produced in association with the National Computing Centre.
Address	Quadrant House, The Quadrant, Sutton SM2 5AS
Telephone	01 661 3122; Telex: 892084; Fax: 01 661 3948

294

Originator	COMPUTER WEEKLY
Title	DP EXPENDITURE AND VERTICAL MARKET SURVEY, annual in a weekly journal
Coverage	Presents a global view of expenditure at approximately 38,000 computer sites in the UK and reviews trends in individual sectors. The results appear in various issues throughout the year.
Availability	Controlled circulation
Cost	Free
Comments	ISSN 0010 4787. Survey undertaken in association with International Data Corporation.
Address	Quadrant House, The Quadrant, Sutton SM2 5AS
Telephone	01 661 3122; Telex: 892084; Fax: 01 661 3948

295

Originator	COMPUTER WEEKLY
Title	DP PROFESSIONALS JOB CHANGING SURVEY, annual in a weekly journal
Coverage	Based on 1,000 questionnaire responses and 150 personal interviews, it examines why people in data processing change jobs and how they find their next job.
Availability	Controlled circulation
Cost	Free
Comments	ISSN 0010 4787. Produced in association with Eastside.
Address	Quadrant House, The Quadrant, Sutton SM2 5AS
Telephone	01 661 3122; Telex: 892084; Fax: 01 661 3948

296

Originator	COMPUTING SERVICES ASSOCIATION
Title	COMPUTING SERVICES ASSOCIATION ANNUAL REPORT, annual
Coverage	Includes the CSA Annual Survey based on voluntary responses from CSA companies (145 companies responded in 1987), with data on their business activities in the preceding 12 months: total revenue, revenue by business sector, revenue per employee, employment trends, profits and future prospects. A detailed commentary supports the statistics.
Availability	General
Cost	Free
Comments	Usually published in October.
Address	Hanover House, 73/74 High Holborn, London WC1V 6LE
Telephone	01 405 2171; Telex: 263224; Fax: 01 404 4119

297

Originator	CONFEDERATION OF BRITISH INDUSTRY (CBI)
Title	CBI/FT SURVEY OF THE DISTRIBUTIVE TRADES, monthly. July 1983–
Coverage	A survey of distributive units in 22 individual sectors with data on sales volume, orders, stocks, employment, investment, prices, business expenditure etc.
Availability	General
Cost	£210, £140 to members
Address	103 New Oxford Street, London WC1A 1DU
Telephone	01 379 7400; Telex: 21332; Fax: 01 240 1578

298

Originator	CONFEDERATION OF BRITISH INDUSTRY (CBI)
Title	ECONOMIC SITUATION REPORT, monthly
Coverage	An economic survey plus a forecast up to 6 months ahead and a comparison of the other major published forecasts. Also a general survey of industrial and regional trends and comparative data for other European countries. Based largely on a combination of CBI data (40%) and Central Government data (48%).
Availability	General
Cost	£163, £108 to members
Address	103 New Oxford Street, London WC1A 1DU
Telephone	01 379 7400; Telex: 21332; Fax: 01 240 1578

299

Originator   CONFEDERATION OF BRITISH INDUSTRY (CBI)

Title   INDUSTRIAL TRENDS SURVEY, quarterly. 1958–
Coverage   Trends for 44 individual industry groups covering orders, stocks, output, capital expenditure, exports, costs, labour etc. for the last 4 months and the next 4 months. Based on a CBI survey of about 1700 companies.

Availability   General
Cost   £184, £115 to members
Comments   Abbreviated data is available in the monthly publication 'Monthly Trends Enquiry' – see below.
Address   103 New Oxford Street, London WC1A 1DU
Telephone   01 379 7400; Telex: 21332; Fax: 01 240 1578

300

Originator   CONFEDERATION OF BRITISH INDUSTRY (CBI)

Title   MONTHLY TRENDS ENQUIRY, monthly
Coverage   Essentially an abbreviated version of the quarterly 'Industrial Trends Survey' with summary statistics on orders, stocks, output, prices etc. A short commentary (15%) accompanies the statistics. Data is based on a survey of companies with responses varying from about 1300 to 1500.

Availability   General
Cost   £156, £104 to members
Comments   Produced on 4 A4 pages.
Address   103 New Oxford Street, London WC1A 1DU
Telephone   01 379 7400; Telex: 21332; Fax: 01 240 1578

301

Originator   CONFEDERATION OF BRITISH WOOL TEXTILES

Title   MONTHLY BULLETIN OF STATISTICS, monthly. January 1950–
Coverage   Production statistics for the wool textile industry with data on combing, weaving, spinning and dyeing and finishing. Also machinery activity and production personnel in the industry. Based entirely on the Confederation's survey.

Availability   General
Cost   £36
Address   60 Toller Lane, Bradford BD8 9BZ
Telephone   0274 491241; Fax: 0274 547320

302

Originator	CONFEDERATION OF BRITISH WOOL TEXTILES
Title	QUARTERLY REVIEW OF UK TRADE STATISTICS, quarterly. December 1981–
Coverage	Imports and exports in the wool textile industry by major products and main markets with additional data on import penetration. Based on Central Government statistics.
Availability	General
Cost	£22
Address	60 Toller Lane, Bradford BD8 9BZ
Telephone	0274 491241; Fax: 0274 547320

303

Originator	CONSENSUS RESEARCH LTD
Title	CONSUMER FINANCE MARKET SEGMENTATION, biennial. 1986–
Coverage	A market study of the personal finance sector and attitudinal segmentation of the consumer market for financial services in the UK. Based on the company's own survey. A commentary accompanies the data (35%).
Availability	General
Cost	On application
Comments	Also publishes an annual survey of the ratings of brokers' analysts amongst senior financial executives.
Address	32 Grosvenor Gardens, London SW1W 0DH
Telephone	01 730 7222; Telex: 296846; Fax: 01 730 6663

304

Originator	CONSENSUS RESEARCH LTD
Title	UNIT TRUST SURVEY, quarterly. 1st quarter 1985–
Coverage	A survey of awareness of and attitudes towards unit trusts amongst unitholders and intermediaries. They are both surveyed every 6 months by the company. A commentary accompanies the data (50%).
Availability	General
Cost	On application
Comments	Also publishes an annual survey of the rating of brokers' analysts amongst senior financial executives.
Address	32 Grosvenor Gardens, London SW1W 0DH
Telephone	01 730 7222; Telex: 296846; Fax: 01 730 6663

305

Originator	CONSTRUCTION NEWS
Title	CONSTRUCTION INDICES, monthly in a weekly journal
Coverage	Cost indices for work and materials in building works, civil engineering and specialist engineering. Based entirely on Central Government statistics.
Availability	General
Cost	£40, or 65p for a single issue
Comments	Also publish an annual review of the top 100 companies in the industry.
Address	International Thomson Publishing, 100 Avenue Road, London NW3 3TP
Telephone	01 935 6611; Telex: 299973; Fax: 01 722 0257

306

Originator	CONSTRUCTION PLANT-HIRE ASSOCIATION
Title	CPA ACTIVITY RATES AND HIRE RATE STUDIES, quarterly. 1979–
Coverage	Activity levels as a percentage and hire rate averages and ranges for a selection of popular plant types. Includes graphs outlining the major trends. Based on returns from about 15% of the membership. Usually produced 2 weeks after the survey.
Availability	Participating members
Cost	Free
Address	28 Eccleston Street, London SW1W 9PY
Telephone	01 730 7117; Fax: 01 730 7110

307

Originator	CONSTRUCTION PLANT-HIRE ASSOCIATION
Title	CPA COST STUDIES, bi-annual. 1977–
Coverage	Plant hire company's costs for machines and drivers with graphs outlining the major trends. Based on a sample survey of members, the sample size varying according to the types of machines surveyed and the types of questions asked. A small amount of supporting text (10%).
Availability	Members and selected non-member organizations
Cost	Free
Comments	Summary data issued as a press release to selected journals.
Address	28 Eccleston Street, London SW1W 9PY
Telephone	01 730 7117; Fax: 01 730 7110

308

Originator	CONTEXT
Title	BUSINESS MICROCOMPUTER INFORMATION SERVICE: ADD-ON BOARDS, 6 issues a year
Coverage	Sales data by value and volume for microcomputer add-on boards with actual figures for the first 2 months and estimates for a third month. Data given on specific types of equipment. Based on a dealer survey by the company.
Availability	General
Cost	On application
Address	435 London House, 26–40 Kensington High St, London W8 4PF
Telephone	01 937 3595

309

Originator	CONTEXT
Title	BUSINESS MICROCOMPUTER INFORMATION SERVICE: DEALER REPORT, 6 issues a year
Coverage	Data on sales of microcomputers and other equipment by dealers. The statistics are based on the data collected for the individual BMIS product reports (see entries below). Based on a survey of dealers by the company.
Availability	General
Cost	On application
Address	435 London House, 26–40 Kensington High St, London W8 4PF
Telephone	01 937 3595

310

Originator	CONTEXT
Title	BUSINESS MICROCOMPUTER INFORMATION SERVICE: HARDWARE, 6 issues a year
Coverage	Sales data by value and volume for computers and related hardware with actual figures for the first 2 months and estimates for a third month. Based on a dealer survey by the company.
Availability	General
Cost	On application
Address	435 London House, 26–40 Kensington High St, London W8 4PF
Telephone	01 937 3595

311

Originator	CONTEXT
Title	BUSINESS MICROCOMPUTER INFORMATION SERVICE: MODEMS, 6 issues a year
Coverage	Sales data by value and volume for modems with actual figures for the first 2 months and estimates for a third month. Data on specific types of modems is given. Based on a dealer survey by the company.
Availability	General
Cost	On application
Address	435 London House, 26–40 Kensington High St, London W8 4PF
Telephone	01 937 3595

312

Originator	CONTEXT
Title	BUSINESS MICROCOMPUTER INFORMATION SERVICE: PRINTERS AND PLOTTERS, 6 issues a year
Coverage	Sales figures by value and volume for printers and plotters with actual figures for the first 2 months and estimates for a third month. Data on specific printers and plotters. Based on a dealer survey by the company.
Availability	General
Cost	On application
Address	435 London House, 26–40 Kensington High St, London W8 4PF
Telephone	01 937 3595

313

Originator	CONTEXT
Title	BUSINESS MICROCOMPUTER INFORMATION SERVICE: SOFTWARE, 6 issues a year
Coverage	Sales figures for microcomputer software by value and volume with actual figures for the first 2 months and estimates for a third month. Data on various types of software. Based on a dealer survey by the company.
Availability	General
Cost	On application
Address	435 London House, 26–40 Kensington High St, London W8 4PF
Telephone	01 937 3595

314

Originator	CONTEXT
Title	BUSINESS MICROCOMPUTER INFORMATION SERVICE PRICING MONITOR, monthly
Coverage	Data on the actual selling prices of a range of microcomputers and related products. Based on a regular survey of computer dealers by the company.
Availability	General
Cost	On application
Address	435 London House, 26–40 Kensington High St, London W8 4PF
Telephone	01 937 3595

315

Originator	CONTRACT CLEANING AND MAINTENANCE ASSOCIATION
Title	CCMA MEMBERSHIP SURVEY, biennial. 1986–
Coverage	A survey of 100 companies in the contract cleaning sector (a 77% response rate out of 130 member companies) with statistics on the size of the market, employment trends, the cleaning industry's purchasing power and membership of the CCMA. A short commentary (18%) accompanies the data. First survey carried out in December 1985 and published in August 1986.
Availability	General
Cost	£2.50
Address	Suite 73/74, Hop Exchange, 24 Southwark Street, London SE1 1TY
Telephone	01 403 2747

316

Originator	CONTRACT JOURNAL
Title	CONSTRUCTION INDICES, monthly in a weekly journal
Coverage	Building costs for civil engineering, building works and specialist engineering. Index figures for the latest month and some earlier months. Based on Central Government data.
Availability	General
Cost	£45
Address	Reed Business Publishing, Carew House, Wallington SM6 0DX
Telephone	01 661 3500; Telex: 892804; Fax: 01 647 4551

317

Originator	COOPERATIVE UNION
Title	COOPERATIVE STATISTICS, annual
Coverage	Retail distribution by individual cooperative society and other information on cooperative wholesaling, banking and insurance activities. Based almost entirely on the Union's own research.
Availability	General
Cost	£50
Address	Holyoake House, Hanover Street, Manchester M60 0AS
Telephone	061 832 4300

318

Originator	COOPERATIVE UNION
Title	ECONOMIC PROSPECTS, annual
Coverage	Covers recent developments in the UK economy plus some data on the world economy. Forecasts for the UK up to 3 years ahead and population forecasts up to 2000+.
Availability	General
Cost	£30
Address	Holyoake House, Hanover Street, Manchester M60 0AS
Telephone	061 832 4300

319

Originator	COOPERS AND LYBRAND (NI) LTD
Title	NORTHERN IRELAND ECONOMY: CURRENT SITUATION AND PROSPECTS, annual
Coverage	A review of business conditions, labour market trends, the economic background, prices and public expenditure. Mainly based on Central Government data (80%) with a large amount of supporting text (65%).
Availability	General
Cost	£25
Address	Fanum House, 108 Great Victoria Street, Belfast BT2 7AX
Telephone	0232 245454; Fax: 0232 242416

320

Originator	CORNWALL COUNTY COUNCIL
Title	BASIC PLANNING STATISTICS, regular. 1970s–

Coverage   A series of loose-leaf sheets on population, employment, incomes, housing, the electorate, tourism and transport for Cornwall and its districts. Based mainly on Central Government data (90%) with some Council material (10%).

Availability General
Cost   Free
Address   Planning Department, County Hall, Truro TR1 3BB
Telephone   0872 74282, x2620; Fax: 0872 70340

321

Originator   CORNWALL COUNTY COUNCIL

Title   ECONOMIC POLICIES AND PROGRAMMES, annual
Coverage   Includes a statistical appendix with data on general trends in the local economy. The remainder of the report looks at national economic policies, EEC policies and local policies and initiatives.

Availability General
Cost   £5
Address   County Hall, Truro TR1 3BB
Telephone   0872 74282; Fax: 0872 70340

322

Originator   COSMETIC WORLD NEWS

Title   LONDON MARKET REPORT, monthly in a monthly journal
Coverage   Prices of specific cosmetics and raw materials in London. Includes essential oils, aroma chemicals, absolutes and concretes, raw materials etc. Based on data collected by the journal.

Availability General
Cost   £52
Comments   ISSN 0305 0319
Address   World News Publications, 130 Wigmore Street, London W1H 0AT
Telephone   01 486 6757; Telex: 817133

323

Originator   COUNCIL FOR NATIONAL ACADEMIC AWARDS (CNAA)

Title   ANNUAL REPORT, annual. 1964–
Coverage   Data on enrolments, awards made and research by type of course and subject. Based on data collected by CNNA with a large amount of supporting text (60%).

Availability General
Cost   Free
Address   344/354 Grays Inn Road, London WC1X 8BP
Telephone   01 278 4411; Fax: 01 833 1012

324

Originator	COUNTY COUNCILS GAZETTE
Title	VARIOUS TITLES, monthly in a monthly journal
Coverage	Every month statistics are published on a different topic, e.g. waste disposal, capital expenditure, rate returns, national parks, small-holdings etc. Statistics are usually by county and are normally taken from CIPFA.
Availability	General
Cost	£9, or 60p for a single issue
Comments	ISSN 0011 0310
Address	ACC, Eaton House, 66A Eaton Square, London SW1W 9BH
Telephone	01 235 1200; Fax: 01 235 8458

325

Originator	COVENTRY CITY COUNCIL
Title	ECONOMIC MONITOR, quarterly. 1975–
Coverage	Review of trends in the local economy covering the job market, industrial trends and the business climate. There are special feature articles in each issue. Mainly based on Central Government data (70%) but also includes statistics from the local authority and other sources. 50% of the monitor is text.
Availability	General
Cost	Free
Address	Economic Development, Much Park Street, Coventry CV1 2PY
Telephone	0203 31222; Fax: 0203 20432

326

Originator	CREMATION SOCIETY OF GREAT BRITAIN
Title	DIRECTORY OF CREMATORIA, annual. 1979/80–
Coverage	Progress of cremation over the last 100 years. Facts and figures section with numbers of crematoria, cremation comparisons between areas, cremations carried out, fees etc. Based on the Society's own survey. Mainly text (90%).
Availability	General
Cost	£11.50
Address	16A Albion Place, Maidstone ME17 1XH
Telephone	0622 688292

327

Originator	CROUDACE CONSTRUCTION
Title	CONSTRUCTION INDUSTRY FORECAST, annual
Coverage	Output forecasts for the construction industry over a 2-3 year period. Gives the company's own forecasts together with those from BMP, NEDO and Savory Milln. Covers starts and orders for public and private housing, industrial and commercial construction, repair and maintenance. Also a summary profile of orders at constant prices and output.
Availability	General
Cost	By negotiation
Address	Croudace House, Caterham CR3 6XQ
Telephone	0883 46464; Telex: 947513; Fax: 0883 49927

328

Originator	CUMBERNAULD DEVELOPMENT CORPORATION
Title	HOUSEHOLD SURVEY REPORT, regular. 1986–
Coverage	Statistics on demography, housing, households and employment based on a 100% survey with a 77% response rate in 1986. A significant amount of text (50%) is included with the data.
Availability	General
Cost	On application
Address	Cumbernauld House, Cumbernauld, Glasgow G67 3JH
Telephone	0236 721155; Telex: 77463; Fax: 0236 739528

329

Originator	CUMBERNAULD DEVELOPMENT CORPORATION
Title	STATISTICAL PROFILE, annual. 1988–
Coverage	Statistics on demography, housing, employment, industry, commerce, social facilities and recreation. Based on a series of 100% surveys carried out by the Corporation with response rates usually over 75%.
Availability	General
Cost	Price to be decided
Address	Cumbernauld House, Cumbernauld, Glasgow G67 3JH
Telephone	0236 721155; Telex: 77463; Fax: 0236 739528

330

Originator	CUMBRIA COUNTY COUNCIL
Title	CUMBRIA MONITOR, monthly. 1980–

Coverage   Statistics and a review of trends in unemployment, redundancies, vacancies etc. by district plus reports of proposed developments and closures. Based on Central Government data.

Availability Mainly internal circulation but available to others on request
Cost   On application
Address   Planning, County Offices, Kendal LA9 4RQ
Telephone   0539 21000

331

Originator   DAIRY TRADE FEDERATION

Title   DAIRY INDUSTRY, annual
Coverage   Statistics covering the prices, consumption and general market for milk and other dairy products. Data from various sources and a large amount of supporting text (80%).

Availability General
Cost   Free
Address   19 Cornwall Terrace, London NW1 4QP
Telephone   01 486 7244; Telex: 262027

332

Originator   DATA STAR

Title   OVERSEAS TRADE STATISTICS, continuous
Coverage   Statistics on the imports and exports of any traded product by value and volume with additional data on country of origin and destination, port of entry and departure etc. Appointed as an official agent of HM Customs and Excise.

Availability General
Cost   On application, depending on the information required
Comments   Data available on disc, microfiche. Data for other countries available on the TRADSTAT on-line database.
Address   DIS Marketing, Plaza Suite, 114 Jermyn Street, London SW1Y 6HJ
Telephone   01 930 5503; Telex: 946240; Fax: 01 930 2581

333

Originator   DATA TRANSCRIPTS

Title   CORRUGATED AND CARTON BULLETIN, 11 issues per year
Coverage   Market trends for corrugated carbon packaging including specific data on products, equipment, processes and company news.

Availability General
Cost   £150
Comments   Data available in machine readable form to subscribers.

Address	PO Box 14, Dorking RH5 4YN
Telephone	0306 884473

334

Originator	DATA TRANSCRIPTS
Title	PACKAGING CONVERTER BULLETIN, 10 issues per year
Coverage	Market trends relating to flexible and semi-rigid packaging with specific data on products, equipment, processes and company news.
Availability	General
Cost	£150
Comments	Data available in machine readable form to subscribers.
Address	PO Box 14, Dorking RH5 4YN
Telephone	0306 884473

335

Originator	DATA TRANSCRIPTS
Title	PLASTICS PACKAGING INDUSTRY MONITOR, 10 issues per year
Coverage	Trends in the plastics packaging market with specific data on products and prices.
Availability	General
Cost	£150
Comments	Data available in machine readable form to subscribers.
Address	PO Box 14, Dorking RH5 4YN
Telephone	0306 884473

336

Originator	DATA TRANSCRIPTS
Title	SELF ADHESIVE MATERIAL AND MARKETS BULLETIN, 10 issues per year
Coverage	Market trends for self-adhesive labels and tapes including data on products, equipment, processes and company news.
Availability	General
Cost	£150
Comments	Data available in machine readable form to subscribers.
Address	PO Box 14, Dorking RH5 4YN
Telephone	0306 884473

337

Originator	DATA TRANSCRIPTS
Title	SPECIALITY PAPERS AND PRODUCTS BULLETIN, 10 issues per year
Coverage	Market trends for speciality papers and boards including specific data on products, equipment, processes and company news.
Availability	General
Cost	£150
Comments	Data available in machine readable form to subscribers.
Address	PO Box 14, Dorking RH5 4YN
Telephone	0306 884473

338

Originator	DEBENHAM, TEWSON AND CHINNOCKS
Title	DIGEST OF PROPERTY STATISTICS, annual
Coverage	Overview of the main variables affecting the property market. Divided into offices, shops, industrial property, agriculture and general. Based on a combination of non-official sources (60%) and Central Government data (40%).
Availability	General
Cost	Free to the general public. A charge may be made to companies
Address	44 Brook Street, London W1A 4NA
Telephone	01 408 1161; Telex: 22105; Fax: 01 491 4593

339

Originator	DEBENHAM, TEWSON AND CHINNOCKS
Title	INDUSTRIAL RENTS AND RATES, annual
Coverage	Levels of industrial rents and rates over a 10 year period in 16 industrial centres. Based on the company's own research.
Availability	General
Cost	£10
Address	44 Brook Street, London W1A 4NA
Telephone	01 408 1161; Telex: 22105; Fax: 01 491 4593

340

Originator	DEBENHAM, TEWSON AND CHINNOCKS
Title	MONEY INTO PROPERTY, annual
Coverage	Examines the amount of bank and institutional money being directed into the property sector.

Availability	General
Cost	£10
Comments	Sources for the individual tables are not given but a general list of sources is given at the end.
Address	44 Brook Street, London W1A 4NA
Telephone	01 408 1161; Telex: 22105; Fax: 01 491 4593

341

Originator	DEBENHAM, TEWSON AND CHINNOCKS
Title	OFFICE FLOORSPACE SURVEY, quarterly
Coverage	Office floorspace availability in Central London based on the company's own research.
Availability	General
Cost	£50
Address	44 Brook Street, London W1A 4NA
Telephone	01 408 1161; Telex: 22105; Fax: 01 491 4593

342

Originator	DEBENHAM, TEWSON AND CHINNOCKS
Title	OFFICE RENTS AND RATES, annual
Coverage	Trends in the level of office rents and rates in the main centres of Great Britain. Based mainly on the company's own research (60%) with additional data from Central Government and other non-official sources.
Availability	General
Cost	£10
Address	44 Brook Street, London W1A 4NA
Telephone	01 408 1161; Telex: 22105; Fax: 01 491 4593

343

Originator	DEBENHAM, TEWSON AND CHINNOCKS
Title	SHOP RENTS AND RATES, annual
Coverage	Trends in the levels of prime shop rents in 20 major centres throughout Great Britain. Based largely on the company's own research (70%), with additional data from Central Government and non-official sources.
Availability	General
Cost	£10
Address	44 Brook Street, London W1A 4NA
Telephone	01 408 1161; Telex: 22105; Fax: 01 491 4593

344

Originator	DECORATIVE LIGHTING ASSOCIATION
Title	TURNOVER ANALYSIS, biennial
Coverage	An analysis of industry sales and imports based on returns from member companies. A small amount of text (10%) accompanies the data.
Availability	Members
Cost	Free
Comments	Recent issues of the analysis have not always appeared because of insufficient responses.
Address	Bryn House, Bryn, Bishops Castle SY9 5LE
Telephone	05884 658

345

Originator	DERBYSHIRE COUNTY COUNCIL
Title	UNEMPLOYMENT IN DERBYSHIRE, annual
Coverage	Commentary and statistics on the unemployment situation and trends in Derbyshire and the districts in the county. Based on Central Government data.
Availability	General
Cost	Free
Address	Planning, County Offices, Matlock DE4 3AG
Telephone	0629 3411; Fax: 0629 57720

346

Originator	DEVON COUNTY COUNCIL
Title	DEVON STATISTICS BULLETIN, regular
Coverage	General statistics on the Devon area including data on population, housing, the economy, transport etc. Mainly based on Central Government data.
Availability	General
Address	Central Information Office, County Hall, Exeter EX2 4QJ
Telephone	0392 77977,x2001; Fax: 0392 51411

347

Originator	DEVON COUNTY COUNCIL
Title	EMPLOYMENT IN DEVON: POLICIES AND PRO-GRAMMES, annual

Coverage	Graphs and tables in the appendix covering employment, earnings, unemployment, industrial development and structure and grants to industry. The main bulk of the report outlines the Council's policies and programmes.
Availability	General
Cost	£2
Address	Lucombe House, Topsham Road, Exeter EX2 4DW
Telephone	0392 77977; Fax: 0392 51411

348

Originator	DIRECT MAIL PRODUCERS ASSOCIATION
Title	SURVEY OF MEMBERS, regular. 1988–
Coverage	Statistics based on members' returns covering business trends, turnover, postage expenditure, future plans etc.
Availability	On application
Cost	On application
Address	34 Grand Avenue, London N10 3BP
Telephone	01 883 7229

349

Originator	DIRECT SELLING ASSOCIATION
Title	DIRECT SELLING IN THE UK – AN OVERVIEW OF THE INDUSTRY, annual
Coverage	Statistics on the value and range of products sold by direct selling, the volume of retail transactions, employment, earnings, selling methods and future prospects. Based on a survey of members (60% of all registered direct selling companies). Some text supports the data (30%).
Availability	General
Cost	£14
Comments	Produced on one sheet of A4 paper.
Address	44 Russell Square, London WC1B 4JP
Telephone	01 580 8433

350

Originator	DORSET COUNTY COUNCIL
Title	ABSTRACT OF STATISTICS FOR DORSET, annual. 1973–
Coverage	General data on the population, area, housing, employment, education, social services, police, libraries, transport, waste disposal, agriculture, oil, the countryside etc. Based on various sources including the Council's own surveys (40%), Central Government data (40%) and other sources (20%).

115 351–353

Availability	General
Cost	£3
Address	Planning Department, County Hall, Dorchester DT1 1XJ
Telephone	0305 204259; Fax: 0305 66120

351

Originator	DRAPERS CHAMBER OF TRADE
Title	MONTHLY SALES FIGURES, annual. 1981–
Coverage	Sales figures by month from a survey of about 200 retail companies. Usually produced 3 months after the end of the year to which it relates.
Availability	Members
Cost	Free
Address	North Bar, Banbury, Oxfordshire
Telephone	0295 53601; Fax: 0295 270062

352

Originator	DRAPERS CHAMBER OF TRADE
Title	OPERATING RESULTS, annual. 1981–
Coverage	Operating results of 5 groups of members according to turnover and type of merchandising sold. For each gives sales index, gross margin and expenses. Based on a survey of about 150 retail companies. Usually produced 6 months after the end of the year to which it relates.
Availability	Members
Cost	Free
Address	North Bar, Banbury, Oxfordshire
Telephone	0295 53601; Fax: 0295 270062

353

Originator	DRINKS RETAILING
Title	DRINKS RETAILING FORECAST, regular in a monthly journal
Coverage	Market trends and forecasts for a few years ahead for mainly alcoholic drinks. Forecasts appear in virtually every issue and a specific drink, e.g. lager, wine, sherry, carbonated water etc. is covered in each forecast. Based mainly on data supplied by the company Adsearch.
Availability	Controlled circulation
Cost	Free
Address	4 Carmelite Street, London EC4Y 0BN
Telephone	01 583 5620

354

Originator	DRIVERS JONAS
Title	ABERDEEN COMMERCIAL AND INDUSTRIAL PROPERTY SURVEY, bi-annual. May 1975–
Coverage	Statistics on the space available, space let or sold and an index of rental levels. Based on the company's own research with some supporting text (50%).
Availability	General
Cost	Free
Address	10 Albyn Terrace, Aberdeen AB1 1YP
Telephone	0224 646931

355

Originator	DRIVERS JONAS
Title	EAST ANGLIA INDUSTRIAL PROPERTY SURVEY, bi-annual. Autumn 1979–
Coverage	Statistics on the space available and space let in the region based on the company's own research. Some supporting text (50%).
Availability	General
Cost	Free
Address	5 Queen Street, Norwich NR2 4SG
Telephone	0603 617338; Telex: 97473

356

Originator	DUN & BRADSTREET LTD
Title	BUSINESS FAILURE STATISTICS, quarterly
Coverage	Company liquidations and bankruptcies analysed by trade and region. Based on the company's own records and accompanied by a large amount of commentary (70%). Usually published 1 week after the results have been compiled.
Availability	General
Cost	Free
Comments	Issued in the form of a press release.
Address	26/32 Clifton Street, London EC2P 2LY
Telephone	01 377 4377; Telex: 886697; Fax: 01 247 3836

357

Originator	DUN & BRADSTREET LTD
Title	KEY BUSINESS RATIOS, annual. 1987–

Coverage	20 key ratios arranged by SIC industry group with data for the latest 3 years available, i.e. the first issue published in 1987 covered 1983–1985. Based on the company's own analysis of company financial data.
Availability	General
Cost	£125
Comments	ISSN 0951 2179. First published in 1987. Usually published in March.
Address	26/32 Clifton Street, London EC2P 2LY
Telephone	01 377 4377; Telex: 886697; Fax: 01 247 3836

358

Originator	EAST SUSSEX COUNTY COUNCIL
Title	HOUSING LAND COMMITMENT, annual. 1974–
Coverage	A summary of outstanding planning permissions for housing developments in the districts of East Sussex plus details of land allocated for housing. Based on the Council's own data.
Availability	General
Cost	On application
Address	Planning, Southover House, Southover Road, Lewes BN7 1YA
Telephone	07916 5400

359

Originator	EAST SUSSEX COUNTY COUNCIL
Title	INDUSTRIAL/OFFICE/RETAIL LAND COMMITMENT, annual. 1975–
Coverage	A summary by local area of the amount of land allocated or with planning permission for industrial, office or retail development. Based on the Council's own data.
Availability	General
Cost	On application
Address	Planning, Southover House, Southover Road, Lewes BN7 1YA
Telephone	07916 5400

360

Originator	ECONOMIC DEVELOPMENT BRIEFING
Title	CHARTERED SURVEYORS SURVEY, annual. 1979–
Coverage	Statistics and trends covering the UK property market, the property professions and the British property media. Based on the company's own survey with a supporting commentary (50%).
Availability	General

Cost   £185
Address   PO Box 625, Hampstead, London NW3 2TZ
Telephone   01 209 1722

361

Originator   ECONOMIST PUBLICATIONS LTD

Title   RETAIL BUSINESS – MARKET REPORTS, monthly
Coverage   Mainly articles on specific products and sectors but the journal also
             contains 2 regular sections. The first is a quarterly forecast of
             consumer spending with forecasts up to 2 years ahead. Quarterly
             product reviews also cover the major sectors in turn, e.g. textiles
             and clothing, food, chemists etc.

Availability General
Cost   £245
Comments   Other regular and one-off reports cover trends in international
             economies and markets.
Address   40 Duke Street, London W1A 1DW
Telephone   01 493 6711; Telex: 266353; Fax: 01 499 9767

362

Originator   ECONOMIST PUBLICATIONS LTD

Title   RETAIL BUSINESS – RETAIL TRADE REVIEWS, quarterly
Coverage   Mainly articles on specific retail sectors and new developments but
             once a year the journal contains an annual review of retailing with
             commentary and statistics on the major trends.

Availability General
Cost   £105
Comments   Other regular and one-off reports published on international eco-
             nomies and markets.
Address   40 Duke Street, London W1A 1DW
Telephone   01 493 6711; Telex: 266353; Fax: 01 499 9767

363

Originator   ECONOMIST PUBLICATIONS LTD

Title   UNITED KINGDOM QUARTERLY ECONOMIC REVIEW,
             quarterly
Coverage   Commentary and statistics on general economic trends and business
             conditions in the UK. Based mainly on Central Government data.

Availability General
Cost   £75
Comments   Quarterly reviews published on various other countries plus a range
             of 'one-off' reports and regular titles.

Address   40 Duke Street, London W1A 1DW
Telephone 01 493 6711; Telex: 266353; Fax: 01 499 9767

364

Originator EDEN VALE

Title   REVIEW OF THE FRESH CHILLED DAIRY PRODUCTS
                MARKET, annual
Coverage   Sections on various dairy products including yoghurt, cream,
                cottage cheese, salad, deserts etc. Covers sales in value and quan-
                tities with projected data for the coming year and historical data for
                comparison. Based on Eden Vale's own figures.

Availability General
Cost   Free
Comments   Prepared for Eden Vale by Cameron, Choat & Partners.
Address   Victoria Road, South Ruislip, Middlesex HA4 0HF
Telephone   01 845 2345; Fax: 01 841 3922

365

Originator EDINBURGH DISTRICT COUNCIL

Title   ECONOMIC AND EMPLOYMENT REVIEW, regular
Coverage   Articles on local economic development issues and specific sectors
                important to the local economy plus some statistics on the local
                economy, employment etc.

Availability General
Cost   Free
Address   375 High Street, Edinburgh EH1 1QE
Telephone   031 225 2424; Telex: 727143

366

Originator ELECTRICAL AND RADIO TRADING

Title   ERT PRICE MONITOR, quarterly in a weekly journal. 1988–
Coverage   Prices and unit sales statistics for various electrical appliances. Data
                for the latest quarter and the previous quarter. Compiled by Philips
                from SEAMA, AGB and Lek-Trak data.

Availability General
Cost   £30, or 60p for a single issue
Comments   ISSN 0013 4228
Address   Quadrant Publishing Services, Quadrant House, Sutton SM2 5AS
Telephone   01 661 8694; Fax: 01 661 8902

367

Originator   ELECTRICAL AND RADIO TRADING

Title   PRODUCT SURVEYS, regular in a weekly journal
Coverage   Regular surveys with a specific domestic electrical appliance cov-
                  ered in each survey, e.g. telephones, cookers, microwaves, videos,
                  televisions etc. A survey usually includes retail sales data taken
                  from surveys by AGB. Each product is usually covered on a number
                  of times per year.

Availability General
Cost   £30, or 60p for a single issue
Comments   ISSN 0013 4228
Address   Quadrant Publishing Services, Quadrant House, Sutton SM2 5AS
Telephone   01 661 8694; Fax: 01 661 8902

368

Originator   ELECTRICAL TIMES

Title   BEAMA INDEX, NEDO INDICES, PRICES OF CABLE-
                  METALS AND MATERIALS, monthly in a monthly journal
Coverage   Labour and material price indices covering electrical equipment
                  and specialized engineering installations plus prices of selected
                  metals and materials. Based on Central Government sources (70%)
                  and non-official sources (30%).

Availability General
Cost   £26.50, or £2.25 for a single issue
Comments   ISSN 0013 4414
Address   Reed Publishing, Quadrant House, The Quadrant, Sutton SM2
                  5AS
Telephone   01 661 3115; Telex: 892084; Fax: 01 661 3948

369

Originator   ELECTRICITY CONSUMERS COUNCIL

Title   ELECTRICITY DISCONNECTIONS, quarterly. 1978–
Coverage   Disconnections of domestic customers by area board with data for
                  the previous year for comparison. Given as a percentage of total
                  accounts and of domestic credit customers. Based on data from the
                  area boards and usually produced 3 months after the quarter to
                  which the data refers.

Availability Selected distribution list
Cost   Free
Comments   Issue tariff levels in different regions annually.
Address   Brook House, 2-16 Torrington Place, London WC1E 7LL
Telephone   01 636 5703

370

Originator	ELECTRICITY COUNCIL
Title	ELECTRICITY SUPPLY INDUSTRY IN ENGLAND AND WALES: PERFORMANCE INDICATORS, annual. 1984–
Coverage	Data on electricity sales, costs, quality of supply, appliances etc. based on the Council's own data.
Availability	General
Cost	£2.50
Comments	ISSN 0951 9351. Also publishes international electricity price data.
Address	30 Millbank, London SW1P 4RD
Telephone	01 834 2333; Telex: 23385; Fax: 01 834 2333

371

Originator	ELECTRICITY COUNCIL
Title	HANDBOOK OF ELECTRICITY SUPPLY STATISTICS, annual
Coverage	Power stations, national grid systems, transmission and distribution, generation finance, commercial data, tariffs, appliances and employment. Historical data is included and there are some comparative figures for other countries. Mainly based on the Council's own data (80%) with some Central Government data (20%).
Availability	General
Cost	Free
Comments	ISSN 0440 1905. Also publishes international electricity prices statistics.
Address	30 Millbank, London SW1P 4RD
Telephone	01 834 2333; Telex: 23385; Fax: 01 834 2333

372

Originator	ELECTRICITY COUNCIL
Title	SUMMARY OF ELECTRICITY TARIFF RATES IN THE UNITED KINGDOM, annual
Coverage	Electricity tariffs for the UK with data on quarterly trends, maximum demand and seasonal time of day. Based on the Council's own data.
Availability	General
Cost	Free
Comments	Also publishes international electricity prices statistics.
Address	30 Millbank, London SW1P 4RD
Telephone	01 834 2333; Telex: 23385; Fax: 01 834 2333

373

Originator	ELECTRONIC ENGINEERING ASSOCIATION
Title	ANNUAL REPORT, annual
Coverage	Mainly commentary on the industry and the Association but some general statistics on aviation electronics, radio communications, space equipment, data systems etc. Based on returns from members.
Availability	General
Cost	Free
Address	8 Leicester Street, London WC2H 7BN
Telephone	01 437 0678; Telex: 263536; Fax: 01 434 3477

374

Originator	ELLIS, RICHARD
Title	PROPERTY INVESTMENT QUARTERLY BULLETIN, quarterly
Coverage	Mainly text but some statistics on property investment trends, projects etc. Each issue usually covers a specific topic, e.g. institutional investment, regional investment etc. Based on the company's own research. Text covers 80%.
Availability	General
Cost	Free
Comments	Occasional reports on property trends in particular cities also produced, e.g. London, Manchester, Glasgow etc.
Address	Berkeley Square House, London W1X 6AN
Telephone	01 629 6290; Telex: 262498; Fax: 01 493 3734

375

Originator	ELLIS, RICHARD
Title	PROPERTY MARKET INDICATORS, annual
Coverage	Indices for regional capital growth rates, rentals in major cities, estimated components of capital growth, changes in equated and prime yields and prime property yields. Based on the company's own database of properties. Some supporting text (10%).
Availability	General
Cost	Free
Comments	Occasional reports on property trends in specific cities also produced, e.g. London, Manchester, Glasgow etc.
Address	Berkeley Square House, London W1X 6AN
Telephone	01 629 6290; Telex: 262498; Fax: 01 493 3734

376

Originator	ELLIS, RICHARD
Title	UK PROPERTY, annual
Coverage	Reviews recent changes in property, construction and professional practice. Covers the past year and outlook for the coming year for office, industrial and shop property. Based mainly on the company's own research (80%) with some Central Government statistics (30%). A large amount of text (80%).
Availability	General
Cost	Free
Comments	Occasional reports on property trends in specific cities published, e.g. London, Manchester, Glasgow etc.
Address	Berkeley Square House, London W1X 6AN
Telephone	01 629 6290; Telex: 262498; Fax: 01 493 3734

377

Originator	ENGINEERING COUNCIL
Title	SURVEY OF CHARTERED AND TECHNICIAN ENGINEERS, biennial. 1967–
Coverage	Employment, incomes, current occupation, field of work, location, qualifications, responsibility, trade unions, fringe benefits, overtime and further training for chartered engineers and technician engineers. Based on the Council's own survey. Usually published within 4 months of the survey.
Availability	General
Cost	£50
Address	10 Maltravers Street, London WC2R 3ER
Telephone	01 240 7891; Telex: 297177; Fax: 01 240 7517

378

Originator	ENGINEERING EMPLOYERS FEDERATION
Title	ENGINEERING ECONOMIC TRENDS, bi-annual
Coverage	Graphs, tables and commentary on engineering output and sales, imports and exports by sector. Forecasts up to 1 year ahead are also included. Mainly based on Central Government data (70%) and text covers 40%.
Availability	General
Cost	On application
Comments	Produced in Spring and Autumn.
Address	Broadway House, Tothill Street, London SW1H 9NQ
Telephone	01 222 7777; Telex: 8814718; Fax: 01 222 2782

379

Originator	ENGINEERING INDUSTRY TRAINING BOARD
Title	EITB ANNUAL REPORT, annual
Coverage	Mainly text but includes a statistical summary covering employment trends in the engineering sector in total plus data by region, occupations, establishments etc. Some statistics on industry trainees and grants. The tables usually give trends over a number of years.
Availability	Available to bona-fide researchers
Cost	On application
Comments	ISSN 0309 2879
Address	54 Clarendon Road, Watford WD1 1LB
Telephone	0923 38441

380

Originator	ENGINEERING INDUSTRY TRAINING BOARD
Title	ENGINEERING INDUSTRY PROFILE REPORTS, bi-annual. 1984–
Coverage	Profiles of specific sectors in the engineering industry updated regularly. Mainly data on employment trends in the sector. Total figures plus statistics by region, occupations etc. Based largely on the Board's own survey (90%) – 100% coverage of firms over 40 employees. Below this total employment is known but estimates made of occupational distribution.
Availability	Available to bona-fide researchers
Cost	On application
Comments	Also produce a regular 'Economic and Industry Monitor' with some statistics. Databank on employment with data from 1978.
Address	54 Clarendon Road, Watford WD1 1LB
Telephone	0923 38441

381

Originator	ENGLISH TOURIST BOARD
Title	BRITAIN'S TOURISM, annual
Coverage	A series of fact sheets on the many aspects of tourism in Britain including figures on holiday tourism, hotel occupancy, business and conference tourism, spending and employment in tourism. Based mainly on the Board's data.
Availability	General
Cost	Free
Comments	Various 'one-off' reports also produced.
Address	Distribution Unit, 4 Bromells Road, London SW4 0BJ
Telephone	01 846 9000; Telex: 266975; Fax: 01 627 5165

382

Originator	ENGLISH TOURIST BOARD
Title	BRITISH HOLIDAY INTENTIONS, annual
Coverage	A survey of a random sample of the British adult population to measure their intentions to have a holiday in the forthcoming season. The survey is usually carried out 2 or 3 weeks before Easter and a short-term forecast based on the survey is published in May.
Availability	General
Cost	£8.50
Comments	Various 'one-off' reports also produced.
Address	Distribution Unit, 4 Bromells Road, London SW4 0BJ
Telephone	01 846 9000; Telex: 266975; Fax: 01 627 5165

383

Originator	ENGLISH TOURIST BOARD
Title	BRITISH TOURISM MARKET – SUMMARY, annual
Coverage	A survey of all trips taken overnight away from home by British people. Information on the trips includes purpose, duration, month, destination, mode of transport, accommodation, party size and an estimate of expenditure. Based on the Board's own survey and data from the British Tourist Board and the Wales Tourist Board.
Availability	General
Cost	£6.50
Comments	Various 'one-off' reports also produced.
Address	Distribution Unit, 4 Bromells Road, London SW4 0BJ
Telephone	01 846 9000; Telex: 266975; Fax: 01 627 5165

384

Originator	ENGLISH TOURIST BOARD
Title	ENGLISH HERITAGE MONITOR, annual
Coverage	Various sections cover visitor trends, admission charges, opening hours and the number of historic buildings. The monitor also contains a general review of conservation and Conservation Areas.
Availability	General
Cost	£9
Comments	Various 'one-off' reports also produced.
Address	Distribution Unit, 4 Bromells Road, London SW4 0BJ
Telephone	01 846 9000; Telex: 266975; Fax: 01 627 5165

385

Originator   ENGLISH TOURIST BOARD

Title   ENGLISH HOTEL OCCUPANCY SURVEY, monthly
Coverage   Statistics on average bed and room occupancy, duration of stay and
                  the proportion of arrivals from overseas. Data for hotels in different
                  locations according to tariff levels and for the 12 ETB regions.
                  There is also an analysis showing mid-week versus weekend occu-
                  pancies. Based on a Board survey of about 550 hotels.

Availability General
Cost   £90, or £10 for one issue
Comments   An annual summary is also available separately for £44. Various
                  'one-off' reports also produced.
Address   Distribution Unit, 4 Bromells Road, London SW4 0BJ
Telephone   01 846 9000; Telex: 266975; Fax: 01 627 5165

386

Originator   ENGLISH TOURIST BOARD

Title   ETB ANNUAL REPORT, annual
Coverage   A review of the Board's work plus statistics on tourism trends in
                  England and tourism developments.

Availability General
Cost   £5
Comments   Various 'one-off' reports also produced.
Address   Distribution Unit, 4 Bromells Road, London SW4 0BJ
Telephone   01 846 9000; Telex: 266975; Fax: 01 627 5165

387

Originator   ENGLISH TOURIST BOARD

Title   NATIONAL FACTS OF TOURISM, annual
Coverage   Key facts about tourism in England covering the volume and value
                  of tourism in England, accommodation use, hotel occupancy, over-
                  seas tourists, visits to selected attractions and tourism in the
                  regions. Based mainly on the Board's data.

Availability General
Cost   Free
Comments   Produced in the form of a reference card. Various 'one-off' reports
                  also produced.
Address   Distribution Unit, 4 Bromells Road, London SW4 0BJ
Telephone   01 846 9000; Telex: 266975; Fax: 01 627 5165

388

Originator	ENGLISH TOURIST BOARD
Title	SIGHTSEEING IN 198., annual
Coverage	An analysis of the usage and capacity of England's attractions for visitors, based on a Board survey of all main tourist sights. Gives data on trends in visitor numbers, opening periods, new attractions, demand relative to capacity, capital expenditure and revenue trends. Also data on employment at attractions.
Availability	General
Cost	£12
Comments	Various 'one-off' reports also produced.
Address	Distribution Unit, 4 Bromells Road, London SW4 0BJ
Telephone	01 846 9000; Telex: 266975; Fax: 01 627 5165

389

Originator	ENGLISH TOURIST BOARD
Title	TOURISM REGIONAL FACT SHEETS, regular
Coverage	Statistics on tourism trends and facilities in 12 English regions based mainly on data collected by the Board. Areas covered are Cumbria, Northumbria, North West, Yorkshire and Humberside, Heart of England, East Midlands, Thames & Chilterns, East Anglia, London, West Country, Southern and South East.
Availability	General
Cost	£25, or £2.50 each
Comments	Various 'one-off' reports also produced.
Address	Distribution Unit, 4 Bromells Road, London SW4 0BJ
Telephone	01 846 9000; Telex: 266975; Fax: 01 627 5165

390

Originator	EQUESTRIAN MANAGEMENT CONSULTANTS LTD
Title	NATIONAL EQUESTRIAN SURVEY, biennial. June 1986–
Coverage	Data on horse riding in the UK including breakdowns by age, sex, class and geographical location. Also includes information on types of riding and horse and pony ownership. Based on the company's own survey with some supporting text (30%).
Availability	General
Cost	£495 + VAT
Address	Wothersome Grange, Bramham, Nr Wetherby LS23 6LY
Telephone	0532 892267

391

Originator	EQUIPMENT LEASING ASSOCIATION
Title	ANNUAL REPORT, annual
Coverage	Contains a statistical section covering assets of members over a 10 year period. Also comparative European figures. Based on a survey of members with a large amount of text (80%).
Availability	General
Cost	Free
Comments	Also publish a quarterly press release with statistics on new assets leased to industry.
Address	18 Upper Grosvenor Street, London W1X 9PB
Telephone	01 491 2783; Fax: 01 629 0396

392

Originator	ESRC DATA ARCHIVE
Title	ESRC DATA ARCHIVE, continuous. 1967–
Coverage	The archive holds surveys from various official and non-official sources. Regular non-official sources covered include Gallup, NOP, the British Social Attitudes Survey and the National Readership Survey.
Availability	General
Cost	Charges for commercial users are now being developed
Comments	Data available on tape, disc and to certain users via the on-line system IRONS.
Address	University of Essex, Colchester CO4 3SQ
Telephone	0206 872319; Telex: 98440; Fax: 0206 873598

393

Originator	ESSEX COUNTY COUNCIL
Title	EMPLOYMENT REPORT, bi-annual. September 1984–
Coverage	National economic indicators plus data on unemployment and vacancies in Essex and industrial and commercial development. Based mainly on Central Government data (80%) with some local authority statistics (20%). Some supporting text (25%).
Availability	General
Cost	£6
Address	Planning, Globe House, New Street, Chelmsford CM1 1LF
Telephone	0245 352232; Fax: 0245 491189

394

Originator   ESSEX COUNTY COUNCIL

Title   ESSEX IN FIGURES, annual. 1984–
Coverage   A fact card outlining the basic statistics for the Essex area and the activities of the County Council. Based on various sources.

Availability   General
Cost   Free
Address   County Hall, Chelmsford CM1 1LX
Telephone   0245 492211; Fax: 0245 352710

395

Originator   ESSEX COUNTY COUNCIL

Title   HOUSING LAND, annual. 1988–
Coverage   Statistics on outstanding dwelling commitments, dwelling completions and supply changes. Analysis by district. Based on County Council data with some supporting text (30%).

Availability   General
Cost   £12.50
Address   Planning, Globe House, New Street, Chelmsford CM1 1LF
Telephone   0245 352232; Fax: 0245 491189

396

Originator   ESSEX COUNTY COUNCIL

Title   MID-YEAR POPULATION ESTIMATES, annual. 1982–
Coverage   Population estimates for various areas including wards, parishes and urban areas in Essex. Based on surveys by the Planning Department.

Availability   General
Cost   £5-£10 depending on the areas required
Address   Planning, Globe House, New Street, Chelmsford CM1 1LF
Telephone   0245 352232; Fax: 0245 491189

397

Originator   ESSEX COUNTY COUNCIL

Title   POPULATION FORECASTS, annual. 1986–
Coverage   Population forecasts for the individual districts in Essex with data to the beginning of the next century. Based on surveys and research by the Planning Department.

Availability   General

Cost	£5
Address	Planning, Globe House, New Street, Chelmsford CM1 1LF
Telephone	0245 352232; Fax: 0245 491189

398

Originator	ESTATES GAZETTE
Title	FACTS AND FIGURES, monthly in a weekly journal. January 1977–
Coverage	General data relating to the property market including house prices, farm prices, rent index, housing starts and completions, land prices, commercial property yields, Agricultural Mortgage Corporation interest rates and compulsory acquisition rates of interest. Mainly non-official sources (65%) with some official data (35%).

Availability	General
Cost	£55, or 75p for a single issue
Comments	ISSN 0014 1240
Address	Estates Gazette Ltd, 151 Wardour Street, London W1V 4BN
Telephone	01 437 0141; Telex: 892751; Fax: 01 437 0141

399

Originator	EUROMONITOR PUBLICATIONS LTD
Title	A-Z OF UK MARKETING DATA, regular
Coverage	General statistics on various consumer markets. Areas covered include sales, production, imports, exports, brand shares etc for various markets. Based on various sources.

Availability	General
Cost	£65
Comments	Various other one-off and international publications produced.
Address	87/88 Turnmill Street, London EC1M 5QU
Telephone	01 251 8024; Telex: 21120; Fax: 01 608 3149

400

Originator	EUROMONITOR PUBLICATIONS LTD
Title	RETAIL MONITOR, monthly
Coverage	News items and retail reviews plus continuously updated statistics on the retail trade. Based on various sources.

Availability	General
Cost	£275
Comments	Also publish 'A–Z of UK Retailing'. Various one-off reports and international publications also produced.
Address	87/88 Turnmill Street, London EC1M 5QU
Telephone	01 251 8024; Telex: 21120; Fax: 01 608 3149

401

Originator EUROMONITOR PUBLICATIONS LTD

Title   UK MARKET REPORTS, regular
Coverage   Regularly updated studies of various industry and market sectors
               with data on sales, production, trade, market size and brand shares
               etc. There are about 50 studies published regularly and based on
               various sources.

Availability General
Cost   On application
Comments   Various one-off and international publications also produced.
Address   87/88 Turnmill Street, London EC1M 5QU
Telephone   01 251 8024; Telex: 21120; Fax: 01 608 3149

402

Originator EUROPEAN PLASTICS NEWS

Title   UK PLASTICS INDUSTRY SURVEY, annual in a monthly
               journal
Coverage   A commentary on the market performance of plastics raw materials
               in the UK with tables on the consumption of major plastics. A
               general outlook for the coming year is given with statistics on the
               previous 2 years.

Availability General
Cost   £50, or £10 for a single issue
Comments   The survey is usually published in the January issue and covers the
                  previous year.
Address   Reed Business Publishing Ltd, Quadrant House, The Quadrant,
                  Sutton M2 5AS
Telephone   01 661 3500; Telex: 892084

403

Originator EXETER AND DISTRICT CHAMBER OF COMMERCE AND
                TRADE

Title   BUSINESS OPINION SURVEY, quarterly
Coverage   Returns from members divided into the following categories:
               manufacturing, primary, retail, services, wholesale, commercial
               and professional. Details of employment, changes in that area,
               changes in trading results and anticipated trading. Some supporting
               text (15%). Latest issue usually covers the previous quarter.

Availability Member and selected others
Cost   Free
Address   Equitable Life House, 31 Southernhay East, Exeter EX1 1NS
Telephone   0392 36641; Telex: 42603; Fax: 0392 50402

404

Originator	EXHIBITION SURVEYS LTD
Title	AUDIENCE PROFILE REPORTS, every 1–3 years (depending on the exhibition)
Coverage	Produce reports for a large number of exhibitions, e.g. Interplas, International Business Show, IPEX, Hevac, Meatex, Boat Show, Commercial Motor Show, Which Computer, Royal Show, Smithfield Show. Analysis of audience, product interests, purchasing role, status, behaviour, opinions, recall, performance of named stands etc. Based on own research with some text (20%).
Availability	Exhibiting companies
Cost	£250 to £350
Address	PO Box 7, Melton Mowbray LE13 0BR
Telephone	0664 67666; Fax: 0664 67528

405

Originator	EXPOTEL EXECUTIVE TRAVEL
Title	UK HOTEL TARIFF SURVEY, annual
Coverage	Figures on the yearly percentage increase of hotel room prices with an analysis of the reasons for and background to these trends. Based on the company's own survey.
Availability	General
Cost	On application
Comments	Data also available on disc.
Address	Banda House, Cambridge Grove, London W6 0LE
Telephone	01 748 8000; Telex: 8811951; Fax: 01 741 7225

406

Originator	FARMLAND MARKET
Title	LAND VALUES, bi-annual in a bi-annual journal. 1973–
Coverage	Farmland auction prices analysed over the last 6 months. Also grass keep and other land values, borrowing charges, rents and land loss in the tenanted sector. Based on a combination of other non-official sources (50%), the journal's own research (20%) and Central Government data (30%).
Availability	General
Cost	£24, or £12 for a single issue
Comments	The journal is published jointly by Farmers Weekly and the Estates Gazette.
Address	Farmers Weekly, Carew House, Wallington SM6 0DX
Telephone	01 661 3500; Telex: 892084

407

Originator	FARMSTAT LTD
Title	FARMSTAT, quarterly
Coverage	Usage of different agricultural inputs on different crops. Covers particularly herbicides, fungicides, fertilizers, growth regulators, insecticides and seed dressings. Based on a survey of 2,000 farms representing about 45,000 fields. Some supporting text (60%). Produced 4-6 weeks after the survey.
Availability	General
Cost	£800-£7,000 depending on the amount of data required
Comments	Also available on-line, on tape and disc. Company also known as Produce Studies Ltd.
Address	Northcroft House, West Street, Newbury RG13 1HD
Telephone	0635 46112; Telex: 849228; Fax: 0635 43945

408

Originator	FAST FACTS LTD
Title	FOOD TRENDS, quarterly
Coverage	Statistics on the consumption trends and patterns for over 200 product categories with data over an 8 year historical period and forecasts up to 2 or 3 years ahead.
Availability	General
Cost	£60 per issue
Address	Walgrave, Northampton NN6 9QF
Telephone	0604 781392

409

Originator	FEDERATION OF BRITISH CREMATION AUTHORITIES
Title	ANNUAL REPORT, annual
Coverage	Includes cremation statistics for individual crematoria over a 5-year period. Data on disposition of ashes. Based on the Federation's own survey. A large amount of supporting text (80%).
Availability	General
Cost	Free
Address	7/17 Lansdowne Road, Croydon CR0 2BX
Telephone	01 688 4422; Fax: 01 681 8186

410

Originator	FEDERATION OF CIVIL ENGINEERING CONTRACTORS
Title	FCEC WORKLOAD SURVEY, quarterly

Coverage	Statistics based on a survey of member companies with data on workload trends and expectations.
Availability	Members and some others on request
Cost	Free
Address	6 Portugal Street, London WC2A 2HH
Telephone	01 404 4020; Telex: 8955101

411

Originator	FEDERATION OF MASTER BUILDERS
Title	FMB STATE OF TRADE SURVEY, quarterly. November 1983
Coverage	Results of a survey of 450 member construction firms in England and Wales with data on workload for the quarter and predictions for the coming quarter. Various topical questions are also included in each survey. Supporting text comprises 50%.
Availability	General
Cost	On application
Address	Gordon Fisher House, 33 John Street, London WC1N 2BB
Telephone	01 242 7583

412

Originator	FEDERATION OF MASTER BUILDERS
Title	MANPOWER IN THE BUILDING INDUSTRY, regular. 1986–
Coverage	Two reports covering recruitment, shortages, training and pay received in the building industry. Based on the Federation's survey of about 2,000 companies with some supporting text (33%).
Availability	General
Cost	On request
Address	33 John Street, London WC1N 2BB
Telephone	01 242 7583

413

Originator	FEDERATION OF OPTHALMIC & DISPENSING OPTICIANS
Title	OPTICS AT A GLANCE, annual. 1982–
Coverage	General statistics on optics including the number of opticians and average spectacle prices. Based on a combination of the Federation's own survey (65%) and Central Government data (35%). Some supporting text (50%).
Availability	General
Cost	Free
Address	40 Portland Place, London W1N 4BA
Telephone	01 637 2507

414

Originator   FEDERATION OF PETROLEUM SUPPLIERS

Title   FPS OIL PRICE REVIEW, weekly. July 1980–
Coverage   Gives the buying prices of various grades of petroleum product, as
             distinct from published wholesale general prices. Based on returns
             from members who subscribe to the Oil Price Review – at present
             about 80 distributors. Some supporting text (20%).

Availability Members
Comments   Produced the day after the figures are collected.
Address   1st Floor, 500 Manchester Road, Worsley, Manchester M28 6NS
Telephone   061 799 5181; Fax: 061 790 2624

415

Originator   FEDERATION OF SMALL MINES OF GREAT BRITAIN

Title   STATISTICS, regular
Coverage   Statistics on the mining sector with data from the Federation's own
             surveys and Central Government statistics.

Availability District Associations
Cost   Free
Address   13A King Street, Newcastle-under-Lyme ST5 1ER
Telephone   0782 614618

416

Originator   FERTILISER MANUFACTURERS ASSOCIATION

Title   FERTILISER REVIEW, annual
Coverage   Covers area of crops, consumption of inorganic fertilizers, straight
             fertilizers and compound fertilizers. Also concentration, appli-
             cation rates and usage of compound fertilizers. Based largely on the
             Association's own research (80%) with additional data from
             Central Government (20%). Most of the review is made up of text
             (90%).

Availability General
Cost   £3
Address   Greenhill House, 90/93 Cowcross Street, London EC1M 6BH
Telephone   01 251 6001; Telex: 94012856

417

Originator   FIFE REGIONAL COUNCIL

Title   FIFE IN FIGURES, regular. 1977–

Coverage	Summary statistics on the population, births, employment, unemployment, dwellings, earnings, car ownership, rates, roads, water, education and social trends. Data for the region and the 3 district councils. Mainly Central Government data (65%) with some Council data (35%).
Availability	General
Cost	Free
Comments	Also available on-line locally via the Council's viewdata service 'Fifeline'.
Address	Planning Department, Rothesay House, North Street, Glenrothes
Telephone	0592 754411; Telex: 727461; Fax: 0592 758582

418

Originator	FIFE REGIONAL COUNCIL
Title	HOUSING REVIEW, regular. 1982–
Coverage	Statistics on housing stock, housing land supply, household projections and future housing requirements. Based on the Council's own surveys with some supporting text (30%).
Availability	General
Cost	£3
Address	Planning Department, Rothesay House, North Street, Glenrothes
Telephone	0592 754411; Telex: 727461; Fax: 0592 758582

419

Originator	FIFE REGIONAL COUNCIL
Title	POPULATION ESTIMATES, annual. 1975–
Coverage	Estimates of the population of every settlement in Fife having more than 100 residents. Also population estimates broken down by other areas, e.g. employment office areas, structure plan sub-areas etc. Based on a survey by the Council with some supporting text (20%).
Availability	General
Cost	Free
Address	Planning Department, Rothesay House, North Street, Glenrothes
Telephone	0592 754411; Telex: 727461; Fax: 0592 758582

420

Originator	FIFE REGIONAL COUNCIL
Title	STRATEGIC PROJECTIONS, regular. 1977–

Coverage	Population projections, household projections and forecasts of labour supply and demand in the region and the 3 district councils. Based on regular surveys by the Council. Supporting text comprises 30%.
Availability	General
Cost	£2.50
Address	Planning Department, Rothesay House, North Street, Glenrothes
Telephone	0592 754411; Telex: 727461; Fax: 0592 758582

421

Originator	FINANCE HOUSES ASSOCIATION
Title	ANNUAL REPORT, annual
Coverage	Contains commentary and statistics on trends in the credit market with data on business lending, consumer lending, analysis of new credit extended by class of goods and base rates. In most tables figures for the last 2 years are given. Based on lending by FHA members.
Availability	General
Cost	Free
Address	18 Upper Grosvenor Street, London W1X 9PB
Telephone	01 491 2783; Fax: 01 629 0396

422

Originator	FINANCIAL TIMES BUSINESS INFORMATION LTD
Title	FT MONTHLY UK STOCK INDICES, monthly
Coverage	Daily information on the FT indices, the main actuary groups and other important indices. Highs, lows and averages for each month and gross redemption figures are also provided. Based on the FT's own data.
Availability	General
Cost	£100
Comments	Data available in other formats through publisher. Also publishes data on world stock indices and currencies.
Address	Bracken House, 10 Cannon Street, London EC4P 4BY
Telephone	01 248 8000; Telex: 8811506; Fax: 01 248 5654

423

Originator	FINANCIAL TIMES BUSINESS INFORMATION LTD
Title	FT-ACTUARIES QUARTERLY INDICES, quarterly. 1962–
Coverage	Mid and end-of-month figures for the index value, earnings yield and dividend yield for each of the FT sub-indices. Based on the FT's own data.

Availability	General
Cost	£100
Comments	Price includes free binder and one year's back data. Also publishes data on world stock indices and currencies.
Address	Bracken House, 10 Cannon Street, London EC4P 4BY
Telephone	01 248 8000; Telex: 8811506; Fax: 01 248 5654

424

Originator	FINANCIAL WEEKLY
Title	BUSINESS CLIMATE, weekly in a weekly journal
Coverage	Graphs and commentary on the general trends in the economy and business. Based largely on official data. Also includes various financial statistics, share prices etc.
Availability	General
Cost	£47 or £1 for a single issue
Address	Financial Weekly Ltd, 14 Greville Street, London EC1N 8SB
Telephone	01 405 2622

425

Originator	FISH TRADER
Title	IMPORTS AND EXPORTS ANALYSIS, quarterly in a weekly journal
Coverage	Imports and exports of fish by volume and value and by type of fish. A short commentary accompanies the data. Based on Customs and Excise data.
Availability	General
Cost	£29.50 or 55p for a single issue
Comments	ISSN 0143 7771
Address	FMJ International, Queensway House, 2 Queensway, Redhill RH1 1QS
Telephone	0737 768611; Telex: 948669; Fax: 0737 761685

426

Originator	FISH TRADER
Title	PORT AND MARKET PRICES/POTATO MARKET REPORT, weekly in a weekly journal
Coverage	Producers' and wholesale prices for potatoes and wholesale fish prices at various markets around the country. Prices are given for various types of fish.
Availability	General
Cost	£29.50 or 55p for a single issue
Comments	ISSN 0143 7771

Address   FMJ International, Queensway House, 2 Queensway, Redhill RH1
                 1QS
Telephone   0737 768611; Telex: 948669; Fax: 0737 761685

427

Originator   FLOWER TRADES JOURNAL

Title   AIPH STATISTICS, annual in a monthly journal. 1981–
Coverage   Cultivation and production data on non-edible horticultural pro-
                 ducts. Based on trade association statistics.

Availability General
Cost   £26 or £1.70 for a single issue
Address   Yewtree Publishing Ltd, 17 Wickham Road, Beckenham BR3 2JS
Telephone   01 658 8688; Telex: 928080; Fax: 01 658 2250

428

Originator   FLYMO LTD

Title   POWER LAWNMOWER MARKET STATISTICS, annual.
                 1983–
Coverage   Tables and graphs on the power lawnmower market with data on
                 total market size, by type of lawnmower, brand shares, lawn
                 numbers and sizes, prices and trends over the last few years. Figures
                 compiled from various market research surveys.

Availability General
Cost   Free
Address   Aycliffe Industrial Estate, Newton Aycliffe DL5 6UP
Telephone   0325 315161; Telex: 58111

429

Originator   FOOD AND DRINK FEDERATION

Title   FDF ANNUAL STATISTICS, annual
Coverage   Production and sales data for individual product sectors in the food
                 and drink industry. Also figures on UK imports and exports of
                 specific products and employment in the UK food industry. Over
                 90% of the data comes from Central Government sources.

Availability General
Cost   £10
Address   6 Catherine Street, London WC2B 5JJ
Telephone   01 836 2460; Telex: 299388; Fax: 01 836 0580

430

Originator	FOOD MANUFACTURER
Title	BRITISH FOOD MACHINERY MARKET, regular in a monthly journal
Coverage	Commentary and statistics on the sales, imports and exports of the major types of food machinery. Usually gives the latest annual figures and includes a brief assessment of the outlook for the sector. Based largely on official data.
Availability	General
Cost	£48 or £4.80 for a single issue
Comments	ISSN 0015 6477
Address	Morgan Grampian, 30 Calderwood Street, London SE18 6QH
Telephone	01 855 7777

431

Originator	FOUNDRY TRADE JOURNAL
Title	UK METAL PRICES, bi-monthly in a bi-monthly journal
Coverage	Prices of ferro-alloy and other metals and non-ferrous metals by type in the UK. Based on various non-official sources.
Availability	General
Cost	£69.75 or £6.60 for a single issue
Comments	Only published monthly in January, August and December.
Address	Fuel and Metallurgical Journals, 2 Queensway, Redhill RH1 1QS
Telephone	0737 768611; Telex: 948669; Fax: 0737 761685

432

Originator	FRASER OF ALLANDER INSTITUTE
Title	QUARTERLY ECONOMIC COMMENTARY, quarterly. 1975–
Coverage	Trends and outlook for the Scottish economy with individual reviews of industrial performance, service sector, labour market and the regions. Also includes feature articles. Based mainly on Central Government data (80%). Commentary covers 50%.
Availability	General
Cost	£20
Comments	ISSN 0306 7866
Address	Strathclyde University, 100 Cathedral Street, Glasgow G4 0LN
Telephone	041 552 4400

433

Originator	FREIGHT INFORMATION SERVICES
Title	EXPORT ANALYSIS AND FORECASTS, quarterly. December 1987–
Coverage	An analysis of UK exports by value, volume and countries of destination. Also includes short term forecasts. Largely based on Central Government data (90%).
Availability	General
Cost	£50
Address	Adelphi Chambers, Hoghton Street, Southport PR9 0NZ
Telephone	0704 38515; Fax: 0704 35133

434

Originator	FREIGHT INFORMATION SERVICES
Title	EXPORT/IMPORT TONNAGES, annual
Coverage	A guide to export and import tonnages to and from the UK and every country in the world. 41 product descriptions and summary tables covering a 4 year period for the major trading areas. A summary of Central Government data.
Availability	General
Cost	£55
Address	Adelphi Chambers, Hoghton Street, Southport PR9 0NZ
Telephone	0704 38515; Fax: 0704 35133

435

Originator	FREIGHT TRANSPORT ASSOCIATION
Title	MANAGERS' FUEL PRICE INFORMATION SERVICE, monthly
Coverage	Prices of derv and fuel oil with a general analysis of market trends. Based on the Association's own survey with some supporting text (60%).
Availability	Members
Cost	£70
Comments	Produced in conjunction with John Hall Associates.
Address	Hermes House, St Johns Road, Tunbridge Wells TN4 9UZ
Telephone	0892 26171; Telex: 957158; Fax: 0892 34989

436

Originator	FREIGHT TRANSPORT ASSOCIATION
Title	MANAGERS' GUIDE TO DISTRIBUTION COSTS, annual with 3 quarterly summary updates
Coverage	Statistics on wages, vehicle operating costs (including cars) and haulage rates. Data on actual costs plus indices to measure trends. Some forecasts are also included and articles on related topics. Largely based on the Association's research (80%) with a large amount of supporting text (90%).
Availability	Members
Cost	£52.50
Address	Hermes House, St Johns Road, Tunbridge Wells TN4 9UZ
Telephone	0892 26171; Telex: 957158; Fax: 0892 34989

437

Originator	FRUIT TRADES JOURNAL
Title	FRESH PRODUCE DESK BOOK, annual
Coverage	A directory of the fruits and flowers industry, also including summary statistics on fruit and flower production, sales and prices.
Availability	General
Cost	£10.50
Address	Lockwood Press, 430/438 Market Towers, London SW8 5NN
Telephone	01 622 6677; Telex: 915149; Fax: 01 720 2047

438

Originator	FRUIT TRADES JOURNAL
Title	MARKET PRICES, weekly in a weekly journal
Coverage	Statistics covering fruit and flower prices in specific UK markets. Prices for specific fruits and flowers and the previous week's prices are given.
Availability	General
Cost	£42
Address	Lockwood Press, 430/438 Market Towers, London SW8 5NN
Telephone	01 622 6677; Telex: 915149; Fax: 01 720 2047

439

Originator	FURNITURE INDUSTRY RESEARCH ASSOCIATION
Title	FURNITURE INDUSTRY IN THE UK: A STATISTICAL DIGEST, annual

Coverage	Statistics on the furniture industry including turnover, sales, deliveries, consumption, imports, exports, prices and advertising. Largely based on Central Government data (70%) with some data from the Association and other non-official sources.
Availability	General
Cost	£90, reduced price to members
Comments	The Association also publishes regular statistics on international markets.
Address	Maxwell Road, Stevenage SG1 2EW
Telephone	0438 313433

440

Originator	FURNITURE INDUSTRY RESEARCH ASSOCIATION
Title	QUARTERLY BULLETIN OF STATISTICS, quarterly
Coverage	Statistics on the UK furniture industry including sales, imports, exports, prices, advertising etc. updating the data in the annual digest (see above). Mainly based on Central Government data.
Availability	General
Cost	£60, reduced prices for members
Comments	The Association also publishes regular statistics on international markets.
Address	Maxwell Road, Stevenage SG1 2EW
Telephone	0438 313433

441

Originator	GALLUP
Title	GALLUP POLITICAL INDEX, monthly. January 1960–
Coverage	Summary data on the various opinion polls carried out by Gallup on political, economic and social issues.
Availability	General
Cost	On application
Comments	ISSN 0435 0812. Gallup data also available on tape, disc.
Address	Social Surveys (Gallup) Ltd, 202 Finchley Road, London NW3 6BL
Telephone	01 794 0461; Telex: 261712

442

Originator	GAS CONSUMERS COUNCIL
Title	AN ANALYSIS OF GAS DISCONNECTIONS, annual. February 1988–

Coverage	Statistics on gas disconnections with national and regional figures. Includes an assessment of the factors leading to the increase in disconnections. Based largely on the Council's own survey (70%), with supporting text (50%).
Availability	General
Cost	£2
Address	6th Floor, Abford House, 15 Wilton Road, London SW1V 1LT
Telephone	01 931 0977; Fax: 01 630 9344

443

Originator	GAS CONSUMERS COUNCIL
Title	ANNUAL REPORT, annual
Coverage	Mainly commentary on events in the gas industry and a report of research undertaken during the year. Includes statistics on complaints and inquiries recieved during the year. Based on the Council's own survey with 80% text.
Availability	General
Cost	Free
Address	6th Floor, Abford House, 15 Wilton Road, London SW1V 1LT
Telephone	01 931 0977; Fax: 01 630 9344

444

Originator	GAS CONSUMERS COUNCIL
Title	EXPENDITURE ON FUELS, annual
Coverage	Secondary analysis of Central Government data from the Family Expenditure Survey giving expenditure on fuels of the various family groups. Some supporting text (40%).
Availability	General
Cost	Free
Address	6th Floor, Abford House, 15 Wilton Road, London SW1V 1LT
Telephone	01 931 0977; Fax: 01 630 9344

445

Originator	GENERAL COUNCIL OF BRITISH SHIPPING
Title	STATISTICAL BRIEF, quarterly. July 1982–
Coverage	General data on the UK and world fleets, shipbuilding, manpower, capital expenditure in shipping and the shipping balance of payments. Based on a range of non-official and Central Government sources with some data from the Council itself (20%).
Availability	General
Cost	£35

Address   30/32 St Mary Axe, London EC3A 8ET
Telephone   01 283 2922; Telex: 884008; Fax: 01 626 8135

446

Originator   GENERAL COUNCIL OF BRITISH SHIPPING

Title   TRAMP TIME CHARTER INDEX, quarterly
Coverage   An index of tramp time charters collated from non-official sources.

Availability General
Cost   Included in the subscription to the previous entry
Address   30/32 St Mary Axe, London EC3A 8ET
Telephone   01 283 2922; Telex: 884008; Fax: 01 626 8135

447

Originator   GENERAL COUNCIL OF BRITISH SHIPPING

Title   TRAMP TRIP CHARTER INDEX, monthly
Coverage   An index of tramp trip charters collated from non-official sources.

Availability General
Cost   £35
Address   30/32 St Mary Axe, London EC3A 8ET
Telephone   01 283 2922; Telex: 884008; Fax: 01 626 8135

448

Originator   GERRARD VIVIAN GRAY LTD

Title   INDUSTRY FORECASTS, monthly
Coverage   Trends and forecasts in various sectors, e.g. building, chemicals,
              materials, engineering etc. Individual reports on specific sectors.

Availability On application
Cost   On application
Address   Ling House, 10/13 Dominion Street, London EC2M 2UE
Telephone   01 638 2888; Telex: 887080

449

Originator   GIN RECTIFIERS AND DISTILLERS ASSOCIATION

Title   RETURNS FOR THE FOUR HALF YEARS ENDED 31ST
              DECEMBER, annual
Coverage   Gives production of gin, home trade sales and export sales to EEC
              countries and non-EEC countries for the last 4 six month periods.
              Based on returns from members.

Availability	General
Cost	Free
Address	37 Waterford House, 110 Kensington Park Road, London W11 2PJ
Telephone	01 229 9222

450

Originator	GLASGOW CHAMBER OF COMMERCE
Title	ECONOMIC SURVEY, quarterly
Coverage	A survey of business activities and expectations in the West o Scotland based on a survey of Chamber members. Supporting tex takes up 50%. Usually published 1 month after the survey.
Availability	General
Cost	Free
Comments	Issued as a press release and also published in the Chamber': journal.
Address	30 George Street, Glasgow G2 1EQ
Telephone	041 204 2121; Telex: 777967; Fax: 041 221 2336

451

Originator	GLASGOW DISTRICT COUNCIL
Title	CITY PROFILE: FACTS AND FIGURES ABOUT GLAS GOW, regular
Coverage	General statistics on the key social and economic indicators includ ing population, economy, industry, housing, unemployment etc Based on a combination of Central Government and other sources
Availability	General
Cost	£4.50
Comments	Latest issue published in 1988.
Address	Planning, 231 George Street, Glasgow G1 1RX
Telephone	041 221 9600

452

Originator	GLASS MANUFACTURERS FEDERATION
Title	BOTTLE BANK PROGRESS REPORT, quarterly. 1979–
Coverage	Data on every bottle bank scheme in the UK based on the Feder ation's own statistics. A small amount of text (5%).
Availability	General
Cost	On application
Address	19 Portland Place, London W1N 4BH
Telephone	01 580 6952; Telex: 27470; Fax: 01 436 4396

453

Originator	GLAZED AND FLOOR TILE HOME TRADE ASSOCIATION
Title	MEMBERS' SALES OF CERAMIC TILES, monthly
Coverage	Sales of ceramic tiles based on a survey of members.
Availability	Members
Cost	Free
Address	Federation House, Station Road, Stoke-on-Trent ST4 2RU
Telephone	0782 747147; Telex: 367446; Fax: 0782 744102

454

Originator	GLAZED AND FLOOR TILE HOME TRADE ASSOCIATION
Title	UK IMPORTS OF CERAMIC TILES, monthly
Coverage	Imports of ceramic tiles based on data from Central Government, HM Customs and Excise.
Availability	Members
Cost	Free
Address	Federation House, Station Road, Stoke-on-Trent ST4 2RU
Telephone	0782 747147; Telex: 367446; Fax: 0782 744102

455

Originator	GORDON SIMMONS RESEARCH LTD
Title	CHAIN STORE INDEX, bi-annual. 1984–
Coverage	Statistics on shopping behaviour, profiles and attitudes for all the major retail chains based on a national quota sample of 3,000 adults.
Availability	General
Cost	From £990
Address	80 St Martins Lane, London WC2N 4AA
Telephone	01 240 0256; Fax: 01 379 5670

456

Originator	GORDON SIMMONS RESEARCH LTD
Title	CONFECTIONERY PROFILES, annual
Coverage	Annual report on the confectionery market covering the total market, data on chocolate and sugar confectionery and brands. Gives consumer expenditure, expenditure profiles, source of purchase, day, time, amount spent per item, pack type, gift market, consumer profiles, childrens market etc. Around 40,000 items checked at 1,000 outlets by the company.

Availability	General
Cost	On application
Address	80 St Martins Lane, London WC2N 2AA
Telephone	01 240 0256; Fax: 01 379 5670

457

Originator	GORDON SIMMONS RESEARCH LTD
Title	IMAGE OF MANUFACTURERS IN THE GROCERY TRADE, annual. 1984–
Coverage	A series of retail studies examining the standing of leading manufac turers among key grocery accounts based on in-depth interview with 20-25 retail buyers per study. 50% of the report is text.

Availability	General
Cost	From £375
Address	80 St Martins Lane, London WC2N 4AA
Telephone	01 240 0256; Fax: 01 379 5670

458

Originator	GORDON SIMMONS RESEARCH LTD
Title	RESTAURANT CHAIN INDEX, bi-annual. 1985–
Coverage	Usage and attitudes towards 14 major restaurant chains based on a national quota sample of 2,000 adults.

Availability	General
Cost	£2,750
Address	80 St Martins Lane, London WC2N 4AA
Telephone	01 240 0256; Fax: 01 379 5670

459

Originator	GORDON SIMMONS RESEARCH LTD
Title	SPORTING AND LEISURE BRANDS, bi-annual. 1985–
Coverage	A study based on a sample of 1,200 adults aged 16-50 years covering awareness of sporting and leisure brands, purchasing preferences advertising awareness, attitudes towards the major brands etc.

Availability	General
Cost	From £650
Address	80 St Martins Lane, London WC2N 4AA
Telephone	01 240 0256; Fax: 01 379 5670

460

Originator	GRAMPIAN REGIONAL COUNCIL
Title	ABERDEEN AREA HOUSING MARKET, quarterly and annual
Coverage	Annual and quarterly summaries of private housing market trends prepared in conjuction with Aberdeen Solicitors Property Centre. Some commentary (30%) supports the statistics.
Availability	General
Cost	£5
Address	Woodhill House, Westburn Road, Aberdeen AB9 2LU
Telephone	0224 682222; Telex: 739277; Fax: 0224 697445

461

Originator	GRAMPIAN REGIONAL COUNCIL
Title	ANNUAL REPORT ON EMPLOYMENT AND UNEMPLOYMENT, annual
Coverage	Provides a detailed review of employment and unemployment in the Grampian region at region, district and local area levels. Based almost entirely on Central Government data, with a supporting commentary (40%).
Availability	General
Cost	£3
Address	Woodhill House, Westburn Road, Aberdeen AB9 2LU
Telephone	0224 682222; Telex: 739277; Fax: 0224 697445

462

Originator	GRAMPIAN REGIONAL COUNCIL
Title	DEVELOPMENT SUMMARIES, annual
Coverage	Summary sheets for 80 settlements in the region containing housing, industrial and commercial information and details of population change, housing stock, waiting lists, education, drainage, water supply and major capital projects. Based on the Council's own data.
Availability	General
Cost	£15
Comments	Also publishes annual housing, industrial and commercial schedules with details on specific sites.
Address	Woodhill House, Westburn Road, Aberdeen AB9 2LU
Telephone	0224 682222; Telex: 739277; Fax: 0224 697445

463

Originator	GRAMPIAN REGIONAL COUNCIL
Title	FORECASTS OF POPULATION, EMPLOYMENT AND HOUSING, annual
Coverage	Forecasts for districts and structure plan areas based upon the latest projections of demographic rates together with an assessment of current market trends, local authority policies and their likely future variations.
Availability	General
Cost	£3
Address	Woodhill House, Westburn Road, Aberdeen AB9 2LU
Telephone	0224 682222; Telex: 739277; Fax: 0224 697445

464

Originator	GRAMPIAN REGIONAL COUNCIL
Title	FUTURE OIL AND GAS PROSPECTS, annual
Coverage	A report assessing the likely offshore developments and interprets these in terms of their probable physical and economic impact upon the region. Mainly based on the Council's own data (70%) with a large amount of supporting commentary (90%).
Availability	General
Cost	£5
Address	Woodhill House, Westburn Road, Aberdeen AB9 2LU
Telephone	0224 682222; Telex: 739277; Fax: 0224 697445

465

Originator	GRAMPIAN REGIONAL COUNCIL
Title	QUARTERLY ECONOMIC SURVEY, quarterly
Coverage	Analysis of trends in the local economy, the labour market and land development over the preceding quarter and reports on developments which are likely to affect future prospects. Published about 3 months after the quarter to which it refers.
Availability	General
Cost	£16 or £5 for a single issue
Address	Woodhill House, Westburn Road, Aberdeen AB9 2LU
Telephone	0224 682222; Telex: 739277; Fax: 0224 697445

466

Originator	GRAMPIAN REGIONAL COUNCIL
Title	SCHOOL ROLL FORECASTS, annual

Coverage   Information on roll, type, capacity and catchment area for each
               school and roll forecasts for the period to 1991. Gives a description
               of the forecasting method.
Availability   General
Cost   £3
Address   Woodhill House, Westburn Road, Aberdeen AB9 2LU
Telephone   0224 682222; Telex: 739277; Fax: 0224 697445

467

Originator   GRAMPIAN REGIONAL COUNCIL

Title   SMALL AREA POPULATIONS, annual
Coverage   Details of current electorate, housing stock and population totals by
               parish and settlement.
Availability   General
Cost   £3
Address   Woodhill House, Westburn Road, Aberdeen AB9 2LU
Telephone   0224 682222; Telex: 739277; Fax: 0224 697445

468

Originator   GRAMPIAN REGIONAL COUNCIL

Title   UNEMPLOYMENT IN GRAMPIAN, monthly
Coverage   A monthly summary of the latest unemployment rates and numbers
               for the travel-to-work areas in Grampian. Based on Central
               Government data with some supporting text (30%).
Availability   General
Cost   £5
Address   Woodhill House, Westburn Road, Aberdeen AB9 2LU
Telephone   0224 682222; Telex: 739277; Fax: 0224 697445

469

Originator   GRAMPIAN TELEVISION PLC

Title   MARKETING FACTS BOOK, biennial
Coverage   Data on population, employment, oil, agriculture, finance, life-
               styles, motoring, leisure and retailing in the Grampian television
               area. Based on a combination of various non-official sources (80%)
               and Central Government data (20%). A small amount of suppor-
               ting text (10%).
Availability   Advertising agencies and selected other organizations
Cost   Free
Address   29 Glasshouse Street, London W1
Telephone   01 439 3141; Telex: 267912; Fax: 01 439 1498

470

Originator	GRANADA TELEVISION LTD
Title	GRANADA MARKET, regular
Coverage	General statistics and commentary on market and social trends in the Granada TV region. Includes data on population, housing spending, ownership of consumer durables, industry, transport etc Based on various sources.
Availability	General
Cost	Free
Comments	Latest edition – 1987.
Address	36 Golden Square, London W1R 4AH
Telephone	01 734 8080; Telex: 27937; Fax: 01 734 2001

471

Originator	GRANADA TELEVISION LTD
Title	GRANADA RETAIL AND SERVICES DIRECTORY, annual. 1980–
Coverage	The number of outlets by type of business in the Granada TV area and for Great Britain as a whole. A detailed breakdown of the major multiple groups both nationally and in the Granada area based on intensive trade inquiries. Largely based on Granada's own surveys (90%). Usually published 3 months after the end of the year to which it relates. A small amount of text (10%).
Availability	General
Cost	Free
Comments	Other directories produced occasionally.
Address	36 Golden Square, London W1R 4AH
Telephone	01 734 8080; Telex: 27937; Fax: 01 734 2001

472

Originator	GREATER MANCHESTER ECONOMIC DEVELOPMENT CORPORATION (GMEDC)
Title	PRESENTATION OF THE FACTS, regular
Coverage	Summary data on the Greater Manchester area and its districts covering population, the economic base, land and property, communications, environment, education etc. Short pieces of text accompany each statistical section.
Availability	General
Cost	Free
Comments	Produced in a loose-leaf folder.
Address	Bernard House, Piccadilly Gardens, Manchester M1 4DD
Telephone	061 236 4412

473

Originator	GREATER MANCHESTER RESEARCH AND INFOR-MATION PLANNING UNIT
Title	MAJOR EMPLOYMENT CHANGES IN GREATER MAN-CHESTER, annual. 1986–
Coverage	A review of employment changes in Greater Manchester with an industry breakdown, redundancy figures and an analysis of press cuttings. Based on Central Government data (50%) and other non-official sources (50%). A large amount of supporting text (60%).
Availability	General
Cost	£1.50
Comments	A similar publication previously published by Greater Manchester County Council.
Address	Metropolitan House, Hobson Street, Oldham OL1 1QD
Telephone	061 678 4178

474

Originator	GREATER MANCHESTER RESEARCH AND INFOR-MATION PLANNING UNIT
Title	MONTHLY UNEMPLOYMENT BULLETIN, monthly. August 1987–
Coverage	Graphical representation of unemployment figures broken down by Greater Manchester district. Based entirely on Central Government data with a small amount of text (10%).
Availability	General
Cost	Free
Comments	A quarterly bulletin to be published shortly will look at age and duration figures in more detail.
Address	Metropolitan House, Hobson Street, Oldham OL1 1QD
Telephone	061 678 4178

475

Originator	GREATER MANCHESTER RESEARCH AND INFOR-MATION PLANNING UNIT
Title	RETAIL DEVELOPMENT DATABASE AND ANALYSIS, annual. June 1987–
Coverage	Information and statistics on retail developments in the 10 district areas of Greater Manchester. Based on data collected by the Unit. A small amount of supporting text (10%).
Availability	General
Cost	£30

Comments	Similar reports being developed for industry and offices.
Address	Metropolitan House, Hobson Street, Oldham OL1 1QD
Telephone	061 678 4178

476

Originator	GREENE, BELFIELD-SMITH
Title	LUXURY COUNTRY HOUSE HOTELS, annual. April 1988–
Coverage	Financial and operating statistics on the luxury country house hotel market. Based on a sample of 75 hotels with a commentary accompanying the data (60%).
Availability	General
Cost	£25
Address	Victoria House, Vernon Place, London WC1B 4DB
Telephone	01 242 3959; Telex: 24292; Fax: 01 831 8626

477

Originator	GREENE, BELFIELD-SMITH
Title	PAY AND BENEFITS IN THE HOTEL AND CATERING INDUSTRY, annual. November 1987–
Coverage	Salaries of management and the wages of non-management staff plus data on benefits packages for all grades of staff in hotels and catering. Based on a survey of about 3,500 salaried employees and about 6,000 wage earners. A commentary (35%) accompanies the data.
Availability	General
Cost	£75
Comments	Also available for use on IBM compatable machines.
Address	Victoria House, Vernon Place, London WC1B 4DB
Telephone	01 242 3959; Telex: 24292; Fax: 01 831 8626

478

Originator	GREENWELL, MONTAGU & CO.
Title	MONETARY BULLETIN, monthly
Coverage	Various figures based on the different definitions of the money supply. Based entirely on Central Government data.
Availability	Primarily clients
Cost	On application
Comments	Also publishes various reports on the equities, gilts markets.
Address	Bow Bells House, Bread Street, London EC4M 9EL
Telephone	01 236 2040; Telex: 883006

479

Originator	GROCER
Title	GROCER PRICE LIST, monthly supplement to a weekly journal
Coverage	A monthly supplement usually produced on the first Saturday of each month giving detailed prices for various foods and grocery products.
Availability	General
Cost	£20
Comments	ISSN 0017 4351. Included as part of the 'Grocer' subscription.
Address	William Reed Ltd, 5 Southwark Street, London SE1 1RQ
Telephone	01 407 6981; Telex: 8812648; Fax: 01 378 6781

480

Originator	GROCER
Title	MARKET PRICES/ MEAT AND PRODUCE PRICES, weekly in a weekly journal
Coverage	Prices of various foods including vegetables, meat, salad, cheese, eggs, butter, lard etc. Based on various non-official sources with some supporting text (15%).
Availability	General
Cost	£20 or 50p for a single issue
Comments	ISSN 0017 4351
Address	William Reed Ltd, 5 Southwark Street, London SE1 1RQ
Telephone	01 407 6981; Telex: 8812648; Fax: 01 378 6781

481

Originator	GWENT COUNTY COUNCIL
Title	ECONOMIC PROGRESS REPORT, quarterly. 1977–
Coverage	Largely concerned with the employment situation in the county with statistics on unemployment, vacancies and redundancies. Also a section on industrial development covering industrial and commercial news and planning permissions. Based mainly on Central Government data (80%) with additional material from the Council (20%). Some supporting text (40%).
Availability	General
Cost	£5
Comments	Replaced publication 'Employment and Industrial Trends' which appeared from 1961 to 1976.
Address	Planning Department, County Hall, Cwmbran NP44 2XF
Telephone	0633 838838,x692; Fax: 0633 838225

482

Originator	HALIFAX BUILDING SOCIETY
Title	HALIFAX HOUSE PRICE INDEX NATIONAL BULLETIN, quarterly. March 1984–
Coverage	Indices of house prices and average prices for all buyers, first-time buyers and former owner-occupiers. Also a general review of mortgage demand. Based on a 100% sample of Halifax mortgage approvals. Some supporting text (30%).
Availability	General
Cost	Free
Comments	From March 1984 to the beginning of 1986 the publication was produced monthly.
Address	Trinity Road, Halifax HX1 2RG
Telephone	0422 65777; Telex: 517441; Fax: 0422 46970

483

Originator	HALIFAX BUILDING SOCIETY
Title	HALIFAX HOUSE PRICE INDEX REGIONAL BULLETIN, quarterly. March 1984–
Coverage	Indices and average prices of different types of houses by economic planning regions. Average prices also by age of property. Based on a 100% sample of Halifax mortgage approvals. Some supporting text (20%).
Availability	General
Cost	Free
Address	Trinity House, Halifax HX1 2RG
Telephone	0422 65777; Telex: 517441; Fax: 0422 46970

484

Originator	HAMPSHIRE COUNTY COUNCIL
Title	EMPLOYMENT NEWSLETTER, bi-annual. September 1981–
Coverage	General labour market news and data on national unemployment trends, Hampshire unemployment and youth unemployment. Based on a combination of the Council's own data (40%) and Central Government statistics (60%). Supporting text covers 60%.
Availability	General
Cost	Free
Address	Planning Department, The Castle, Winchester SO23 8UJ
Telephone	0962 846792; Fax: 0962 67273

485

Originator	HAMPSHIRE COUNTY COUNCIL
Title	HAMPSHIRE EDUCATION STATISTICS, annual
Coverage	Pupil numbers, teaching staff, further education student numbers, student awards, special education numbers, external examination statistics and career details for young people. Based on a combination of sources with about 50% from the Council's own surveys. A small amount of text (5%).
Availability	General
Cost	Free
Address	Education Department, The Castle, Winchester SO23 8UJ
Telephone	0962 846363; Fax: 0962 67273

486

Originator	HAMPSHIRE COUNTY COUNCIL
Title	HAMPSHIRE FACTS AND FIGURES, annual. 1977–
Coverage	Summary of trends in the county including sections on population, employment, housing, transport, social services, education, other services and finance. Each issue has a 'special topic' section. Based mainly on the Council's own data (75%) with some Central Government statistics (25%). Some supporting text (60%).
Availability	General
Cost	£6 plus 50p p+p
Address	Planning Department, The Castle, Winchester SO23 8UE
Telephone	0962 846363; Fax: 0962 67273

487

Originator	HAMPSHIRE COUNTY COUNCIL
Title	HOUSING NEWSLETTER, bi-annual. 1982–
Coverage	Statistics on the housing market in the county based on a combination of Council data (40%) and Central Government statistics (60%). A large amount of supporting text (70%).
Availability	General
Cost	Free
Address	Planning Department, The Castle, Winchester SO23 8UJ
Telephone	0962 846784; Fax: 0962 67273

488

Originator	HAMPSHIRE COUNTY COUNCIL
Title	SMALL AREA POPULATION AND DWELLINGS FORE-CASTS, biennial. 1983–
Coverage	Population and dwellings forecasts at county, district and ward/parish level. Based largely on the Council's own data (80%) supported by Central Government statistics (20%).
Availability	General
Cost	£2.50 plus 50p p+p
Comments	Latest edition – 1985–1992.
Address	Planning Department, The Castle, Winchester SO23 8UE
Telephone	0962 841841; Fax: 0962 67273

489

Originator	HARDWARE TODAY
Title	TODAY'S TRADING TRENDS, quarterly in a monthly journal
Coverage	Performance trends, i.e. profits, sales, wages, stocks etc. in 3 hardware sectors: homecentres, merchants and retailers. Based on voluntary returns from members of the British Hardware Federation. Figures usually relate to the previous quarter. Some supporting text (30%).
Availability	General
Cost	£10
Address	BHF, 20 Harborne Road, Edgbaston, Birmingham B15 3AB
Telephone	021 454 4385; Telex: 338024; Fax: 021 455 8670

490

Originator	HARDWARE TRADE JOURNAL
Title	BUSINESS NEWS, monthly in a weekly journal. 1983–
Coverage	Average price movements in hardware, paint, paper, glass, pottery, DIY and garden products. Based mainly on Central Government statistics (80%) and the journal's own survey (20%). Prices usually relate to the previous month.
Availability	General
Cost	£42 or 80p for a single issue
Comments	ISSN 0017 7741
Address	Benn Publications, Sovereign Way, Tonbridge TN9 1RW
Telephone	0732 364422; Telex: 95132; Fax: 0732 361534

491

Originator   HARDWARE TRADE JOURNAL

Title   PRICEWATCH, monthly in a weekly journal. 1983–
Coverage   Retail prices in the major DIY multiples based on the journal's own
                survey. Published 1 week after the survey.

Availability General
Cost   £42 or 80p for a single issue
Comments   ISSN 0017 7741
Address   Benn Publications, Sovereign Way, Tonbridge TN9 1RW
Telephone   0732 364422; Telex: 95132; Fax: 0732 364422

492

Originator   HARINGEY WOMEN'S EMPLOYMENT PROJECT

Title   WOMENS' EMPLOYMENT IN HARINGEY: FACTS AND
                FIGURES, regular. 1987–
Coverage   Commentary and statistics on various areas including occupations,
                industries, unemployment, education, training, wages, equal
                opportunities and trade unions. Based on various sources, mainly
                official.

Availability General
Comments   First published in 1987 but if it is well received further issues are
                  planned.
Address   1B Ringslade Road, Wood Green, London N22 4TE
Telephone   01 889 6599

493

Originator   HARVEST INFORMATION SERVICES LTD

Title   MARKET REPORTS, regular. 1985–
Coverage   Regular reports on request covering over 100 consumer markets
                with data on market size and development, market segmentation,
                market shares, new products, distribution, prices, consumers,
                advertising plus forecasts. Based on the company's own research
                (50%), Central Government data (15%) and other non-official
                sources (35%). Reports contain 66% text.

Availability General
Cost   £7,000 subscription per year for all reports
Comments   Available via Viewdata.
Address   63 St Martin's Lane, London WC2N 4JT
Telephone   01 836 8633

494

Originator	HATRA
Title	KNITSTATS, annual. 1976–
Coverage	UK production, imports, exports, sales, yarn consumption, capacity, wages and hours of working for the UK knitting industry. Based mainly on Central Government statistics (70%) with some data from HATRA (10%) and other non-official sources (20%). Some supporting text (25%). Usually published 9-12 months after the year to which it relates.
Availability	General
Cost	£20
Comments	ISSN 0260 8855
Address	7 Gregory Boulevard, Nottingham NG7 6LD
Telephone	0602 623311; Telex: 378230; Fax: 0602 625450

495

Originator	HAY MANAGEMENT CONSULTANTS LTD
Title	BOARDROOM REMUNERATION GUIDE, annual
Coverage	A survey focusing on the remuneration of top management and directors with data on over 4,000 top jobs (including 1,200 directors) from over 325 companies. Based on salary data collected for the Hay Remuneration Comparison (see entry below) with additional data on share options, cars, pensions and other benefits. Survey in July each year.
Availability	Participants
Cost	£590
Comments	Participants receive analysis showing their practice in relation to the market. International surveys also available.
Address	52 Grosvenor Gardens, London SW1W 0AU
Telephone	01 730 0833; Telex: 296922; Fax: 01 730 8193

496

Originator	HAY MANAGEMENT CONSULTANTS LTD
Title	CBI/HAY TOP JOB REWARDS, quarterly. 1984–
Coverage	A survey of pay and entitlements of Executive and Non-Executive directors in CBI affiliated companies. The survey has over 225 participating companies with data on pay and main benefits. Analyses of pay by sector can also be provided. Each participating company receives guidance on the position of their top jobs in relation to the market. Survey in October.
Availability	Participants
Cost	£185 plus entry fee and quarterly updates

Comments	Updates on 1 January, 1 April and 1 July. International surveys and special analysis also available.
Address	52 Grosvenor Gardens, London SW1W 0AU
Telephone	01 730 0833; Telex: 296922; Fax: 01 730 8193

497

Originator	HAY MANAGEMENT CONSULTANTS LTD
Title	HAY CHANNEL ISLANDS SURVEYS, annual and bi-annual
Coverage	Bi-annual surveys of pay for all levels of employees in the financial sectors in Jersey and Guernsey and an annual survey of salaries and benefits for all levels of staff in industrial and service organizations in Guernsey. The bi-annual surveys are carried out on 1 May and 1 November with the annual survey on 1 July.
Availability	Participants
Cost	£800 bi-annual surveys, £500 annual surveys
Comments	International surveys and special analyses also available.
Address	52 Grosvenor Gardens, London SW1W 0AU
Telephone	01 730 0833; Telex: 296922; Fax: 01 730 8193

498

Originator	HAY MANAGEMENT CONSULTANTS LTD
Title	HAY DATA PROCESSING SURVEY, bi-annual
Coverage	Covers all types of DP jobs from DP managers to programmers, analysts, technical support and operations staff. There are about 75 participants and pay data is analysed by location, function and by industrial, service and financial sector splits. Survey dates are 1 April and 1 October. Participants own practices can be compared with the general trends.
Availability	Participants
Cost	£475
Comments	International surveys and special analysis also available.
Address	52 Grosvenor Gardens, London SW1W 0AU
Telephone	01 730 0833; Telex: 296922; Fax: 01 730 8193

499

Originator	HAY MANAGEMENT CONSULTANTS LTD
Title	HAY REGIONAL SURVEYS, annual
Coverage	Salaries for over 50 secretarial, clerical, accounts, computer and other office and support positions in various centres in the UK. Existing surveys cover Basingstoke, Bournemouth, North of England and Tunbridge Wells/Sevenoaks/Tonbridge. Surveys are planned for Birmingham, Nottingham, Bristol and Central Scotland.

Availability	Participants
Cost	£295 to £325
Comments	International surveys and special analysis also available.
Address	52 Grosvenor Gardens, London SW1W 0AU
Telephone	01 730 0833; Telex: 296922; Fax: 01 730 8193

500

Originator   HAY MANAGEMENT CONSULTANTS LTD

Title   HAY REMUNERATION COMPARISON, quarterly
Coverage   Statistics and analysis on the salaries and main benefits of executive, managerial and supervisory positions. Analysis by major industrial or service sector, location and function. Based on a quarterly updated database of over 480 companies and 80,000 jobs. Survey dates are 1 July, 1 October, 1 January and 1 April.

Availability	Participants
Cost	£895 main report, other costs for quarterly updates/other reports
Comments	International surveys and special analyses can be conducted using the Hay database.
Address	52 Grosvenor Gardens, London SW1W 0AU
Telephone	01 730 0833; Telex: 296922; Fax: 01 730 8193

501

Originator   HAY MANAGEMENT CONSULTANTS LTD

Title   HAY SURVEY OF EMPLOYEE BENEFITS, annual
Coverage   Detailed analysis and comparisons on pensions, cars and car allowances, sickness and insurance, holidays, incentive schemes and other employment conditions. 290 companies participate and the results are published in 2 volumes – Industrial and Service and Financial.

Availability	Participants
Cost	£495 for new participants, £425 existing participants
Comments	International surveys and special analysis also available.
Address	52 Grosvenor Gardens, London SW1W 0AU
Telephone	01 730 0833; Telex: 296922; Fax: 01 730 8193

502

Originator   HAY MANAGEMENT CONSULTANTS LTD

Title   HOME COUNTIES INDUSTRIAL AND OFFICE PAY SURVEY, bi-annual

Coverage   Covers 4 job categories of secretarial/clerical, craft and operative, supervisory and junior technical jobs in an area around 50 miles from Central London. Analyses for individual job and by location, usually county. There are currently 30 participants. Surveys carried out on 1 July and 1 January.

Availability   Participants
Cost   £325 per edition
Comments   International surveys and special analysis also available.
Address   52 Grosvenor Gardens, London SW1W 0AU
Telephone   01 730 0833; Telex: 296922; Fax: 01 730 8193

503

Originator   HAY MANAGEMENT CONSULTANTS LTD

Title   INVESTMENT FUND MANAGERS, bi-annual
Coverage   Covers the pay and benefits of investment fund managers and related jobs down to the level of investment analysts. Analyses are provided by sector, e.g. insurance, banking, industrial and service etc. and geographical location. Analysis shows participants' jobs against the 'average' practice of all jobs in the survey. Surveys on 1 October and 1 April.

Availability   Participants
Cost   £375 for Hay-evaluated firms, £710 for others + £95 for updates
Comments   International surveys and special analysis also available.
Address   52 Grosvenor Gardens, London SW1W 0AU
Telephone   01 730 0833; Telex: 296922; Fax: 01 730 8193

504

Originator   HAY MANAGEMENT CONSULTANTS LTD

Title   LONDON OFFICE STAFF SALARY SURVEY, bi-annual
Coverage   Covers a range of 56 secretarial, clerical, accounts, computer and other office and support jobs in the London area. Analyses provided for 2 London areas, Inner London and Outer London, and by individual job. There are 80 participants. Second issue of the year contains a section on benefits. Participants' practices shown against the total. Surveys on 1 May and 1 November.

Availability   Participants
Cost   £350 per edition
Comments   International surveys and special analysis also available.
Address   52 Grosvenor Gardens, London SW1W 0AU
Telephone   01 730 0833; Telex: 296922; Fax: 01 730 8193

505

Originator	HAY MANAGEMENT CONSULTANTS LTD

Title STORE MANAGERS AND BUYERS IN RETAIL, annual
Coverage Analyses the pay, benefits and conditions of employment of shop/ store managers and buying jobs in 40 leading companies within the retail sector. The survey is carried out on 1 October.

Availability Participants
Cost £400
Comments International surveys and special analysis also available.
Address 52 Grosvenor Gardens, London SW1W 0AU
Telephone 01 730 0833; Telex: 296922; Fax: 01 730 8193

506

Originator HAY MANAGEMENT CONSULTANTS LTD

Title SURVEY OF LARGE IBM MAINFRAME USERS (ITEX), bi-annual
Coverage Salaries and benefits of staff in organisations with substantial IBM installations in the South East of England. Surveys carried out on 1 April and 1 October. Twice-yearly analysis combined with discussion meetings for participants.

Availability Participants
Cost £845
Comments International surveys and special analysis also available.
Address 52 Grosvenor Gardens, London SW1W 0AU
Telephone 01 730 0833; Telex: 296922; Fax: 01 730 8193

507

Originator HEALEY AND BAKER

Title PRIME, bi-annual
Coverage Commentary and statistics on the trends in property rents with data for industrial, office and retail property. Figures for the standard regions and a table of summary data covering a 10 year period. Based on the company's own research with a supporting text (50%).

Availability General
Cost Free
Address 29 George Street, Hanover Square, London W1A 3BG
Telephone 01 629 9292; Telex: 21800; Fax: 01 355 4299

508

Originator	HEALEY AND BAKER
Title	QUARTERLY INVESTMENT REPORT, quarterly
Coverage	Data on investment trends in the retail, office and industrial property sectors. Commentary supported by various tables.
Availability	General
Cost	Free
Address	29 George Street, Hanover Square, London W1A 3BG
Telephone	01 629 9292; Telex: 21800; Fax: 01 355 4299

509

Originator	HEATING AND VENTILATING CONTRACTORS ASSOCIATION
Title	COSTING SURVEY, annual
Coverage	Statistics on the profitability and accounting ratios for the heating and ventilating sectors based on a survey by the Association.
Availability	Members
Cost	Free
Address	34 Palace Court, Bayswater, London W2 4JG
Telephone	01 229 2488; Telex: 27929; Fax: 01 727 9268

510

Originator	HEATING AND VENTILATING CONTRACTORS ASSOCIATION
Title	MARKETPLACE BULLETIN, monthly. 1984–
Coverage	Statistics and market information on construction, heating, air conditioning, ventilation and refrigeration.
Availability	General
Cost	£74.75p
Address	34 Palace Court, Bayswater, London W2 4JG
Telephone	01 229 2488; Telex: 27929; Fax: 01 727 9268

511

Originator	HEATING AND VENTILATING CONTRACTORS ASSOCIATION
Title	STATE OF TRADE ENQUIRY, bi-annual
Coverage	Current and anticipated volume of work in the heating and ventilating sectors based on a survey of members.
Availability	Members

Cost	Free
Address	34 Palace Court, Bayswater, London W2 4JG
Telephone	01 229 2488; Telex: 27929; Fax: 01 727 9268

512

Originator	HENLEY CENTRE
Title	COSTS AND PRICES, quarterly
Coverage	Statistics and forecasts of cost and price movements of energy, metal, freight, packaging and property. Covers cost and price changes in 26 industrial sectors with data on budgeting, cost control, pricing, purchasing and marketing policy. Forecasts up to 5 years ahead.
Availability	General
Cost	£450
Comments	Other reports produced on international economies and currencies. CENTREX database available to clients.
Address	2/4 Tudor Street, Blackfriars, London EC4Y 0AA
Telephone	01 353 9961; Telex: 298817; Fax: 01 353 2899

513

Originator	HENLEY CENTRE
Title	DIRECTORS GUIDE, monthly
Coverage	A digest providing a regular review of economic and social trends and forecasts up to 2 years ahead. A commentary analyses the implications of changes in the business environment.
Availability	General
Cost	£125
Comments	Other reports produced on international economies and currencies. CENTREX database available to clients.
Address	2/4 Tudor Street, Blackfriars, London EC4Y 0AA
Telephone	01 353 9961; Telex: 298817; Fax: 01 353 2899

514

Originator	HENLEY CENTRE
Title	FRAMEWORK FORECASTS FOR THE UK ECONOMY, monthly
Coverage	Statistics and forecasts of the UK economy. Forecasts up to 5 years ahead for national income, business trends, consumer spending, costs and prices, output, money and the stock market. Based on Central Government data (50%) with Henley forecasts (50%) and some supporting text (50%).

Availability	General
Cost	£750
Comments	Other reports produced on international economies and currencies. CENTREX database available to clients.
Address	2/4 Tudor Street, Blackfriars, London EC4Y 0AA
Telephone	01 353 9961; Telex: 298817; Fax: 01 353 2899

515

Originator	HENLEY CENTRE
Title	LEISURE FUTURES, quarterly
Coverage	Statistics and forecasts up to 5 years ahead for leisure spending in total and for specific leisure sectors. Data on leisure time use, activities and spending patterns.
Availability	General
Cost	£715
Comments	Other reports published on international economies and currencies. CENTREX database available to clients.
Address	2/4 Tudor Street, Blackfriars, London EC4Y 0AA
Telephone	01 353 9961; Telex: 298817; Fax: 01 353 2899

516

Originator	HENLEY CENTRE
Title	MEASURES OF HEALTH, continuous
Coverage	A continuous survey covering attitudes to health and health related issues, shopping habits relating to health care products, health demographics and eating and drinking habits. Based on a weekly quota survey of 800 adults producing an annual sample of 40,000 respondents.
Availability	General
Cost	On application
Comments	Other reports produced on international economies and currencies. CENTREX database available to clients.
Address	2/4 Tudor Street, Blackfriars, London EC4Y 0AA
Telephone	01 353 9961; Telex: 298817; Fax: 01 353 2899

517

Originator	HENLEY CENTRE
Title	PLANNING CONSUMER MARKETS, quarterly
Coverage	Statistics and forecasts of consumers' income and expenditure and social trends with a regional analysis. Forecasts by quarter up to 18 months and annually up to 5 years.

Availability	General
Cost	£625
Comments	Other reports produced on international economies and currencies. CENTREX database available to clients.
Address	2/4 Tudor Street, Blackfriars, London EC4Y 0AA
Telephone	01 353 9961; Telex: 298817; Fax: 01 353 2899

518

Originator   HENLEY CENTRE

Title   PLANNING FOR SOCIAL CHANGE, annual
Coverage   Statistics, forecasts and analysis of changes in social attitudes and trends and their economic significance. Available as a complete service or via customized summaries on major 'spheres'. The sphere reports cover spending and saving, travel and holidays, entertainment, shopping, health/fitness, homes, personal appearance, food and hospitality/social venues.

Availability	General
Cost	On application
Comments	Other reports produced on international economies and currencies. CENTREX database available to clients.
Address	2/4 Tudor Street, Blackfriars, London EC4Y 0AA
Telephone	01 353 9961; Telex: 298817; Fax: 01 353 2899

519

Originator   HIGHLAND REGIONAL COUNCIL

Title   HIGHLAND ECONOMIC REVIEW, regular
Coverage   Commentary and statistics on the local economy and details of local schemes and initiatives. Most issues also contain a special feature on a relevant topic.

Availability	General
Cost	On application
Address	Regional Buildings, Glenurquhart Road, Inverness IV3 5NX
Telephone	0463 234121; Fax: 0463 223201

520

Originator   HIGHLANDS AND ISLANDS DEVELOPMENT BOARD

Title   HIDB ANNUAL REPORT, annual. 1967–
Coverage   A review of HIDB activities and the Highland economy with statistical appendices on population, unemployment, HIDB aid etc. Based on various official and non-official sources.

Availability   General

Cost	Free
Address	20 Bridge Street, Inverness 1V1 1QR
Telephone	0463 234171; Telex: 75267; Fax: 0463 244469

521

Originator	HIGHLANDS AND ISLANDS DEVELOPMENT BOARD
Title	NUMERICALLY SPEAKING, annual. December 1987–
Coverage	Annual statistics on the Highlands and Islands of Scotland with data on the economy, population, employment etc. Based mainly on Central Government sources (60%) plus the Board's own data (30%) and other sources (10%). A small amount of text (10%).

Availability	General
Cost	Free
Address	20 Bridge Street, Inverness 1V1 1QR
Telephone	0463 234171; Telex: 75267; Fax: 0463 244469

522

Originator	HILLIER PARKER
Title	CENTRAL LONDON SHOPS SURVEY, every 2 or 3 years
Coverage	Data on the number of shops by types, general trading trends and the number of shops and their characteristics in 4 main shopping districts within the capital. Based on research by the company.

Availability	General
Cost	Free
Comments	Various 'one-off' surveys also published.
Address	77 Grosvenor Street, London W1A 2BT
Telephone	01 629 7666; Telex: 267683; Fax: 01 409 3016

523

Originator	HILLIER PARKER
Title	FORECAST OF INDUSTRIAL RENTS, annual
Coverage	Forecasts of industrial rents up to 18 months ahead based on the company's surveys in various major industrial centres around the country.

Availability	General
Cost	Free
Comments	Various 'one-off' reports also published.
Address	77 Grosvenor Street, London W1A 2BT
Telephone	01 629 7666; Telex: 267683; Fax: 01 409 3016

524

Originator	HILLIER PARKER
Title	FORECAST OF SHOP RENTS, annual
Coverage	Forecasts of shop rents up to 18 months ahead in various retailing centres around the country. Based largely on the company's survey (80%) supplemented by some Central Government data (20%).
Availability	General
Cost	Free
Comments	Various 'one-off' reports also produced.
Address	77 Grosvenor Street, London W1A 2BT
Telephone	01 629 7666; Telex: 267683; Fax: 01 409 3016

525

Originator	HILLIER PARKER
Title	ICHP RENT INDEX, bi-annual
Coverage	Statistics on the general rents for shops, offices and industrial premises with data over a 5 year period and a regional breakdown. Based on the company's own survey.
Availability	General
Cost	£5
Comments	Produced in association with the 'Investors Chronicle' which includes summary data. Various 'one-off' surveys published.
Address	77 Grosvenor Street, London W1A 2BT
Telephone	01 629 7666; Telex: 267683; Fax: 01 409 3016

526

Originator	HILLIER PARKER
Title	INDUSTRIAL RENT AND YIELDS CONTOURS, regular
Coverage	Various maps showing trends in industrial rents and yields across the country. Contour lines show the major rental trends. Based on the company's own survey.
Availability	General
Cost	Free
Comments	Various 'one-off' surveys also produced.
Address	77 Grosvenor Street, London W1A 2BT
Telephone	01 629 7666; Telex: 267683; Fax: 01 409 3016

527

Originator	HILLIER PARKER
Title	OFFICE RENT AND YIELD CONTOURS, regular

Coverage   Various maps showing the trends in office rents and yields across the
                 country. Contour lines show the trends in rents and yields. Based on
                 the company's own survey.

Availability General
Cost   Free
Comments   Various 'one-off' surveys also produced.
Address   77 Grosvenor Street, London W1A 2BT
Telephone   01 629 7666; Telex: 267683; Fax: 01 409 3016

528

Originator   HOME GROWN CEREALS AUTHORITY

Title   ANNUAL REPORT, annual
Coverage   Mainly a general commentary on the cereals sector but includes
                  some general statistics on production, supplies, trade etc.

Availability General
Comments   A telephone information service on prices is also available.
Address   Hamlyn House, Highgate Hill, London N19 5PR
Telephone   01 263 3391; Telex: 27615

529

Originator   HOME GROWN CEREALS AUTHORITY

Title   CEREAL QUALITY SURVEY, annual
Coverage   A national survey of the quality of wheat and barley crops. Based on
                  the Authority's own survey in association with a number of agricul-
                  tural organizations.

Availability General
Cost   £3
Comments   A daily telephone information service on prices is also available.
Address   Hamlyn House, Highgate Hill, London N19 5PR
Telephone   01 263 3391; Telex: 27615

530

Originator   HOME GROWN CEREALS AUTHORITY

Title   CEREAL STATISTICS, annual
Coverage   Production and supplies of specific types of cereals plus data on
                  prices and imports and exports. Some international comparisons
                  are included. One section gives historical data over a 100 year
                  period. Based mainly on Central Government data (65%) with
                  additional material from the Authority and other non-official
                  sources (35%)

Availability General

Cost	£8
Comments	A daily telephone information service on prices is also available.
Address	Hamlyn House, Highgate Hill, London N19 5PR
Telephone	01 263 3391; Telex: 27615

531

Originator	HOME GROWN CEREALS AUTHORITY
Title	CEREALS MARKET INFORMATION, monthly
Coverage	Statistics on grain usage, supplies and consumption. Based on a combination of Central Government data (50%) and the Authority's own research and other non-official sources (50%).
Availability	General
Cost	Free
Comments	Issued as a press release. A daily telephone information service on prices is also available.
Address	Hamlyn House, Highgate Hill, London N19 5PR
Telephone	01 263 3391; Telex: 27615

532

Originator	HOME GROWN CEREALS AUTHORITY
Title	WEEKLY BULLETIN, weekly
Coverage	Statistics on prices, imports, exports and the futures market for cereals. International data is also included.
Availability	General
Cost	£17.50
Comments	A daily telephone information service on prices is also available.
Address	Hamlyn House, Highgate Hill, London N19 5PR
Telephone	01 263 3391; Telex: 27615

533

Originator	HOME GROWN CEREALS AUTHORITY
Title	WEEKLY DIGEST, weekly
Coverage	Statistics on cereal output, prices, grain fed to livestock and compound feed production. Based on a combination of Central Government statistics (50%) and data from the Authority and other non-official sources (50%).
Availability	General
Cost	£12.50
Comments	A daily telephone information service on prices is also available.
Address	Hamlyn House, Highgate Hill, London N19 5PR
Telephone	01 263 3391; Telex: 27615

534

Originator	HORTICULTURE WEEK
Title	MARKET REPORTS, weekly in a weekly journal. 1968–
Coverage	Wholesale prices for cut flowers, foliage plants and flowering pot plants by type of flower and plant.
Availability	General
Cost	£41 or 70p for a single issue
Comments	Once a year the journal contains the results of the MAFF Census of horticultural holdings. Also publish monthly horticultural share prices.
Address	Haymarket Publishing, 38/42 Hampton Road, Teddington TW11 0JE
Telephone	01 977 8787; Telex: 8952440

535

Originator	HORWATH & HORWATH (UK) LTD
Title	UK HOTEL INDUSTRY, annual
Coverage	Part of a worldwide survey of first class hotels comparing London, provincial England and Scotland. 280 hotels respond representing 44,041 rooms. Covers room occupancy and rates, analysis of guests, methods of payment, distribution of revenue and expenses, operational data, food and drink and departmental revenues, expenses. Includes previous year's data.
Availability	General
Cost	£25
Address	8 Baker Street, London W1M 1DA
Telephone	01 486 5191; Telex: 299489; Fax: 01 935 5465

536

Originator	HP INFORMATION PLC
Title	DATE OF AGREEMENT ANALYSIS – PRIVATE CARS AND COMMERCIAL VEHICLES, quarterly
Coverage	Analysis of hire purchase and other finance arrangements by date of agreement for private cars and commercial vehicles and by manufacturer. Based on HPI's own records.
Availability	On application
Cost	On application
Comments	Also produces market share data for individual registering companies.
Address	PO Box 61, Dolphin House, New Street, Salisbury SP1 2TB
Telephone	0722 413434; Telex: 47445

537

Originator	HP INFORMATION PLC

Title   HPI RECEIPTS REPORTS, monthly
Coverage   Analysis of hire purchase and other finance agreements received by HPI each month from finance companies for consumer goods and including cars and commercial vehicles.

Availability   On application
Cost   On application
Comments   Also produces market share data for individual registering companies.
Address   PO Box 61, Dolphin House, New Street, Salisbury SP1 2TB
Telephone   0722 413434; Telex: 47445

538

Originator	HP INFORMATION PLC

Title   TYPE OF FINANCE AGREEMENT ANALYSIS, quarterly
Coverage   Analysis of finance agreement registrations for new/used cars by finance agreement type – HP, lease, conditional sale, credit sale, personal loan and miscellaneous. Total market figures and figures for individual registering companies. Based on the company's own records.

Availability   On application
Cost   On application
Comments   Also produces market share data for individual registering companies.
Address   PO Box 61, Dolphin House, New Street, Salisbury SP1 2TB
Telephone   0722 413434; Telex: 47445

539

Originator	HTV

Title   HTV MARKETING HANDBOOK, regular
Coverage   General statistics on the HTV area covering population, agriculture, communications, living standards, leisure, financial trends and retailing. Based on various sources.

Availability   General
Cost   On application
Comments   Latest issue published – 1988.
Address   Marketing & Planning, 99 Baker Street, London W1M 2AJ
Telephone   01 486 4311

540

Originator	HULL CITY COUNCIL
Title	MONITORING THE LOCAL ECONOMY, quarterly
Coverage	Local economic and employment trends, the general outlook and company news. Includes a commentary with the statistics.
Availability	General
Cost	Free
Address	Industrial Development, 77 Lowgate, Hull HU1 1HP
Telephone	0482 222694

541

Originator	HUMBERSIDE COUNTY COUNCIL
Title	HUMBERSIDE ECONOMIC DEVELOPMENT MONITOR, monthly
Coverage	General news items and graphs and tables on economic trends in the county, unemployment and vacancies. Based mainly on Central Government data.
Availability	General
Cost	Free
Comments	ISSN 0266 0547
Address	County Hall, Beverley HU17 9BA
Telephone	0482 867131; Fax: 0482 867335

542

Originator	HUMBERSIDE COUNTY COUNCIL
Title	HUMBERSIDE FACTS AND FIGURES, annual. 1973–
Coverage	Basic statistics on the county plus specific data on services and communications, economic development, financial assistance, labour, population, housing and the administrative background. Based on various sources including the Council's own data (40%) and Central Government statistics (50%). Some supporting text (30%).
Availability	General
Cost	On application
Comments	ISSN 0262 5555. Usually published in Spring each year.
Address	County Hall, Beverley HU17 9BA
Telephone	0482 867131; Fax: 0482 867335

543

Originator	INCOMES DATA SERVICES LTD
Title	IDS PAY DIRECTORY, 3 issues per year
Coverage	The directory covers about 250 job titles with data on pay rates and employment conditions. Also lists the main industry agreements and Wages Councils with details of weekly rates, shift rates, guaranteed pay and the number of employees. Based on data collected from various sources by IDS.
Availability	General
Comments	Various other reports on pay and conditions published.
Address	193 St John Street, London EC1V 4LS
Telephone	01 250 3434

544

Originator	INCOMES DATA SERVICES LTD
Title	IDS TOP PAY UNIT REVIEW, monthly
Coverage	A briefing on the salaries and benefits of executive and professional staff with data from a wide range of salary surveys, research and other reports. The review also looks at the recruitment market and special topics are covered in regular features.
Availability	General
Comments	Various other reports on pay and conditions are also produced.
Address	193 St John Street, London EC1V 4LS
Telephone	01 250 3434

545

Originator	INCORPORATED SOCIETY OF BRITISH ADVERTISERS LTD
Title	EXHIBITION EXPENDITURE SURVEY, annual
Coverage	Expenditure by UK exhibitors on trade and consumer exhibitions, by venue and by media. Data on agricultural shows, private exhibitions and overseas exhibition expenditure by UK firms. Includes an index of media rate increases. Based on a survey of about 2,000 exhibitors at various types of exhibitions. Some supporting text (10%).
Availability	General
Cost	£15
Address	44 Hertford Street, London W1Y 8AE
Telephone	01 499 7502; Telex: 22525; Fax: 01 629 5355

546

Originator   INDEPENDENT HOSPITALS ASSOCIATION

Title   SURVEY OF ACUTE HOSPITALS IN THE INDEPENDENT
              SECTOR, biennial
Coverage   With data on ownership, beds, closures and proposed hospitals and
              expansions. Regional data is included. Based on information from
              IHA members. List of hospitals is included.

Availability General
Cost   £15
Address   Africa House, 64/78 Kingsway, London WC2B 6BD
Telephone   01 430 0537

547

Originator   INDEPENDENT SCHOOLS INFORMATION SERVICE (ISIS)

Title   ISIS ANNUAL CENSUS, annual. 1974–
Coverage   General statistical information about the number of pupils in ISIS
              schools, current trends in independent education, education spend-
              ing etc. Based on a regular ISIS survey.

Availability General
Cost   Free
Address   56 Buckingham Gate, London SW1E 6AG
Telephone   01 630 8793; Fax: 01 630 5013

548

Originator   INDICES LTD

Title   THE NEW GREY LIST, monthly
Coverage   Market prices for over 30,000 hardware and DIY products based on
              a survey by Indices of prices throughout the country.

Availability General
Cost   £65
Address   22 Northfield Avenue, Ealing, London W13 9RL
Telephone   01 579 5629

549

Originator   INDUSTRIAL ROBOT

Title   ROBOT STATISTICS, annual in a monthly journal
Coverage   The UK robot population and an analysis of robot use by sector,
              based on data collected by the British Robot Association (see entry
              142). Some international comparisons also included.

Availability	General
Cost	£69
Comments	Latest figures at the time of writing – June 1988. Some other robot surveys are published throughout the year.
Address	IFS Publications, 35/39 High Street, Kempston MK42 7BT
Telephone	0234 853605; Telex: 825489; Fax: 0234 854499

550

Originator	INDUSTRIAL SOCIETY
Title	CATERING PRICES, COSTS AND SUBSIDIES AND OTHER INFORMATION, biennial
Coverage	Analysis by location of companies, number of meal sales, day/shift working etc., based on the Society's own survey. Details of the statistical techniques used are included. The statistics are usually one year old at the time of publication.
Availability	General
Cost	£12
Comments	A survey supplement is issued between main surveys to update the data – £3.50
Address	Peter Runge House, 3 Carlton House Terrace, London SW1Y 5DG
Telephone	01 839 4300; Fax: 01 930 7558

551

Originator	INFORMATION RESEARCH LTD
Title	A PROFILE OF THE UK PAINT INDUSTRY, biennial. 1969–
Coverage	Text and statistics on trends in raw materials, paint market segmentation, employment, industry structure, servicing the industry, marketing and companies. Based on data from various sources.
Availability	General
Cost	£97.50
Comments	Latest edition – 1987. Also publishes a regular report on the European paint industry and 'one-off' reports.
Address	262 Regent Street, London W1R 5DA
Telephone	01 434 4536; Telex: 24224

552

Originator	INSTITUTE OF ADMINISTRATIVE MANAGEMENT
Title	OFFICE SALARIES ANALYSIS, annual
Coverage	Salary data for office staff in all industries, analysed by area industry and size of establishment. Based on a survey of about 400 UK companies. Supporting text comprises 30%.

Availability	General
Cost	£175, discount for participants
Comments	ISSN 0307 0727
Address	40 Chatsworth Parade, Petts Wood, Orpington BR5 1RW
Telephone	0689 75555; Telex: 8952569; Fax: 0689 70891

553

Originator	INSTITUTE OF ADMINISTRATIVE MANAGEMENT
Title	OFFICE TREND REPORT, annual
Coverage	Summary of the annual 'Office Salaries Analysis' – see above. Data on salary scales, hours, holidays, benefits and general trends. Based on a survey of about 400 companies with some supporting text (45%).
Availability	General
Cost	£25, free to participants
Comments	ISSN 0307 0727
Address	40 Chatsworth Parade, Petts Wood, Orpington BR5 1RW
Telephone	0689 75555; Telex: 8952569; Fax: 0689 70891

554

Originator	INSTITUTE OF DIRECTORS
Title	BUSINESS OPINION SURVEY, bi-monthly. October 1983–
Coverage	Results of an opinion survey of 200 business leaders asking for comments on UK economic trends, company performance, the state of confidence in British boardrooms and future government action wanted. Published a few weeks after the survey. Some supporting text (30%).
Availability	General
Cost	£30
Comments	Summary results are published in a press release.
Address	116 Pall Mall, London SW1Y 5ED
Telephone	01 839 1233; Telex: 21614; Fax: 01 930 1949

555

Originator	INSTITUTE OF GROCERY DISTRIBUTION
Title	ECONOMIC BULLETIN, monthly
Coverage	Commentary on recent economic developments and a review and interpretation of economic forecasts. Also includes a summary of relevant economic statistics. Based mainly on Central Government data (75%) with the remainder made up of Institute figures and data from other non-official sources (25%).

Availability	General
Cost	£90, £35 to company members, £70 to individual members
Address	Letchmore Heath, Watford WD2 8DQ
Telephone	09276 7141; Telex: 881158

556

Originator	INSTITUTE OF GROCERY DISTRIBUTION

Title	FOOD INDUSTRY STATISTICS DIGEST, monthly
Coverage	Retailing trends by sector, company, region and the number and size of shops. Costs, profits, employment, stocks and capital are also included along with summary economic indicators and consumption and expenditure patterns. A combination of Central Government sources (50%) and data from the Institute and other non-official sources (50%).

Availability	General
Cost	£90, £35 to company members, £90 to individual members
Comments	Loose-leaf format with binder.
Address	Letchmore Heath, Watford WD2 8DQ
Telephone	09276 7141; Telex: 881158

557

Originator	INSTITUTE OF INFORMATION SCIENTISTS

Title	IIS REMUNERATION SURVEY, annual
Coverage	Salary statistics for Institute members in full time employment. Analysis by grade of membership, age and industries/sectors of employment. A commentary (50%) accompanies the data.

Availability	General
Cost	£5, free to members
Address	44 Museum Street, London WC1A 1LY
Telephone	01 831 8003

558

Originator	INSTITUTE OF MATHEMATICS AND ITS APPLICATIONS

Title	REMUNERATION SURVEY, every 2/3 years
Coverage	A survey of members which includes an analysis of occupations by grade and age, employment of women by age and sector, remuneration by age and grade for all occupations in selected employment groups and remuneration by age up to 29 years. Based on a survey of members.

Availability	General
Cost	Free

Address	Maitland House, Warrior Square, Southend SS1 2JY
Telephone	0702 612177; Fax: 0702 612610

559

Originator	INSTITUTE OF PETROLEUM
Title	INSTITUTE OF PETROLEUM PRESS RELEASE, quarterly
Coverage	Statistics on deliveries of petroleum products in the UK, Scotland and Northern Ireland – specific press releases for each area. Gives percentage change over previous year. Based on the Institute's own statistics with a small amount of supporting text (10%).
Availability	Press, interested companies etc.
Cost	Free
Comments	Various reports, booklets and datasheets produced on the UK and world oil industry.
Address	61 New Cavendish Street, London W1M 8AR
Telephone	01 636 1004; Telex: 264380; Fax: 01 255 1472

560

Originator	INSTITUTE OF PETROLEUM
Title	UK PETROLEUM INDUSTRY STATISTICS: CONSUMPTION AND REFINERY PRODUCTION, annual
Coverage	Deliveries, end use and production of petroleum products with data for the latest 2 years. Based on the Institute's own data with a small amount of supporting text (10%).
Availability	General
Cost	Free
Comments	ISSN 0141 4305. Various other reports, booklets and datasheets produced on the UK and world oil industry.
Address	61 New Cavendish Street, London W1M 8AR
Telephone	01 636 1004; Telex: 264380; Fax: 01 255 1472

561

Originator	INSTITUTE OF PHYSICS
Title	REMUNERATION SURVEY, annual. 1948–
Coverage	Analysis of salaries of members by age, sex, class of membership, type of work etc. Based on a survey of members with a small commentary (10%).
Availability	General
Cost	Free
Comments	Available in house journal ' Physics Bulletin' or as an offprint.
Address	47 Belgrave Square, London SW1X 8QX
Telephone	01 235 6111; Telex: 918453

562

Originator	INSTITUTE OF PHYSICS
Title	STATISTICS RELATING TO PHYSICS AND EDUCATION, every 5-6 years. 1979–
Coverage	Data on physics education at all levels from CSE to postgraduate, covering entrants, passes and employment. Based mainly on Central Government sources (80%) with other material from the Institute (10%) and non-official sources (10%). Some supporting text (20%).
Availability	General
Cost	£5
Comments	Most recent edition – 1986.
Address	47 Belgrave Square, London SW1X 8QX
Telephone	01 235 6111; Telex: 918453

563

Originator	INSTITUTE OF PRACTITIONERS IN ADVERTISING
Title	IPA AGENCY CENSUS, annual. Pre-1960–
Coverage	Estimated number of people employed in IPA member advertising agencies by location, size of agency and staff category. Based on the IPA's own survey with a small amount of supporting text (10%). Usually produced 4-5 months after the year to which it refers.
Availability	General
Cost	£30, free to members
Address	44 Belgrave Square, London SW1X 8QS
Telephone	01 235 7020; Telex: 918352; Fax: 01 245 9904

564

Originator	INSTITUTE OF PRACTITIONERS IN ADVERTISING
Title	IPA ANNUAL ANALYSIS OF AGENCY COSTS, annual. 1960–
Coverage	Turnovers, costs, profits, payroll and capital in percentage terms and by size of agency. Based on a survey of IPA members.
Availability	Members
Cost	Free to participants, £100 to non-participating members
Address	44 Belgrave Square, London SW1X 8QS
Telephone	01 235 7020; Telex: 918352; Fax: 01 245 9904

565

Originator	INSTITUTE OF PRACTITIONERS IN ADVERTISING
Title	IPA SALARIES ANALYSIS, annual

Coverage   Numbers of staff at various salary levels by position, size and location of agencies. Based on the IPA's own survey. Usually produced 3 months after the year to which it relates.

Availability Participating member agencies
Cost   Free
Address   44 Belgrave Square, London SW1X 8QS
Telephone 01 235 7020; Telex: 918352; Fax: 01 245 9904

566

Originator   INSTITUTION OF CHEMICAL ENGINEERS

Title   REMUNERATION SURVEY, bi-annual
Coverage   Remuneration and employment trends for members of the Institution based on the organization's own survey.

Availability General
Cost   £25, free to members
Address   G E Davis Building, 165/171 Railway Terrace, Rugby CV21 3HQ
Telephone   0788 78214; Telex: 311780; Fax: 0788 60833

567

Originator   INSTITUTION OF CIVIL ENGINEERS

Title   ICE SALARY SURVEY, every 2 or 3 years
Coverage   An analysis by employer, age, type of work, overtime payments, location, firm size, qualifications etc. Based on a survey of members.

Availability General
Cost   On application
Comments   Some results usually published in the Institution's journal 'New Civil Engineer' (see entry 728).
Address   1/7 Great George Street, London SW1P 3AA
Telephone   01 222 7722; Telex: 935637; Fax: 01 222 7500

568

Originator   INSTITUTION OF ELECTRICAL ENGINEERS (IEE)

Title   IEE SALARY SURVEY, annual. 1976–
Coverage   A random sample (about 40%) of members, analysed by age, position, class and field of employment, type of work, levels of responsibilty, size of work, qualifications, location of employment, fringe benefits etc. A small amount of supporting text (15%).

Availability General
Cost   £35

Comments	Published in March. IEE main office is at Savoy Place, London WC2R 0BL but the survey is available from the address below.
Address	Station House, Nightingale Road, Hitchin SG5 1RJ
Telephone	0462 53331; Telex: 825962; Fax: 01 240 7735

569

Originator	INSTITUTION OF ENVIRONMENTAL HEALTH OFFICERS
Title	ENVIRONMENTAL HEALTH REPORT, annual
Coverage	With a statistical section covering food, working environment, pollution control, noise control, housing, ports etc. Based on data collected by the Institution.
Availability	General
Cost	£7
Address	Chadwick House, Rushworth Street, London SE1 0RB
Telephone	01 928 6006

570

Originator	INSTITUTION OF MECHANICAL ENGINEERS
Title	SALARY SURVEY, biennial
Coverage	Salary survey of the members of the Institution with data by type of member, sector of work and location. Other data on fringe benefits and overtime. Usually published 3 or 4 months after the survey.
Availability	General
Cost	£35
Comments	Latest survey – April 1988.
Address	1 Birdcage Walk, London SW1H 9JJ
Telephone	01 222 7899; Telex: 917944; Fax: 01 222 4557

571

Originator	INSURANCE PERSONNEL SELECTION GROUP LTD
Title	LONDON INSURANCE MARKET SALARIES REPORT, annual
Coverage	A guide to salaries paid by employers to insurance staff employed in London. Average salaries by age from 16 to 35 and a projected norm salary for each age in the coming year. Also data on senior management and directors' salaries. About 500 people are placed in new posts in London annually and a sample of at least 25 applicants per age group is used. Text 50%.
Availability	London broking houses, Lloyds and London insurance companies
Cost	£25
Address	Lloyds Avenue House, 6 Lloyds Avenue, London EC3N 3ES
Telephone	01 481 8111; Telex: 8951182; Fax: 01 480 6178

572

Originator	INTER COMPANY COMPARISONS LTD (ICC)
Title	INDUSTRIAL PERFORMANCE ANALYSIS, annual. 1975–
Coverage	The financial situation and trends in 170 production, distribution and service sectors with data on industry balance sheets, sales , profits and growth trends. Data for earlier years given. Statistics usually cover a period 12-18 months before the publication date. Based on an analysis of company accounts by ICC. A brief commentary is included (5%).
Availability	General
Cost	£59
Comments	ISSN 0262 3684. More detailed reports on the individual sectors are also available.
Address	Field House, 72 Oldfield Road, Hampton, Middlesex TW12 2HQ
Telephone	01 783 0977; Fax: 01 783 1940

573

Originator	INTERMARKET RESEARCH PUBLICATIONS
Title	LONG HAUL TRAVEL MONITOR, quarterly. August 1986–
Coverage	Statistics reviewing long haul visits to and from the UK. Long haul is defined as transatlantic, south of Sahara or east of Iran. Based largely on Central Government data (90%) with some supporting text (50%).
Availability	General
Cost	£300
Comments	There are plans to publish a monitor covering all travel, i.e. long, short, medium haul, in 1988.
Address	Tower House, Southampton Street, London WC2 7HN
Telephone	01 379 6017; Telex: 8953744; Fax: 01 836 2052

574

Originator	INTERNATIONAL STOCK EXCHANGE OF THE UNITED KINGDOM
Title	STOCK EXCHANGE FACT SHEET, monthly
Coverage	Statistics on the daily market trends for the month plus data on equities, gilts, renewable issues, traded options etc., based on a regular review of Stock Exchange activities.
Availability	General
Cost	£28
Address	Fact Service, Stock Exchange, London EC2N 1HP
Telephone	01 588 2355; Telex: 884782; Fax: 01 588 2355

575

Originator	INTERNATIONAL STOCK EXCHANGE OF THE UNITED KINGDOM
Title	STOCK EXCHANGE QUALITY OF MARKETS, quarterly
Coverage	A commentary followed by a statistical section covering funds, turnover, new work, sector analysis etc., based on statistics maintained by the Stock Exchange.
Availability	General
Cost	£48 or £15 for a single issue
Address	Fact Service, Stock Exchange, London EC2N 1HP
Telephone	01 588 2355; Telex: 884782; Fax: 01 588 2355

576

Originator	INVESTMENT PROPERTY DATABANK (IPD)
Title	IPD ANNUAL REVIEW, annual. 1986–
Coverage	Presents and interprets statistics about current trends in the commercial property market covering 4 areas: property institutions; property investment activity; property returns; fund returns. Utilizes information from 9000 records of individual properties worth over £14bn in the IPD. A large amount of text (70%).
Availability	General
Cost	£70
Comments	Also takes telephone inquiries to the Databank charged at an hourly rate.
Address	7/8 Greenland Place, London NW1 0AP
Telephone	01 482 5149; Telex: 923753; Fax: 01 267 0208

577

Originator	INVESTORS CHRONICLE
Title	ANNUAL STATISTICAL SUMMARY, annual in a weekly journal
Coverage	Covers the number of new issues and the total amount raised, BES issues, rights issues, the number of vendor placings and the total amounts raised and the number of takeover bids and the total value. Based on data collected by Investors Chronicle from company prospectuses, news items, press releases etc.
Availability	General
Cost	£62 or £1.20 for a single issue
Comments	ISSN 0261 3115. The above data is also included in the Annual review available separately from the journal for £10.
Address	FT Business Information, Fetter Lane, London EC4A 1ND
Telephone	01 405 6969; Telex: 883694; Fax: 01 405 5276

578

Originator	INVESTORS CHRONICLE
Title	MARKET INDICATORS/ECONOMIC INDICATORS, weekly in a weekly journal
Coverage	'Market Indicators' covers UK and international stockmarkets, interest rates, exchange rates and commodity indices. 'Economic Indicators' covers output, demand, prices and trade plus a summary of the main economic forecasts. A combination of Central Government and various non-official sources.
Availability	General
Cost	£62 or £1.20 for a single issue
Comments	ISSN 0261 3115. Various one-off statistics produced and an Annual Review with some statistics published separately at £10.
Address	FT Business Information, Fetter Lane, London EC4A 1ND
Telephone	01 405 6969; Telex: 883694; Fax: 01 405 5276

579

Originator	JOHNSEN JORGENSEN & WETTRE LTD
Title	DIGEST OF UNITED KINGDOM WOODPULP IMPORTS AND PRICE REVIEW, annual. March 1964–
Coverage	Woodpulp imports and prices on a running 10-year basis, with comment on the UK market situation and the consumption and production of paper and board. Based on the company's own survey. Some supporting text (15%).
Availability	Limited circulation at the discretion of the company
Cost	Free
Address	Johnsen House, Wellington Road, Wokingham RG11 2LB
Telephone	0734 793033; Telex: 848308; Fax: 0734 794197

580

Originator	JOINT INDUSTRY COMMITTEE FOR NATIONAL READERSHIP SURVEYS (JICNARS)
Title	NATIONAL READERSHIP SURVEY, annual. 1968–
Coverage	Statistics on the readership of national newspapers and various consumer magazines based on a stratified random sample of about 28,500 individuals. Results are published about 3 months after the completion of the survey. Some supporting text (20%).
Availability	General
Cost	£920
Comments	Also available on-line and batch via a computer bureau.
Address	44 Belgrave Square, London SW1X 8QS
Telephone	01 235 7020; Telex: 918352

581

Originator	JONES LANG WOOTTON
Title	50 CENTRES: A GUIDE TO OFFICE AND INDUSTRIAL RENTAL TRENDS IN ENGLAND AND WALES, bi-annual. 1984–
Coverage	Statistics on 53 main urban centres in England and Wales. A supplement covers 3 centres in Scotland. Based on JLW's 50 Centres Database which records transactions at the top end of the prime property market within specified floorspace ranges. Supporting text covers 20%.
Availability	General
Cost	Free
Address	22 Hanover Square, London W1A 2BN
Telephone	01 493 6040; Telex: 23858; Fax: 01 408 0220

582

Originator	JONES LANG WOOTTON
Title	CENTRAL LONDON OFFICES RESEARCH, bi-annual. 1982–
Coverage	Commentary and statistics on the Central London office market including supply and take-up trends. Covers 3 main study areas: the City, Midtown and the West End. The data is derived from JLW's computerised database with information on over 2,500 offices at all stages of the development cycle. Text covers 20%.
Availability	General
Cost	£50
Address	22 Hanover Square, London W1A 2BN
Telephone	01 493 6040; Telex: 23858; Fax: 01 408 0220

583

Originator	JONES LANG WOOTTON
Title	GREATER LONDON OFFICES RESEARCH, annual. 1983–
Coverage	Trends in the Greater London office market, demand, supply, starts, proposals, occupier mix etc. Four geographical sectors are covered with an analysis by borough. The information is derived from JLW's computerized database containing data on over 2,500 offices at all stages of the development cycle. Supporting text covers 20%.
Availability	General
Cost	£100
Address	22 Hanover Square, London W1A 2BN
Telephone	01 493 6040; Telex: 23858; Fax: 01 408 0220

584

Originator   JONES LANG WOOTTON

Title   JLW PROPERTY INDEX, quarterly. 1979–
Coverage   Analysis of the returns to property by type and comparisons with
                 other investments. Figures given over a 10-year period and portfo-
                 lio statistics by region. Data calculated from various sources,
                 including FT indices. Some supporting text (20%).

Availability General
Cost   Free
Address   22 Hanover Square, London W1A 2BN
Telephone   01 493 6040; Telex: 23858; Fax: 01 408 0220

585

Originator   KENT COUNTY COUNCIL

Title   ECONOMIC DEVELOPMENT REVIEW, annual
Coverage   Commentary and statistics covering general economic trends,
                 employment, unemployment, industrial land, office floorspace and
                 trends in the major industrial and service sectors locally.

Availability General
Address   Planning, County Hall, Maidstone ME14 1XQ
Telephone   0622 671411; Telex: 965212

586

Originator   KEYNOTE PUBLICATIONS LTD

Title   KEYNOTE REPORTS, annual
Coverage   Commentary and statistics on various markets, each covered by a
                 specific report updated annually and usually containing a 5-year run
                 of figures and some short-term forecasts. Based on a combination of
                 Central Government data, non-official sources and original
                 research. Text covers 70%.

Availability General
Cost   £89 per report
Comments   Also publishes a few European reports.
Address   Field House, 72 Oldfield Road, Hampton, Middlesex TW12 2HQ
Telephone   01 783 0755; Fax: 01 783 1940

587

Originator   KING AND COMPANY

Title   INDUSTRIAL FLOORSPACE SURVEY, 3 issues per year.
                 1975–

Coverage   Details of the availability of industrial property (warehouses and factories) for England and Wales with regional breakdowns and historical comparisons. Based on the company's own research with some supporting text (25%).

Availability General
Cost   Free
Address   70 Grosvenor Street, London W1X 7SB
Telephone   01 491 2771; Telex: 885485

588

Originator   KIRKLEES AND WAKEFIELD CHAMBER OF COMMERCE AND INDUSTRY

Title   STATE OF TRADE SURVEY, quarterly
Coverage   Figures on the economic position and performance of member firms based on a sample survey of members. Usually published 2 weeks after the date of the survey.

Availability Members
Cost   Free
Address   New North Road, Huddersfield, West Yorkshire HD1 5PJ
Telephone   0484 26591; Telex: 51458; Fax: 0484 514199

589

Originator   KIRKLEES AND WAKEFIELD CHAMBER OF COMMERCE AND INDUSTRY

Title   WAGES SURVEY, bi-annual
Coverage   A survey of wage rates, hours of work and overtime rates in industries locally based on a survey of members. Usually published 1 month after the date of the survey.

Availability General
Cost   £100, £30 to participants
Address   New North Road, Huddersfield, West Yorkshire HD1 5PJ
Telephone   0484 26591; Telex: 51458; Fax: 0484 514199

590

Originator   KLUWER PUBLISHING LTD

Title   BRITISH INSURANCE INDUSTRY, biennial. 1982–
Coverage   General data on the insurance market and performance data on companies licensed to transact business in the UK. Based largely on Central Government data (70%) with some original data (20%) and data from other non-official sources (10%). Some supporting text (35%).

191

Availability	General
Cost	£150
Comments	Also publishes a directory of all businesses entitled to transact insurance business in the UK.
Address	1 Harlequin Avenue, Great West Road, Brentford
Telephone	01 568 6441; Telex: 917490; Fax: 01 847 2610

591

Originator	KNIGHT, FRANK & RUTLEY
Title	DOCKLANDS: COMMERCIAL AND RESIDENTIAL DEVELOPMENTS, bi-annual. March 1987–
Coverage	Commercial and residential development markets and prospects in London docklands. Based on the company's own research with a large amount of supporting text (75%).
Availability	General
Cost	Free
Address	20 Hanover Square, London W1A 2BN
Telephone	Telex: 265384; Fax: 01 493 4114

592

Originator	KORN/FERRY INTERNATIONAL
Title	BOARDS OF DIRECTORS STUDY, annual
Coverage	Information on the composition of company boards, special committees, salaries, fringe benefits, days served, period of services, issues and government policies important to board members, pay rises etc. Broken down by company type, business, market and number of employees. Compiled from questionnaires sent to the Times 1000 companies.
Availability	General
Cost	£50
Address	Norfolk House, 31 St James Square, London SW1Y 4JL
Telephone	01 930 4334; Telex: 914860; Fax: 01 730 8085

593

Originator	KP FOODS LTD
Title	SNACK FOOD REVIEW, annual
Coverage	Summary of the snack food market with market share figures and an analysis of specific markets for crisps, nuts and savoury snacks. Also sales by outlet, products, packaging and growth prospects. A large amount of supporting text (60%).
Availability	General

Cost	Free
Comments	Available from Hillert Knowlton at the address and telephone number below.
Address	11A West Halkin Street, London SW1X 8JL
Telephone	01 235 7040

594

Originator	LABOUR RESEARCH
Title	BARGAINING REPORT SPECIAL ISSUE, annual in a monthly journal. 1980–
Coverage	Analysis of collective bargaining developments with data on wage rates, hours, holidays etc., covering the private and public sectors and manual and non-manual workers. Based on a questionnaire to about 800 workplace contacts. Response rate varies – response has been 40%.
Availability	General
Cost	£19.50 or £1.95 for a single issue
Comments	ISSN 0023 7000. Also publishes London weighting figures and shift pay data.
Address	78 Blackfriars Road, London SE1 8HF
Telephone	01 928 3649; Fax: 01 928 0621

595

Originator	LABOUR RESEARCH
Title	ECONOMIC NOTES, monthly in a monthly journal
Coverage	General economic statistics taken mainly from Central Government statistical series. One table included at the back of the journal.
Availability	General
Cost	£19.50 or £1.95 for a single issue
Comments	ISSN 0023 7000. Also publishes an occasional survey of directors' pay.
Address	78 Blackfriars Road, London SE1 8HF
Telephone	01 928 3649; Fax: 01 928 0621

596

Originator	LAING AND CRUIKSHANK
Title	BUILDING MATERIALS AND CONSTRUCTION QUARTERLY REVIEW, quarterly. 1980–
Coverage	A summary of construction output plus an industry outlook including financial data on relevant companies plus share price graphs and statistics.

Availability	Clients
Cost	Free
Comments	Other reports produced on specific sectors, mainly giving a company analysis.
Address	Piercy House, 7 Copthall Avenue, London EC2R 7BE
Telephone	01 588 2800; Telex: 888397; Fax: 01 588 5819

597

Originator	LAING AND CRUIKSHANK
Title	PRIVATE HOUSEBUILDING ANNUAL REVIEW, annual
Coverage	Mainly company data but a summary section gives statistics and commentary on trends in housebuilding.
Availability	Clients
Cost	Free
Comments	Produces various other sector reports mainly giving company financial data.
Address	Piercy House, 7 Copthall Avenue, London EC2R 7BE
Telephone	01 588 2800; Telex: 888397; Fax: 01 588 5819

598

Originator	LANCASHIRE COUNTY COUNCIL
Title	LANCASHIRE 198.: AN ECONOMIC SITUATION REPORT, annual
Coverage	Commentary and statistics on the local economic situation and trends in specific industrial and service sectors. Detailed information on the local labour market and industry structure.
Availability	General
Cost	On application
Address	Planning, East Cliff, County Offices, Preston PR1 3EX
Telephone	0772 54868

599

Originator	LEATHER
Title	MARKET REPORT, monthly in a monthly journal
Coverage	Data on slaughterings and hide prices. One table per issue usually providing data for 3-4 weeks earlier.
Availability	General
Cost	£44 or £4.20 for a single issue
Comments	Also contains data on the international price of hides etc.
Address	Benn Publications, Sovereign Way, Tonbridge TN9 1RW
Telephone	0732 364422; Telex: 95132; Fax: 0732 361534

600

Originator	LEEDS CHAMBER OF COMMERCE AND INDUSTRY
Title	LOCAL ECONOMIC SURVEY, quarterly
Coverage	Data on the economic performance of member companies based on the Chamber's survey of these companies. Some supporting text is included (40%).
Availability	Members
Cost	Free
Address	Commerce House, St Albans Place, Wade Lane, Leeds LS2 8HZ
Telephone	0532 430491; Telex: 55293; Fax: 0532 430504

601

Originator	LEISURE CONSULTANTS
Title	LEISURE FORECASTS, annual
Coverage	A review of the key leisure markets, e.g. media leisure, hobbies and pastimes, entertainment and sport, catering and holidays. Forecasts are given for 5 years ahead for consumer spending, prices and key market indicators. Based largely on the company's own research (80%) with some supporting text (50%).
Availability	General
Cost	£160. Reduced rates available for academic institutions
Address	Lint Growis, Foxearth, Sudbury CO10 7JX
Telephone	0787 75777

602

Originator	LIBRARY ASSOCIATION RECORD
Title	PERIODICAL PRICES, annual in a monthly journal
Coverage	Average prices of periodicals analysed by subject and country of origin and based on a survey by Blackwell's Periodical Division.
Availability	General
Cost	£53, free to Library Association members
Comments	ISSN 0024 2195. Survey usually appears in the May issue.
Address	7 Ridgmount Street, London WC1E 7AE
Telephone	01 636 7543; Telex: 21897; Fax: 01 436 7218

603

Originator	LIVERPOOL COTTON ASSOCIATION LTD
Title	WEEKLY RAW COTTON REPORT, weekly

Coverage	The Liverpool market for cotton, UK cotton supply and consumption, futures markets, conference freight rates to Liverpool and world raw cotton markets.
Availability	General
Cost	£19.50. £14 to members
Address	620 Cotton Exchange Building, Edmund Street, Liverpool L3 9LH
Telephone	051 236 6041; Telex: 627849

604

Originator	LIVERPOOL MACROECONOMIC RESEARCH LTD, UNIVERSITY OF LIVERPOOL
Title	MERSEYSIDE ECONOMIC PROSPECT, bi-annual. February 1986–
Coverage	Commentary and statistics on economic and business trends on Merseyside, based mainly on Central Government statistics (85%). A large commentary is included (75%).
Availability	General
Cost	£15
Comments	ISSN 0952 0732. Data also available in machine readable form.
Address	Economics & Accounting Department, PO Box 147, Liverpool L69 3BX
Telephone	051 709 6022; Telex: 627095; Fax: 051 708 6502

605

Originator	LIVERPOOL MACROECONOMIC RESEARCH LTD, UNIVERSITY OF LIVERPOOL
Title	QUARTERLY ECONOMIC BULLETIN, quarterly. 1981–
Coverage	Economic trends and forecasts for the UK economy with additional data on world trends. Central Government data forms the basis of the forecasts produced. A large amount of commentary is included in the bulletin (75%).
Availability	General
Cost	£85
Comments	ISSN 0952 0274. Data also available in machine readable form.
Address	Economics & Accounting Department, PO Box 147, Liverpool L69 3BX
Telephone	051 709 6022; Telex: 627095; Fax: 051 708 6502

606

Originator	LIVESTOCK AUCTIONEERS' MARKET COMMITTEE FOR ENGLAND AND WALES
Title	THROUGHPUT AND TURNOVER LIVESTOCK AUCTION MARKETS, annual. 1975–
Coverage	Sales of cattle, sheep, pigs and calves for store and for slaughter. Statistics are given for the last 5 years. Based on the Committee's survey of markets. Detailed text and statistics.
Availability	Members and some others
Cost	Free
Address	Norden House, Basing View, Basingstoke, Hampshire RG21 2HN
Telephone	04862 64934

607

Originator	LIVESTOCK MARKETING COMMISSION FOR NORTHERN IRELAND
Title	ANNUAL REPORT, annual. 1968–
Coverage	A report of the activities of the LMC which includes statistics on livestock numbers, slaughterings, exports etc. Includes a commentary on the cattle and sheep trade. Based mainly on Central Government statistics (80%).
Availability	General
Cost	Free
Address	57 Malone Road, Belfast BT9 6SA
Telephone	0232 381022; Telex: 747117

608

Originator	LIVESTOCK MARKETING COMMISSION FOR NORTHERN IRELAND
Title	LMC BULLETIN, weekly. 1968–
Coverage	A weekly review of the cattle and sheep trade with statistics on Northern Ireland deadweight and auction cattle and sheep prices plus other statistics at regular intervals. A combination of LMC data (25%), Central Government statistics (25%) and data from other non-official sources (50%).
Availability	General
Cost	Free
Address	57 Malone Road, Belfast BT9 6SA
Telephone	0232 381022; Telex: 747117

609

Originator	LIVESTOCK MARKETING COMMISSION FOR NORTHERN IRELAND
Title	MEAT RETAILER, monthly. July 1985–
Coverage	A review with statistics on the retail prices of meat in Northern Ireland, based on the LMC's own surveys.
Availability	General
Cost	Free
Address	57 Malone Road, Belfast BT9 6SA
Telephone	0232 381022; Telex: 747117

610

Originator	LIVINGSTON DEVELOPMENT CORPORATION
Title	FACTS AND FIGURES, annual
Coverage	Information on population, housing, employment, industrial premises, shops, offices, education and leisure. The sources of the statistics are not acknowledged.
Availability	General
Cost	Free
Address	Sidlaw House, Almondvale, Livingston, West Lothian EH54 6QA
Telephone	0506 414177; Telex: 727178; Fax: 0506 33018

611

Originator	LIVINGSTON DEVELOPMENT CORPORATION
Title	LIVINGSTON EMPLOYMENT SURVEY, annual
Coverage	Statistics on employment trends and characteristics in Livingston based on the Corporation's own survey.
Availability	General
Cost	Free
Address	Sidlaw House, Almondvale, Livingston, West Lothian EH54 6QA
Telephone	0506 414177; Telex: 727178; Fax: 0506 33018

612

Originator	LIVINGSTON DEVELOPMENT CORPORATION
Title	LIVINGSTON POPULATION PROFILE, biennial. 1985–
Coverage	Statistics on the population structure and household composition in Livingston based on the Corporation's own survey.
Availability	General
Cost	Free

Address	Sidlaw House, Almondvale, Livingston, West Lothain EH54 6QA
Telephone	0506 414177; Telex: 727178; Fax: 0506 33018

613

Originator	LIVINGSTON DEVELOPMENT CORPORATION
Title	QUARTERLY STATISTICAL ABSTRACT, quarterly
Coverage	Information on the population, housing, employment, industrial premises, shops and offices. The sources of the statistics are not acknowledged.
Availability	General
Cost	Free
Address	Sidlaw House, Almondvale, Livingston, West Lothian EH54 6QA
Telephone	0506 414177; Telex: 727178; Fax: 0506 33018

614

Originator	LLOYDS BANK PLC
Title	BRITISH ECONOMY IN FIGURES, annual
Coverage	National income, production, balance of payments, adult earnings, public expenditure and the purchasing power of the £. Basic data from mainly Central Government sources.
Availability	General
Cost	Free
Comments	Also produce 'Scottish Economy in Figures' and 'Welsh Economy in Figures'.
Address	Box 95, Hays Lane House, Hays Lane, London SE1 2HN
Telephone	01 407 1000; Telex: 888301; Fax: 01 237 2467

615

Originator	LLOYDS BANK PLC
Title	ECONOMIC PROFILE OF BRITAIN, annual
Coverage	General statistics on economic trends in Britain using data mainly from Central Government sources (70%). A detailed commentary (65%) supports the statistics.
Availability	General
Cost	Free
Address	Box 95, Hays Lane House, Hays Lane, London SE1 2HN
Telephone	01 407 1000; Telex: 888301; Fax: 01 237 2467

616

Originator LONDON AND SOUTH EAST REGIONAL PLANNING CONFERENCE (SERPLAN)

Title HOUSING LAND SUPPLY IN THE SOUTH EAST (OUTSIDE LONDON), annual. 1981–
Coverage Statistics by county based on the structure plans produced by the specific local authorities. A commentary (50%) accompanies the statistics.

Availability General
Cost £5
Address 8th Floor, 50/64 Broadway, London SW1H 0DB
Telephone 01 799 2191; Fax: 01 799 2075

617

Originator LONDON AND SOUTH EAST REGIONAL PLANNING CONFERENCE (SERPLAN)

Title REGIONAL TRENDS IN THE SOUTH EAST – THE SOUTH EAST REGIONAL MONITOR, annual. 1981–
Coverage Commentary and statistics on general trends in the South East with specific chapters on demography, housing and economy and employment. Figures mainly from Central Government sources with some data broken down by county and various tables giving figures for previous years. Text covers 65%.

Availability General
Cost £25
Address 8th Floor, 50/64 Broadway, London SW1H 0DB
Telephone 01 799 2191; Fax: 01 799 2075

618

Originator LONDON AND SOUTH EAST REGIONAL PLANNING CONFERENCE (SERPLAN)

Title WASTE DISPOSAL IN THE SOUTH EAST REGION, biennial. 1986–
Coverage Statistics on each of the counties of South East England plus Greater London including an assessment of the number and nature of void spaces. Based on SERPLAN's own survey with a supporting commentary (40%).

Availability General
Cost £5
Address 8th Floor, 50/64 Broadway, London SW1H 0DB
Telephone 01 799 2191; Fax: 01 799 2075

619

Originator	LONDON BANKS' PERSONNEL MANAGEMENT GROUP
Title	LONDON BANKS CLERICAL SALARY SURVEY, bi-annual
Coverage	Data on 90 clerical and supervisory positions in various functions including banking, investment banking, communications, personnel, graduate entry, data processing etc. Based on data supplied by participants.
Availability	Participants and new members
Cost	£67.50 + VAT
Comments	Produced for the Group by the Wyatt Company (UK) Ltd at the address below.
Address	21 Tothill Street, Westminster, London SW1H 9LL
Telephone	01 222 8033; Telex: 916283; Fax: 01 222 9182

620

Originator	LONDON BANKS' PERSONNEL MANAGEMENT GROUP
Title	LONDON BANKS MANAGEMENT SALARY SURVEY, bi-annual
Coverage	Data on 57 management positions including foreign exchange and money management, lending, corporate finance, investment banking, accounts, operations, administration, data processing and property lending. Based on returns from 146 participants.
Availability	Participants and new members
Cost	£67.50 + VAT
Comments	Produced for the Group by the Wyatt Company (UK) Ltd at the address below.
Address	21 Tothill Street, Westminster, London SW1H 9LL
Telephone	01 222 8033; Telex: 916283; Fax: 01 222 9182

621

Originator	LONDON BANKS' PERSONNEL MANAGEMENT GROUP
Title	SURVEY OF SALARY ADMINISTRATION PRACTICES AND BENEFITS IN LONDON BANKS, bi-annual
Coverage	Data on salary administration practices, overtime, shifts, hours of work, compensation practices etc. Also information on benefits found in international banks. Based on returns from 157 participants.
Availability	Participants and new members
Cost	£40 + VAT
Comments	Produced for the Group by the Wyatt Company (UK) Ltd at the address below.
Address	21 Tothill Street, Westminster, London SW1H 9LL
Telephone	01 222 8033; Telex: 916283; Fax: 01 222 9182

622

Originator   LONDON BOROUGH OF EALING

Title   EALING ECONOMY, quarterly
Coverage   Mainly text with some statistics on local economic development trends but includes appendices with statistics on unemployment, the economically active population, employment structure etc.

Availability   General
Cost   Free
Address   Economic Development, Civic Centre, Uxbridge W5
Telephone   01 579 2924; Fax: 01 579 0410

623

Originator   LONDON BOROUGH OF HAMMERSMITH AND FULHAM

Title   UNEMPLOYMENT BULLETIN, regular. 1987–
Coverage   Articles and statistics on employment and unemployment trends in the borough, based mainly on Central Government data.

Availability   General
Cost   Free
Address   Research & Information, Town Hall, King Street, London W6 9JU
Telephone   01 748 3020

624

Originator   LONDON BUSINESS SCHOOL

Title   LBS ECONOMIC OUTLOOK, monthly
Coverage   3 major forecasts and 9 intermediate forecast releases per annum. A forecast summary is followed by the forecast in detail and topical articles. The major reports also have a financial and sector analysis. Forecasts usually up to 3 years ahead. The commentary covers about 50%.

Availability   General
Cost   £120
Comments   Published by Gower Publishing at the address and telephone number below.
Address   Gower House, Croft Road, Aldershot GU11 3HR
Telephone   0252 331551

625

Originator   LONDON CHAMBER OF COMMERCE

Title   LONDON CHAMBER ECONOMIC REPORT AND SURVEY, quarterly

Coverage	A review of economic and business trends in London including statistics on export and domestic business, investment and profitability and recruitment difficulties. 70% of the data is based on a regular survey of about 250 companies employing 250,000 in London. Additional data from Central Government sources (30%). Published 1 month after the survey is completed.
Availability	General
Cost	£38, £26 to members
Address	69 Cannon Street, London EC4N 5AB
Telephone	01 248 4444; Telex: 888941; Fax: 01 489 0391

626

Originator	LONDON CORN CIRCULAR
Title	MARKET PRICES, weekly in a weekly journal. 1843–
Coverage	Prices of cereals and various other crops with forecasts of future prices.
Availability	General
Cost	£45
Address	Dittonfern, 54 Wentworth Crescent, Ash Vale, Aldershot GU12 5LF
Telephone	0252 29082

627

Originator	LONDON REGIONAL TRANSPORT
Title	ANNUAL REPORT AND ACCOUNTS, annual. 1984–
Coverage	Includes data on traffic, unit costs, waiting times, tickets issued, staff, assets, grants received etc. Based on the organization's own surveys. Text covers 50%.
Availability	General
Cost	£2
Comments	Also produces an annual Business Plan which includes some statistics.
Address	55 Broadway, London SW1H 0BD
Telephone	01 222 5600; Telex: 893633; Fax: 01 222 5719

628

Originator	LONDON RESEARCH CENTRE
Title	ANNUAL ABSTRACT OF GREATER LONDON STATISTICS, annual. 1966–

Coverage Demographic, economic and social statistics, with historical data in a number of tables, for Greater London as a whole and for the individual London boroughs. Based on a combination of Central Government and local government data.

Availability General
Cost £30 plus p+p
Comments Previously published by the Greater London Council (GLC).
Address Room 508A, County Hall, London SE1 7PB
Telephone 01 633 8447; Fax: 01 633 8236

629

Originator LONDON RESEARCH CENTRE

Title HOUSE PRICE BULLETIN, quarterly
Coverage Price trends for housing in Greater London with statistics for the individual London boroughs.

Availability General
Cost £16 or £5 per issue plus p+p
Comments Various 'one-off' statistical surveys also produced.
Address County Hall, London SE1 7PB
Telephone 01 633 8447; Fax: 01 633 8236

630

Originator LONDON RESEARCH CENTRE

Title LONDON HOUSING STATISTICS, annual
Coverage Various sections covering population, households, dwelling stock and condition, owner-occupied houses, local authority dwellings, homelessness, ethnic records, racial harrassment and new house building. Data is given for the individual London boroughs. Based on a combination of Central Government and local government data.

Availability General
Cost £15 plus p+p
Comments Various 'one-off' statistical surveys also produced.
Address Room 508A, County Hall, London SE1 7PB
Telephone 01 633 8447; Fax: 01 633 8236

631

Originator LONDON TOURIST BOARD AND CONVENTION BUREAU

Title LONDON'S TOURIST STATISTICS, annual

Coverage	Facts about London, volume and value of tourism, purpose of visit and accommodation used, hotel occupancy, known stock of tourist accommodation, day trips to London and visitors to selected attractions. Based mainly on Central Government data (70%) with other material from the Board (20%) and other non- official sources (10%).
Availability	General
Cost	£8
Address	26 Grosvenor Gardens, London SW1W 0DU
Telephone	01 730 3450; Telex: 919041; Fax: 01 730 9367

632

Originator	LONDON TOURIST BOARD AND CONVENTION BUREAU
Title	SURVEY AMONG OVERSEAS VISITORS TO LONDON, annual
Coverage	A survey by the Board of 1,200 overseas visitors to London every July and August. Data on visitor profiles, usage of facilities, services and attitudes. Includes a commentary (50%).
Availability	General
Cost	£12
Address	26 Grosvenor Gardens, London SW1W 0DU
Telephone	01 730 3450; Telex: 919041; Fax: 01 730 9367

633

Originator	LONDON WEEKEND TELEVISION LTD (LWT)
Title	LWT INVESTOR: A SURVEY AMONG HOLDERS AND NON-HOLDERS OF STOCKS AND SHARES IN THE LWT AREA, regular. 1986–
Coverage	Results of interviews by NOP with 433 people contrasting awareness, knowledge and opinions about different savings methods between holders and non-holders of stocks and shares. A large amount of commentary (70%) supports the statistics.
Availability	General
Cost	On application
Comments	2 surveys have been carried out so far in 1986 and 1987. Also publishes a regular 'Marketing Review' with some statistics.
Address	South Bank Television Centre, London SE1 9LT
Telephone	01 261 3434; Telex: 918123; Fax: 01 928 6941

634

Originator	LONDON WEEKEND TELEVISION LTD (LWT)
Title	LWT MARKETING MANUAL, regular. 1980–

Coverage   General market data on the LWT area including population trends, TV equipment, durables and vehicles, incomes, savings and expenditure, education and employment, leisure, retailing and the standard of living. Based on a variety of non-official sources (75%) and Central Government data (25%).

Availability Controlled circulation at LWT's discretion
Cost   Free
Comments   Also produce a regular 'Marketing Review' which occasionally features the results of statistical surveys.
Address   South Bank Television Centre, London SE1 9LT
Telephone   01 261 3434; Telex: 918123; Fax: 01 928 6941

635

Originator   LYONS MAID LTD

Title   ICE CREAM IN THE 80s, annual. 1987–
Coverage   Market trends and figures for 3 sectors: confectionery lines, e.g. cones, wafers, lollies; grocery products, e.g. packs; in-hand and bulk products. Most of the data comes from other non-official sources with additional data from Lyons Maid and Central Government. Approximately half of the report contains a general commentary.

Availability General
Cost   £35
Comments   Produced for Lyons Maid by Gerry Coveney & Associates.
Address   Glacier House, Oldfield Lane North, Greenford UB6 0BA
Telephone   01 575 2004; Telex: 8955495

636

Originator   McCARTHY INFORMATION LTD

Title   FT STATS FICHE, weekly. October 1983–
Coverage   Statistics from the Financial Times produced on fiche including authorized unit trusts, insurances, overseas and money funds, share prices, foreign exchanges, money markets, FT Actuaries Indices, world value of the £ etc.

Availability General
Cost   £310 plus VAT
Comments   Also produces company reports (MIRAC) and overseas financial data on fiche. On-line service via FINSTAT on 01 925 2323.
Address   Manor House, Ash Walk, Warminster, Wiltshire BA12 8PY
Telephone   0985 215151; Fax: 0985 217479

637

Originator	MACHINE TOOL TRADES ASSOCIATION
Title	BASIC FACTS, annual. 1977–
Coverage	Summary data on the machine tool industry taken from Central Government sources (80%) and various non-official sources (20%).
Availability	General
Cost	Free
Comments	Produced in pocket book format.
Address	62 Bayswater Road, London W2 3PS
Telephone	01 402 6671; Telex: 27829; Fax: 01 724 7250

638

Originator	MACHINE TOOL TRADES ASSOCIATION
Title	MACHINE TOOL STATISTICS, annual. 1980–
Coverage	Machine tool production, orders, imports, exports, population, prices and employment. Based on Central Government sources (80%) and various non-official sources (20%), and data for a number of years is usually given. Some supporting text (20%).
Availability	General
Cost	£25
Address	62 Bayswater Road, London W2 3PS
Telephone	01 402 6671; Telex: 27829; Fax: 01 724 7250

639

Originator	MACLEAN HUNTER
Title	BRITISH RATE AND DATA (BRAD), monthly. 1954–
Coverage	Details of all UK media advertising rates, subscription rates, cover prices, circulation trends etc. Based on data collected by BRAD.
Availability	General
Cost	£230
Address	Maclean Hunter House, Cockfosters Rd., Barnet EN4 0BU.
Telephone	01 441 6644; Telex: 299072; Fax: 01 441 1361

640

Originator	MAIL ORDER TRADERS ASSOCIATION
Title	TURNOVER FIGURES, annual
Coverage	Mail order sales and the share of total retail and of non-food retail. Some estimates for the coming year and some general economic data. No details on how the figures are prepared.

Availability	General
Cost	Free
Comments	Produced in the form of an information sheet.
Address	25 Castle Street, Liverpool L2 4TD
Telephone	051 236 7581; Telex: 628169; Fax: 051 227 2584

641

Originator	MANAGEMENT CONSULTANCIES ASSOCIATION
Title	MCA ANNUAL REPORT AND CHAIRMAN'S STATEMENT, annual. 1970–
Coverage	An analysis of the turnover of member firms over the past year and the Chairman's view of market trends and prospects for the coming year. Based on returns from members.
Availability	General
Cost	Free
Address	11 West Halkin Street, London SW1X 8JL
Telephone	01 235 3897; Fax: 01 235 0825

642

Originator	MANCHESTER CHAMBER OF COMMERCE AND INDUSTRY
Title	ECONOMIC REVIEW, quarterly. 1980–
Coverage	Statistics on deliveries, orders, production, stocks, cash flow, investment and business confidence in both the manufacturing and service sectors. Based on a survey of about 250 local member firms. Includes some text (33%).
Availability	Mainly participating members and the press
Cost	Free
Address	56 Oxford Street, Manchester M60 7HJ
Telephone	061 236 3210; Telex: 667822; Fax: 061 236 4160

643

Originator	MANCHESTER POLYTECHNIC, DEPARTMENT OF CLOTHING DESIGN AND TECHNOLOGY
Title	HOLLINGS APPAREL INDUSTRY REVIEW, 3 issues per year
Coverage	The Spring and Autumn issues contain a wide range of statistical data covering production, expenditure, prices, sales, employment, trade, turnover, wages, stoppages, finance and regional trends in the clothing industry. The journal also contains articles and relevant papers. All statistics used are from Central Government sources.
Availability	General

Cost	£20
Address	Hollings Faculty, Old Hall Lane, Manchester M14 6HR
Telephone	061 224 7341

644

Originator	MAN-MADE FIBRES INDUSTRY TRAINING ADVISORY BOARD
Title	ANNUAL REPORT AND ACCOUNTS, annual. 1982–
Coverage	Contains production data for the industry, numbers employed in occupational groups, new entrants to the workforce, apprentice data and financial information. Mainly based on the Board's own data (90%) with a large amount of text (60%).
Availability	General
Cost	Free
Address	Gable House, 40 High Street, Rickmansworth WD3 1ER
Telephone	0923 778371; Fax: 0923 896043

645

Originator	MANPOWER LTD
Title	SURVEY OF EMPLOYMENT PROSPECTS, quarterly. 1969–
Coverage	Short-term forecasts of employment for specific sectors in manufacturing, services and the public sector. Based on the stated intentions of about 1600 companies selected by the various Manpower offices as the largest employers in their category. Also gives data by region and covers special topics occasionally. A supporting commentary (50%).
Availability	General
Cost	Free
Comments	ISSN 0260 8146
Address	Manpower House, 270/272 High Street, Slough SL1 1LJ
Telephone	0753 73111; Telex: 848704; Fax: 0753 824524

646

Originator	MANUFACTURING CHEMIST
Title	AEROSOL REVIEW, annual and as a separate item from the journal
Coverage	Listing of all aerosols filled in the UK and imported. Also lists all types of aerosols filled by company, brand name, type etc. Based on non-official sources.
Availability	General
Cost	£18

Comments	ISSN 0568 062X
Address	Morgan-Grampian Ltd, 30 Calderwood Street, London SE18 69H
Telephone	01 855 7777; Telex: 896238; Fax: 01 854 7476

647

Originator	MARKET AND OPINION RESEARCH INTERNATIONAL (MORI)
Title	BRITISH PUBLIC OPINION, 10 issues per year
Coverage	A digest of recent MORI polls published with summary statistics and commentary, including a summary of polls produced by other polling organizations. Text covers about 60%.
Availability	General
Cost	£50
Comments	ISSN 0265 6175. Available from Page Systems at the address below.
Address	Page Systems, 11/13 Macklin Street, London WC2B 5NH
Telephone	01 831 0961

648

Originator	MARKET ASSESSMENT PUBLICATIONS
Title	GROWTH MARKETS, quarterly. July 1987–
Coverage	2 volumes covering food growth markets and non-food growth markets respectively. Each volume includes 48 specific markets with trends over the last few years and forecasts for 5 years ahead.
Availability	General
Cost	£480 per volume
Address	2 Duncan Terrace, London N1 8BZ
Telephone	01 278 9517; Fax: 01 278 6246

649

Originator	MARKET ASSESSMENT PUBLICATIONS
Title	MARKET ASSESSMENT'S TOP 400 MARKETS, annual. 1987–
Coverage	A 1-page summary is provided on each of the top 400 UK consumer, retail and office markets. The summary includes market value for the latest 2 years, import penetration, brand shares, advertising and general market trends. Based on various sources.
Availability	General
Cost	£250
Address	2 Duncan Terrace, London N1 8BR
Telephone	01 278 9517; Fax: 01 278 6246

650

Originator	MARKET ASSESSMENT PUBLICATIONS

Title	MARKET FORECASTS, annual
Coverage	Forecasts over 5-year period of trends in 250 markets with historical data over a 5 year period. The forecasts are based on the views of over 1,000 senior executives coupled with an interpretation of business prospects. One volume covers food, drink and personal care products and a second covers non-food products.

Availability	General
Cost	£250
Address	2 Duncan Terrace, London N1 8BZ
Telephone	01 278 9517; Fax: 01 278 6246

651

Originator	MARKET ASSESSMENT PUBLICATIONS

Title	MARKET SECTOR REPORTS, annual
Coverage	60 individual reports on specific consumer, retail and office markets. Each contains a market overview, sales data and production data over a 6 year period, imports and exports and statistics on market segmentation, brand shares, advertising, distribution and consumer profiles. Forecasts up to 5 years ahead are included.

Availability	General
Cost	£185-£400 per report
Address	2 Duncan Terrace, London N1 8BZ
Telephone	01 278 9517; Fax: 01 278 6246

652

Originator	MARKET LOCATION LTD

Title	STATISTICAL ANALYSIS OF BRITISH INDUSTRY, bi-annual
Coverage	Tables and maps giving the distribution of industry and industrial profiles for each of 73 separate geographic areas. Industry in each area is analysed by activity and size of unit and indexed to show any divergence from the national average. Based on the company's continuous surveys.

Availability	General
Cost	£75 per issue
Address	1 Warwick Street, Leamington Spa CV32 5LW
Telephone	0926 450388; Fax: 0926 450592

653

Originator	MARKETING DIRECTION LTD
Title	YOUTH FACTS, biennial. 1986–
Coverage	Commentary and statistics relating to the teenage population covering demographic characteristics, education, employment, income, health, leisure activities, product use by type, media use, attitudes etc. Mainly based on the company's own research.
Availability	General
Cost	£150
Comments	2nd edition, September 1988.
Address	1 Palace Gate, Hampton Court Road, Hampton Court KT8 9BN
Telephone	01 979 0936; Telex: 263158; Fax: 01 941 3407

654

Originator	MARKETING WEEK
Title	DATABASE, weekly in a weekly journal
Coverage	Summary statistics with different topics covered each week including consumer spending, consumer profiles, audience surveys, population trends, market shares etc. Based largely on various non-official sources (80%).
Availability	General
Cost	£55, free controlled circulation to selected organizations
Address	Centaur Publications, 50 Poland Street, London W1V 4AX
Telephone	01 439 9381; Fax: 01 439 9669

655

Originator	MARKETPOWER LTD
Title	CATERING SCENARIOS, annual
Coverage	Statistics for the latest 5 years and forecasts for the next 5 years for 32 factors likely to have an effect on the catering sector. Based on the company's own research.
Availability	General
Cost	On application
Comments	Various other services also available.
Address	82/84 Uxbridge Road, London W13 8RA
Telephone	01 840 5252; Telex: 858623

656

Originator	MARPLAN
Title	OMNIBUS SURVEY, regular

Coverage	A survey of approximately 1,500 persons with data on consume: spending, goods purchased, advertising awareness etc.
Availability	General
Cost	On application
Comments	Various other services and analyses available.
Address	41/45 Goswell Road, London EC1V 7DN
Telephone	01 251 4000

657

Originator	MEAT TRADES JOURNAL
Title	MARKETS INFORMATION, weekly in a weekly journal. 1965–
Coverage	Production and stock data for specific meats and livestock and live wholesale and retail prices for different types of meat and livestock in various cities in the UK. Data is usually 7 days old.
Availability	General
Cost	50p per issue
Address	International Thomson Publishing Ltd, 100 Avenue Road, London NW3 3TP
Telephone	01 935 6611; Telex: 299973; Fax: 01 586 5799

658

Originator	MEDIA EXPENDITURE ANALYSIS LTD (MEAL)
Title	ADVERTISEMENT ANALYSIS, monthly
Coverage	A record of each press and television advertisement placed during the month. Total expenditure and sub-totals for press and television are shown for each brand/product. Reports are available for each o MEAL's product groups or brands and the complete analysis i available on fiche. Produced within 7 days of the end of the month covered. Based on MEAL's research.
Availability	General
Cost	On application
Comments	Various specialized services available. MEALINK is available on line. Data on microfiche for any period from 1974.
Address	63 St Martin's Lane, London WC2N 4JT
Telephone	01 240 1903; Fax: 01 240 2602

659

Originator	MEDIA EXPENDITURE ANALYSIS LTD (MEAL)
Title	BRAND EXPENDITURE BY AREA, monthly

Coverage   Covers television and press. The areas are defined by TV regions
            and the allocation of press expenditure is according to JICNARS
            readership profiles. Gives data for the latest month and the total
            latest year. Reports for each product group and the complete
            analysis on fiche. Based on MEAL's research.

Availability General
Cost   On application
Comments   Various specialized services available. MEALINK available on-
              line. Data on microfiche for any period from 1974.
Address   63 St Martin's Lane, London WC2N 4JT
Telephone   01 240 1903; Fax: 01 240 2602

660

Originator   MEDIA EXPENDITURE ANALYSIS LTD (MEAL)

Title   BRAND EXPENDITURE BY MEDIA GROUP, monthly
Coverage   Shows the allocation across various media groups. Expenditure is in
             £000s for the previous month and in total for the last year. Profiles
             by media group. Reports available for each product group and a
             complete analysis is on fiche. Produced within 7 days of the end of
             the month covered. Based on MEAL's research.

Availability General
Cost   On application
Comments   Various specialized services available. MEALINK available on-
              line. Data on microfche for any period from 1974.
Address   63 St Martin's Lane, London WC2N 4JT
Telephone   01 240 1903; Fax: 01 240 2602

661

Originator   MEDIA EXPENDITURE ANALYSIS LTD (MEAL)

Title   BRAND EXPENDITURE BY MEDIUM, monthly
Coverage   Television and press expenditure during each of the previous 12
             months and in total for the period. For each brand the expenditure
             is shown in £000s for each month. Reports are available for each of
             MEAL's product groups or brands and the complete analysis is on
             fiche. Produced within 7 days of the end of the month covered.
             Based on MEAL's own research.

Availability General
Cost   On application
Comments   Various specialized services available. MEALINK is available on-
              line. Data on microfiche available for any period from 1974.
Address   63 St Martin's Lane, London WC2N 4JT
Telephone   01 240 1903; Fax: 01 240 2602

662

Originator	MEDIA EXPENDITURE ANALYSIS LTD (MEAL)
Title	BRAND EXPENDITURE BY TELEVISION REGIONS, monthly
Coverage	Gives total television expenditure, by channel and by TV region. Reports are available for each of MEAL's product groups and the complete analysis is available on fiche. Based on MEAL's research and dispatched within 7 days of the previous month.
Availability	General
Cost	On application
Comments	Various specialized services available. MEALINK available on-line. Data on microfiche available from 1974.
Address	63 St Martin's Lane, London WC2N 4JT
Telephone	01 240 1903; Fax: 01 240 2602

663

Originator	MEDIA EXPENDITURE ANALYSIS LTD (MEAL)
Title	BRAND EXPENDITURE ON RADIO, monthly
Coverage	Results compiled from 10 major radio contractors in 6 primary marketing areas accounting for about 70% of ILR's revenue. Data is given for the latest month and the total year. Dispatched within 7 days after the end of the month covered. Reports available for each product group and the complete analysis is on microfiche.
Availability	General
Cost	On application
Comments	Various specialized services available. MEALINK available on-line. Data on microfiche for any period from 1974.
Address	63 St Martin's Lane, London WC2N 4JT
Telephone	01 240 1903; Fax: 01 240 2602

664

Originator	MEDIA EXPENDITURE ANALYSIS LTD (MEAL)
Title	TRI-MEDIA DIGEST OF BRANDS AND ADVERTISERS, quarterly
Coverage	The combined television and press advertising expenditure for brands spending at least £60,000 in the previous 12 months. The data covers the latest quarter, each month in the quarter and the total for the previous 12 months. Also shows the split between television and press expenditure for each brand/product over the last 12 months. Based on MEAL's research.
Availability	General
Cost	£580

Comments   Various specialized services available. MEALINK is available on-
line. Data also on microfiche for any period from 1974.
Address   63 St Martin's Lane, London WC2N 4JT
Telephone 01 240 1903; Fax: 01 240 2602

665

Originator   MERRILL LYNCH

Title   ANNUAL STUDY OF EMPLOYEE RELOCATION POLICIES
AMONG MAJOR UK COMPANIES, annual
Coverage   Statistics on the size and nature of the relocation market in the UK
and overseas plus information on the attitudes to relocation and
corporate policies. Based on interviews with executives in 300
companies.

Availability General
Cost   On application
Comments   The survey is carried out by the Harris Research Centre.
Address   136 New Bond Street, London W1Y 9FA
Telephone   01 629 82222

666

Originator   MESSEL & CO

Title   ECONOMIC OUTLOOK, monthly
Coverage   Commentary and statistics on the key economic indicators and
short-term forecasts, based largely on Central Government data.

Availability General
Cost   On application
Comments   Also publishes a weekly 'Economic Monitor'.
Address   1 Finsbury Avenue, London EC2M 2QE
Telephone   01 377 0123; Telex: 883004; Fax: 01 247 8278

667

Originator   METAL PACKAGING MANUFACTURERS ASSOCIATION

Title   ANNUAL REPORT, annual
Coverage   Includes a review of the year with statistics on sales of packaging
materials and end users. Based on data collected by the Associ-
ation.

Availability General
Cost   Free
Address   19 Elmshott Lane, Cippenham, Slough SL1 5QS
Telephone   06286 5203; Telex: 846782

668

Originator	METALWORKING PRODUCTION
Title	SURVEY OF MACHINE TOOLS AND PRODUCTION EQUIPMENT IN BRITAIN, every 5 years published separately from the journal. 1961–
Coverage	Trends in sales and use of the various types of machine tools with a detailed breakdown by industrial sector and a regional analysis. The latest survey (1988) is based on returns from 4,754 companies and covers 767,000 machine tools. Based on fieldwork carried out in 1987 and various introductory sections provide a commentary (20%).
Availability	General
Comments	The latest survey (1988) is the sixth edition.
Address	Morgan Grampian, 30 Calderwood Street, Woolwich, London SE18 6QH
Telephone	01 855 7777

669

Originator	MID-GLAMORGAN COUNTY COUNCIL
Title	MID-GLAMORGAN IN FIGURES, annual. 1975–
Coverage	Summary data on the county covering population, employment, households, housing, unemployment, education, socio-economic groups etc. 30 tables from various sources.
Availability	General
Cost	Free
Address	Room 406, Council Offices, Greyfriars Road, Cardiff CF1 3LG
Telephone	0222 820073; Fax: 0222 820777

670

Originator	MILK MARKETING BOARD
Title	DAIRY FACTS AND FIGURES, annual. 1962–
Coverage	Data on producers, dairy farming, milk supplies, utilization, prices, advertising, transport, expenditure, consumption and trade. Historical figures are given in most tables and some EEC figures are included. Based on the Board's own data (75%) and some Central Government statistics (25%).
Availability	General
Cost	£7.50
Comments	The publication is jointly produced by the Milk Marketing Boards. The Board also runs the Dairyfax viewdata service.
Address	Thames Ditton, Surrey KT7 0EL
Telephone	01 398 4101; Telex: 8956671; Fax: 01 398 4101

671

Originator   MILK MARKETING BOARD

Title   KEY MILK FIGURES IN ENGLAND AND WALES, annual
Coverage   Basic figures for sales by region, consumption, utilization, regional
                 prices, realization for milk manufactured, EEC prices, producer
                 numbers, livestock numbers, transport and milk quality.

Availability General
Cost   Free
Comments   Produced in card format. The Board also runs the Dairyfax
                 viewdata service.
Address   Thames Ditton, Surrey KT7 0EL
Telephone   01 398 4101; Telex: 8956671; Fax: 01 398 4101

672

Originator   MILK MARKETING BOARD

Title   MILK PRODUCER, monthly
Coverage   A monthly journal with news items and statistics covering producer
                 prices, supplies and milk sales by region.

Availability General
Cost   £9, free to milk producers
Comments   The Board also runs the Dairyfax viewdata service.
Address   Thames Ditton, Surrey KT7 0EL
Telephone   01 398 4101; Telex: 8956671; Fax: 01 398 4101

673

Originator   MILK MARKETING BOARD

Title   NATIONAL MILK RECORDS: ANNUAL REPORTS, annual
Coverage   Milk production and quality by leading cows and herds in 4 different
                 areas of England and Wales: North, Midlands and Wales, East and
                 South East, West.

Availability General
Cost   £12 for 4 volumes or £3.50 per volume
Comments   Published as a 4-volume set. The Board also runs a Dairyfax
                 viewdata service.
Address   Thames Ditton, Surrey KT7 0EL
Telephone   01 398 4101; Telex: 8956671; Fax: 01 398 4101

674

Originator	MILK MARKETING BOARD
Title	REPORT OF THE BREEDING AND PRODUCTION ORGANISATION, annual
Coverage	Results of a survey of trends throughout the country with data on specific livestock. Survey carried out by the Board.
Availability	General
Cost	£3.50
Comments	The Board also runs the Dairyfax viewdata service.
Address	Thames Ditton, Surrey KT7 0EL
Telephone	01 398 4101; Telex: 8956671; Fax: 01 398 4101

675

Originator	MILK MARKETING BOARD FOR NORTHERN IRELAND
Title	ANNUAL REPORT, annual. 1956–
Coverage	Includes a statistical section with data on the number of registered milk producers, production, herd sizes, prices, yields and sales. Mainly commentary (80%).
Availability	General
Cost	Free
Address	456 Antrim Road, Belfast BT15 5GD
Telephone	0232 770123; Telex: 747136

676

Originator	MILK MARKETING BOARD FOR NORTHERN IRELAND
Title	KEY MILK FIGURES IN NORTHERN IRELAND, annual. 1978–
Coverage	Statistics on milk production, utilization, producer prices, dairy herds, milk quality, EEC prices etc. Based largely on data collected by the Board (90%) with some Central Government statistics (10%).
Availability	General
Cost	Free
Comments	Produced in a card format.
Address	456 Antrim Road, Belfast BT15 5GD
Telephone	0232 770123; Telex: 747136

219

677

Originator	MILLS, ROWENA & ASSOCIATES
Title	STATISTICAL AND ECONOMIC REVIEW OF THE UK PACKAGING INDUSTRY, annual. 1970–
Coverage	A detailed commentary plus a retail attitudes survey and a statistical section with over 250 tables on specific products. The detailed commentary appears every 2 years but the statistics are published annually. Based on data from Central Government and various non-official sources.
Availability	General
Cost	£450, or £175 for the statistical update without the commentary
Comments	The complete review with a commentary will be published again in 1989. Published in association with PIRA.
Address	PO Box 594, London W8 7DE
Telephone	01 937 4035

678

Originator	MILPRO LTD
Title	NATIONAL VETERINARY INDEX, bi-annual. 1966–
Coverage	Estimates of purchases of animal health products by veterinary practices. The data is collected from a panel of 480 practices representative of total practices in England, Scotland and Wales.
Availability	Subscribers only
Cost	Price varies according to the data required
Address	1/2 Berners Street, London W1P 3AG
Telephone	01 637 1444; Telex: 25206; Fax: 01 631 4819

679

Originator	MILPRO LTD
Title	PRESCRIBING TRENDS, monthly. October 1975–
Coverage	Monitor of trends in general practitioners' prescribing. Data available for 14 therapeutic groups and 300 specific products within these groups. Based on a survey of a panel of GPs with quota controls for area and size of practice. Published 2 weeks after the survey.
Availability	Subscribers only
Cost	On application
Address	1/2 Berners Street, London W1P 3AG
Telephone	01 637 1444; Telex: 25206; Fax: 01 631 4819

680

Originator	MINING JOURNAL
Title	METAL ORE MARKETS, weekly in a weekly journal
Coverage	A brief tabulation of London Metal Exchange prices, stocks, turnovers and monthly average prices. Tabulation of selection of main non-ferrous metals and ore prices. Based on figures collected by the journal and other non-official sources.
Availability	General
Cost	£108
Address	60 Worship Street, London EC2A 2HD
Telephone	01 377 2020; Fax: 01 247 4100

681

Originator	MINTEL
Title	LEISURE INTELLIGENCE, quarterly
Coverage	Mainly feature articles on specific leisure areas but each issue also contains a ' Leisure Trends' section with regular data on DIY activity, gardening and audio-visual activities.
Availability	General
Cost	£545
Comments	Various other surveys published.
Address	KAE House, 7 Arundel Street, London WC2R 3DR
Telephone	01 836 1814; Telex: 21405; Fax: 01 836 1682

682

Originator	MINTEL
Title	MINTEL MONTHLY DIGESTS, monthly
Coverage	A range of specific digests with regularly updated statistics and commentary on various products in the foods, retailing, transport, vehicles and financial services sectors.
Availability	General
Cost	£150 each
Comments	Various other surveys published.
Address	KAE House, 7 Arundel Street, London WC2R 3DR
Telephone	01 836 1814; Telex: 21405; Fax: 01 836 1682

683

Originator	MINTEL
Title	RETAIL INTELLIGENCE, quarterly

221   **684–686**

Coverage   Mainly feature articles on specific retailing topics but includes
               regular sections with statistics on the major areas of retailing, e.g.
               household/DIY retailing, clothing and footwear retailing etc.

Availability General
Cost   £545
Comments   Various other surveys published.
Address   KAE House, 7 Arundel Street, London WC2R 3DR
Telephone   01 836 1814; Telex: 21405; Fax: 01 836 1682

                684

Originator   MIRROR GROUP NEWSPAPERS 86 LTD

Title   MGN MARKETING MANUAL OF THE UK, regular
Coverage   Compilation of various sources of marketing data covering popu-
                 lation, social and economic trends, consumers, media trends,
                 advertising and market data on over 100 different products. Based
                 on a range of official and non-official sources.

Availability General
Cost   £75
Comments   Published annually up to 1979 then a gap until 1986. At the time of
                 writing this is still the latest issue.
Address   Holborn Circus, London EC1P 1DQ
Telephone   01 353 0246; Fax: 01 353 3429

                685

Originator   MONKS PUBLICATIONS

Title   TOP MANAGEMENT REMUNERATION, bi-annual. 1978–
Coverage   Pay and benefits of directors and senior managers in all industries
                 and sectors. Based on the company's own research with a small
                 amount of supporting text (10%).

Availability General
Cost   £200, reduced rates for participants
Comments   Database covering 1200 mainly quoted companies and special
                 analyses of the database available on request. Published in October
                 and March.
Address   Debden Green, Saffron Walden, CB11 3LX
Telephone   Telephone; 0371 830939

                686

Originator   MORGAN GRENFELL SECURITIES LTD

Title   BUILDING BULLETIN, 1 or 2 issues per month
Coverage   Commentary and statistics on the building industry and companies
                 in the construction sector.

Availability On application
Cost On application
Address PO Box 479, 20 Finsbury Circus, London EC2M 7BB
Telephone 01 256 6278; Telex: 9390222; Fax: 01 256 6870

687

Originator MORGAN GRENFELL SECURITIES LTD

Title DRINKS MONITOR, 1 or 2 issues per month
Coverage Commentary and statistics on the drinks industry and drinks companies. An annual issue gives prospects for the year ahead.

Availability On application
Cost On application
Address PO Box 479, 20 Finsbury Circus, London EC2M 7BB
Telephone 01 256 6278; Telex: 9390222; Fax: 01 256 6870

688

Originator MORGAN GRENFELL SECURITIES LTD

Title UK ECONOMIC OUTLOOK, monthly
Coverage A commentary and statistics on general trends with some statistics on the short-term outlook, largely based on Central Government data.

Availability On application
Cost On application
Address PO Box 479, 20 Finsbury Circus, London EC2M 7BB
Telephone 01 256 6278; Telex: 9390222; Fax: 01 256 6870

689

Originator MORRELL, JAMES AND ASSOCIATES

Title BUSINESS FORECASTS, 3 issues per year. 1980–
Coverage Summary forecasts for the main economic variables plus output in 15 sectors, consumer spending in 11 sectors, property trends, regional data and population and life-style trends. Forecasts up to 10 years ahead. A commentary (50%) supports the data.

Availability General
Cost £133
Address 1 Paternoster Row, St Pauls, London EC4M 7DH
Telephone 01 236 6950

690

Originator	MOTHERWELL DISTRICT COUNCIL
Title	MOTHERWELL ECONOMIC REVIEW 198., annual
Coverage	Commentary and statistics on the local economy with data on unemployment, vacancies etc. Also outlines district council policies. Mainly based on Central Government data.
Availability	General
Cost	£6
Address	Planning, PO Box 14, Civic Centre, Motherwell ML1 1TW
Telephone	0698 66166

691

Originator	MOTOR CYCLE ASSOCIATION OF GREAT BRITAIN
Title	ESTIMATED RUNNING COSTS, annual
Coverage	Covers various types of powered two wheelers, e.g. cycles, scooters, mopeds etc., based on data collected by the Association.
Availability	General
Cost	Free
Comments	More detailed figures available to members.
Address	Starley House, Eaton Road, Coventry CV1 2FH
Telephone	0203 27427; Telex: 31590; Fax: 0203 29175

692

Originator	MOTOR CYCLE ASSOCIATION OF GREAT BRITAIN
Title	FIRST REGISTRATIONS OF POWERED TWO AND THREE WHEELED VEHICLES IN THE UK, monthly
Coverage	Data by make, model and geographical area and divided into the various two and three wheeled types, e.g. mopeds, scooters, cycles etc.
Availability	General
Cost	Free
Comments	More detailed information available to members.
Address	Starley House, Eaton Road, Coventry CV1 2FH
Telephone	0203 27427; Telex: 31590; Fax: 0203 29175

693

Originator	MOTOR CYCLE ASSOCIATION OF GREAT BRITAIN
Title	IMPORT/EXPORT OF POWERED TWO-WHEELERS, monthly

Coverage	Imports and exports of various types of powered two-wheelers, e.g. mopeds, scooters, cycles, sidecars etc. Based on Central Government data.
Availability	General
Cost	Free
Comments	More detailed information available to members.
Address	Starley House, Eaton Road, Coventry CV1 2FH
Telephone	0203 27427; Telex: 31590; Fax: 0203 29175

694

Originator	MOTOR CYCLE ASSOCIATION OF GREAT BRITAIN
Title	MARKETING AND INFORMATION SERVICE, monthly
Coverage	Various statistics on the industry covering new registrations by style and by area, data on the characteristics of purchasers of new machines, the motorcycle parc, imports, exports and a dealer directory with a geographical breakdown of dealers. A number of tables give data for earlier years and months.
Availability	General
Cost	£3 per issue, free to members
Address	Starley House, Eaton Road, Coventry CV1 2FH
Telephone	0203 27427; Telex: 31590; Fax: 0203 29175

695

Originator	MOTOR CYCLE ASSOCIATION OF GREAT BRITAIN
Title	UK MOTOR CYCLE INDUSTRY IN A NUTSHELL, annual
Coverage	Summary statistics on production, imports, exports, vehicles in use and general sales. Based on a combination of the Association's own data (60%) and Central Government statistics (40%).
Availability	General
Cost	On application
Comments	More detailed figures available to members.
Address	Starley House, Eaton Road, Coventry CV1 2FH
Telephone	0203 27427; Telex: 31590; Fax: 0203 29175

696

Originator	MOTOR TRADER
Title	REGISTRATIONS AND DATACHECK, monthly in a weekly journal

225   **697–699**

Coverage	Breakdown of new car registrations in the UK and trends in the market shares of car manufacturers and importers. One table per month based on non-official sources, mainly the Society of Motor Manufacturers and Traders. Data usually refers to the previous month.
Availability	General
Cost	£45
Address	Reed Publishing, Quadrant House, The Quadrant, Sutton SM2 5AS
Telephone	01 661 3276; Telex: 892084; Fax: 01 661 3705

697

Originator	MOTOR TRANSPORT
Title	COST TABLES, quarterly in a weekly journal. 1965–
Coverage	Commercial vehicles in a range of weight categories giving standing costs and costs for a range of annual mileages. Based mainly on the journal's own research (90%).
Availability	General
Cost	£44, free to transport operators
Address	Reed Publishing, Quadrant House, The Quadrant, Sutton SM2 5AS
Telephone	01 661 3500; Telex: 892084; Fax: 01 661 3705

698

Originator	MOTOR TRANSPORT
Title	TRENDS AND FORECASTS, bi-annual. March 1988–
Coverage	Commentary and statistics on the road haulage sector with statistics and forecasts on new registrations of trucks and goods moved by road. Data from 1975 to 1991.
Availability	General
Cost	£44, free to transport operators
Comments	First published in March 1988 with the second feature in July 1988. Prepared by the research company MMD.
Address	Reed Publishing, Quadrant House, The Quadrant, Sutton SM2 5AS
Telephone	01 661 3500; Telex: 892084; Fax: 01 661 3705

699

Originator	MS SURVEYS AND PROMOTIONAL SERVICES LTD
Title	MERCHANDISING AND PROMOTIONAL INTELLIGENCE, monthly

Coverage	A review of promotional activity in various consumer markets with statistics on the level of activity. Based on the company's own survey.
Availability	General
Cost	£150
Address	Hesketh House, Portman Square, London W1H 0JH
Telephone	01 486 5111

700

Originator	MS SURVEYS AND PROMOTIONAL SERVICES LTD
Title	PROMOTION 8, annual
Coverage	Statistics on promotional activity and new promotions with data on types of promotions by product area, product activity and new products. A supporting text covers 40%.
Availability	General
Cost	£55
Address	Hesketh House, Portman Square, London W1H 0JH
Telephone	01 486 5111

701

Originator	MUSHROOM GROWERS ASSOCIATION
Title	MUSHROOM GROWERS ASSOCIATION INDUSTRY SURVEY, annual. 1979–
Coverage	Production and manpower figures for the sector plus a cost analysis, methods of growing and industry yield figures. Based on a survey of members with supporting text (50%). Usually published 1–2 months after the year to which it relates.
Availability	Members
Address	Agriculture House, Knightsbridge, London SW1X 7NJ
Telephone	01 235 5077; Telex: 919669; Fax: 01 235 3526

702

Originator	MUSIC PUBLISHERS ASSOCIATION LTD
Title	SUMMARY OF PRINTED MUSIC SALES, bi-annual
Coverage	UK and overseas sales with data for the latest year and the previous year. Based on a survey by the Association with a small amount of supporting text (20%). Published 4-5 months after the end of the year to which it relates.
Availability	General
Cost	Free
Address	7th Floor, Kingsway House, 103 Kingsway, London WC2B 6QX
Telephone	01 831 7591; Fax: 01 242 0612

703

Originator   NABISCO GROUP LTD

Title   NABISCO VIEW OF THE BISCUIT MARKET, every 2 or 3
                 years. 1984–
Coverage   Commentary and statistics with data from various sources. A large
                 amount of text (75%) supports the data.

Availability General
Cost   Free
Address   121 Kings Road, Reading RG1 3EF
Telephone   0734 583535; Telex: 848360; Fax: 0734 589428

704

Originator   NATIONAL AND LOCAL GOVERNMENT OFFICERS
                 ASSOCIATION (NALGO)

Title   NALGO RESEARCH, monthly
Coverage   News items and statistics on the economy and public sector devel-
                 opments with data on unemployment, retail prices, the tax and
                 price index, earnings and recent public sector pay settlements.

Availability Members and some others
Cost   Free
Address   1 Mabledon Place, London WC1H 9AJ
Telephone   01 388 2366

705

Originator   NATIONAL ASSOCIATION OF PENSION FUNDS LTD

Title   ANNUAL SURVEY OF OCCUPATIONAL PENSION
                 SCHEMES, annual. 1975–
Coverage   A survey of 91 public and 888 private sector schemes. Covers
                 income and expenditure and size of fund, the nature of the schemes,
                 benefits provided and the Social Security Pensions Act 1975. The
                 data is collected via a postal survey to all members of the associ-
                 ation. A supporting commentary is included with the statistics.

Availability General
Cost   £50, £25 to members
Comments   ISSN 0309 0078
Address   12/18 Grosvenor Gardens, London SW1W 0DH
Telephone   01 730 0588; Telex: 28557; Fax: 01 730 2595

706

Originator	NATIONAL ASSOCIATION OF STEEL STOCKHOLDERS
Title	ANNUAL REPORT, annual
Coverage	Statistical appendix gives domestic supplies, deliveries to stockholders from the UK, production, imports and the share of imported steel products in the domestic markets of the ECSC countries. Based on a combination of the Association's data (65%) and Central Government data (35%). Text accounts for 80%.
Availability	General
Cost	Free
Address	Gateway House, High Street, Birmingham B4 7SY
Telephone	021 632 5821; Telex: 335908; Fax: 021 643 6645

707

Originator	NATIONAL ASSOCIATION OF STEEL STOCKHOLDERS
Title	BUSINESS TRENDS, monthly
Coverage	Summary of executive opinion on a range of topics, e.g. the economy, sales trends, stock levels, buying and selling prices, processing and credit. Trends surveys carried out for a range of products. Based on a survey of members with some supporting text (10%).
Availability	Members
Cost	Free
Address	Gateway House, High Street, Birmingham B4 7SY
Telephone	021 632 5821; Telex: 335908; Fax: 021 643 6645

708

Originator	NATIONAL BEDDING FEDERATION
Title	BEDDING SALES STATISTICS, regular
Coverage	General statistics abstracted from Central Government figures.
Availability	Members
Cost	Free
Address	251 Brompton Road, London SW3 2EZ
Telephone	01 589 4888

709

Originator	NATIONAL BOOK TRUST
Title	LIBRARY BOOK SPENDING IN UNIVERSITIES, POLYTECHNICS AND COLLEGES, biennial. 1982–

Coverage   University expenditure on books as a percentage, whole expenditure on books per full-time equivalent student in polytechnics and as a percentage of total expenditure and expenditure on books in further education by local authority. Based largely on non-official sources (about 70%), with some supporting text.

Availability General
Cost   Free with the inclusion of a stamped addressed envelope
Address   Book House, 45 East Hill, London SW18 2QZ
Telephone 01 870 9055

710

Originator NATIONAL BOOK TRUST

Title   PUBLIC LIBRARY SPENDING IN ENGLAND AND WALES, annual. 1981–
Coverage   Actual and estimated expenditure per head of population by county and metropolitan district. Includes data on publishers turnover. Some supporting text is included with the statistics. Half of the data comes from non-official sources with the remaining unacknowledged.

Availability General
Cost   Free with the inclusion of a stamped addressed envelope
Address   Book House, 45 East Hill, London SW18 2QZ
Telephone 01 870 9055

711

Originator NATIONAL BUSINESS EQUIPMENT SURVEY

Title   NATIONAL BUSINESS EQUIPMENT SURVEY, continuous
Coverage   Continuous sample survey of users of various product groups, including general office equipment, word processors, microfilms, copiers etc.

Availability General
Cost   On application
Address   71 Quickswood, London NW3 3RT
Telephone 01 586 0403

712

Originator NATIONAL CARPET INDEX/NATIONAL FURNITURE INDEX

Title   NATIONAL BEDDING INDEX, annual. 1982–

Coverage	Market data based on 400 retailers. Statistics on the total market, market shares, distribution, sales by type, prices and price points, display trends and best selling models. Based on original research by the company.
Availability	General
Cost	£7,000
Comments	Data in machine readable form available by arrangement.
Address	Sinclair House, The Avenue, West Ealing, London W13 8NT
Telephone	01 997 4619

713

Originator	NATIONAL CARPET INDEX/NATIONAL FURNITURE INDEX
Title	NATIONAL CARPET INDEX & NATIONAL UNDERLAY INDEX, annual. 1971–
Coverage	A survey of the UK markets based on 400 retailers. Data on the market, market shares, distribution, wholesaling, product styles, prices and price points, display trends and best selling designs. Based on original research by the company.
Availability	General
Cost	£7,000
Comments	Data in machine readable form available by arrangement.
Address	Sinclair House, The Avenue, West Ealing, London W13 8NT
Telephone	01 997 4619

714

Originator	NATIONAL CAVITY INSULATION ASSOCIATION
Title	ANNUAL STATISTICS, annual
Coverage	The industry based on a survey of members.
Availability	Members
Address	PO Box 12, Haslemere, Surrey GU27 3AN
Telephone	0428 54011; Telex: 858819; Fax: 0428 51401

715

Originator	NATIONAL COUNCIL OF BUILDING MATERIAL PRODUCERS
Title	BMP FORECASTS, 3 issues per year
Coverage	Forecasts 3 years ahead for housing starts and completions, other new work and repair, maintenance and improvement. Based on the Council's own forecasts with a large amount of supporting commentary (80%).

Availability	General
Cost	£50
Comments	Usually published in March, July and November.
Address	10 Great George Street, London SW1P 3AE
Telephone	01 222 5315

716

Originator	NATIONAL COUNCIL OF BUILDING MATERIAL PRO-DUCERS
Title	BMP STATISTICAL BULLETIN, monthly
Coverage	Covers housebuilding starts and completions, renovations, prices, mortgages, architects' workload, value of new orders and output, capital expenditure, building material production, prices and trade. Based on a combination of Central Government data (50%) and various non-official sources (50%). Data is usually 2 months old.
Availability	General
Cost	£50
Address	10 Great George Street, London SW1P 3AE
Telephone	01 222 5315

717

Originator	NATIONAL DOCK LABOUR BOARD
Title	ANNUAL REPORT AND ACCOUNTS, annual
Coverage	Includes a section of statistical tables covering the labour force, registers, training, education, welfare, pensions etc. The report also contains financial accounts. Based on the Board's own data.
Availability	General
Cost	£1
Address	22/26 Albert Embankment, London SE1 7TE
Telephone	01 735 7271; Fax: 01 735 5967

718

Originator	NATIONAL FARMERS UNION
Title	UK AGRICULTURE: ITS IMPORTANCE AND RELATION-SHIP TO THE ECONOMY AS A WHOLE, annual
Coverage	Includes statistics on factors of production, agricultural output, technical and economic efficiency, self-sufficiency and trends in ancillary industries. The sources of the statistics are not given. Text covers about 40%.
Availability	Members
Cost	Free

Comments	Published as a duplicated 5–6-page leaflet.
Address	Agriculture House, Knightsbridge, London SW1X 7NJ
Telephone	01 235 5077; Telex: 919669; Fax: 01 235 3526

719

Originator	NATIONAL HOUSE BUILDING COUNCIL
Title	PRIVATE HOUSE BUILDING STATISTICS, quarterly. 1981–
Coverage	Covers dwelling starts and completions, prices, market share of timber frame, first time buyers ability to buy and some regional trends. Largely based on the Council's own survey (90%) plus some Central Government data. Usually published 2 to 3 weeks after the end of the quarter.
Availability	General
Cost	£10
Address	Chiltern Avenue, Amersham, Buckinghamshire HP6 5AP
Telephone	0494 434477; Fax: 0494 434477

720

Originator	NATIONAL HOUSING AND TOWN PLANNING COUNCIL
Title	HOUSING AND PLANNING REVIEW, 6 issues per year
Coverage	Includes various statistics and features based on a variety of sources.
Availability	General
Cost	£13
Address	14/18 Old Street, London EC1V 9AB
Telephone	01 251 2363

721

Originator	NATIONAL INSTITUTE OF ECONOMIC AND SOCIAL RESEARCH (NIESR)
Title	NATIONAL INSTITUTE ECONOMIC REVIEW, quarterly
Coverage	General commentary on the home and world economy with forecasts usually up to 18 months ahead. Special articles on relevant topics. A separate statistical section plus various tables included in the text (80%). Statistics mainly from NIESR based on official statistics.
Availability	General
Cost	£45, £15 to students
Comments	ISSN 0027 9501. NIESR macroeconomic analysis package available in machine readable form – £800 plus VAT per year.
Address	2 Dean Trench Street, Smith Square, London SW1P 3HE
Telephone	01 222 7665

722

Originator	NATIONAL SULPHURIC ACID ASSOCIATION LTD
Title	ANNUAL REPORT AND FINANCIAL STATEMENTS, annual
Coverage	A statistical section covers the production of sulphuric acid in the UK, the import of sulphur, use of raw materials, acid consumption by major industries in the UK and trade uses of the acid. The remainder of the report provides a commentary on the sector, annual accounts and a list of members.
Availability	Primarily members, but generally available on request
Cost	Free
Address	140 Park Lane, London W1Y 4DT
Telephone	01 495 0414; Telex: 21724; Fax: 01 409 0209

723

Originator	NATIONAL SULPHURIC ACID ASSOCIATION LTD
Title	ANNUAL SUMMARY OF MONTHLY RETURNS, annual
Coverage	Production and consumption of sulphuric acid, oleum and sulphur raw materials. Based on a survey of members and produced 2–3 months after the end of the year. Produced on one sheet of paper.
Availability	General
Cost	Free
Address	140 Park Lane, London W1Y 4DT
Telephone	01 495 0414; Telex: 21724; Fax: 01 409 0209

724

Originator	NATIONAL SULPHURIC ACID ASSOCIATION LTD
Title	QUARTERLY SUMMARY OF MONTHLY RETURNS, quarterly
Coverage	Production and consumption of sulphuric acid, oleum and sulphur raw materials. Statistics based on a survey of members and published on one sheet of paper 1–2 months after the survey.
Availability	General
Cost	Free
Address	140 Park Lane, London W1Y 4DT
Telephone	01 495 0414; Telex: 21724; Fax: 01 409 0209

725

Originator	NATIONAL UTILITY SERVICES LTD
Title	UTILITY NEWSBRIEFS, quarterly

Coverage	Essentially a newsletter on energy and telecommunications with a regular section on the costs of energy, water and telecommunications by industrial sector and region. Based on their own survey.
Availability	Clients and special organizations
Cost	Free
Address	Carolyn House, Dingwall Road, Croydon CR9 3LX
Telephone	01 681 2500; Telex: 917363; Fax: 01 688 7229

726

Originator	NATIONWIDE ANGLIA BUILDING SOCIETY
Title	HOUSE PRICES, quarterly. 1955–
Coverage	By region and by type of house, with general indices of house prices, housebuilding costs, retail prices and earnings. Other data on the relationship between house prices, mortgage advances, incomes and repayments and previous owner occupiers. Based mainly on the Society's own data (90%). Some supporting text (10%).
Availability	General
Cost	Free
Comments	ISSN 0263 3639
Address	Chesterfield House, Bloomsbury Way, London WC1V 6PW
Telephone	01 242 8822; Telex: 264549; Fax: 01 242 8822

727

Originator	NATIONWIDE ANGLIA BUILDING SOCIETY
Title	LOCAL AREA HOUSING STATISTICS, regular. January 1985–
Coverage	A detailed analysis of the Society's borrowers in a particular local area in each issue. Covers previous tenure, age, income, distance moved, sex etc. and property characteristics such as age, prices, housetype, amenities etc. 50% of each report is text.
Availability	General
Cost	Free
Comments	Usually 2 or 3 reports on various county and regional areas each month.
Address	Chesterfield House, Bloomsbury Way, London WC1V 6PW
Telephone	01 242 8822; Telex: 264549; Fax: 01 242 8822

728

Originator	NEW CIVIL ENGINEER
Title	CONSTRUCTION INDICES, monthly in a weekly journal
Coverage	Price indices for labour, materials and building work in the civil engineering sector with data for the latest month and comparative data for some earlier months. Based on Central Government data.

Availability	General
Cost	£67 or £1.50 for a single issue
Comments	ISSN 0307 7683. The journal of the Institution of Civil Engineers.
Address	1 Heron Quay, London E14 9XF
Telephone	01 987 6999; Telex: 298105; Fax: 01 538 4656

729

Originator	NEW CIVIL ENGINEER
Title	ICE SALARY SURVEY, every 2 or 3 years in a weekly journal
Coverage	A summary of the salary survey by the Institution of Civil Engineers (see entry 567) with data by employer, age, qualifications, location, type of work etc. The survey is based on members of the Institution.
Availability	General
Cost	£67 or £1.50 for a single issue
Comments	ISSN 0307 7683. The journal of the Institution of Civil Engineers.
Address	1 Heron Quay, London E14 9XF
Telephone	01 987 6999; Telex: 298105; Fax: 01 538 4656

730

Originator	NEWCASTLE UNDER LYME BOROUGH COUNCIL
Title	HOUSING DEVELOPMENT MONITORING REPORTS, annual. 1982–
Coverage	Examination of recent housebuilding activity in the borough, progress being made towards satisfying housing needs and land supply for private sector housebuilding. Based largely on a local authority survey (90%) with some supporting text (60%).
Availability	General
Cost	Free
Comments	Also various reports on the Census and population change.
Address	Civic Offices, Merrial Street, Newcastle under Lyme ST5 2AG
Telephone	0782 717717; Telex: 20959; Fax: 0782 711032

731

Originator	NEWCASTLE-UPON-TYNE METROPOLITAN DISTRICT COUNCIL
Title	CITY PROFILES, regular
Coverage	Economic and social data for Newcastle-upon-Tyne based mainly on Central Government sources such as the census, General Household Survey etc. plus some Council surveys.
Availability	General
Cost	£6

Address	Civic Centre, Newcastle-upon-Tyne NE1 8QN
Telephone	091 232 8520, x5035

732

Originator	NEWCASTLE-UPON-TYNE METROPOLITAN DISTRICT COUNCIL
Title	ECONOMIC PROFILES, regular
Coverage	General data covering employment, unemployment, industry etc. based on Central Government data. New issues appear when new Central Government surveys are published.
Availability	General
Cost	£2.50
Address	Civic Centre, Newcastle-upon-Tyne NE1 8QN
Telephone	091 232 8520, x5035

733

Originator	NEWPORT BOROUGH COUNCIL
Title	EMPLOYMENT TRENDS, quarterly. 1987–
Coverage	A review of local and national trends and information on local planning permissions. A combination of Central Government data and the Council's own data, with a supporting text (50%).
Availability	General
Cost	Free
Comments	Replaces the publication 'Industrial and Employment Monitor' published from 1980 to 1986.
Address	Development Department, Civic Centre, Newport, Gwent NP9 4UR
Telephone	0633 244491; Telex: 497385; Fax: 0633 244721

734

Originator	NIELSEN MARKETING RESEARCH
Title	CASH AND CARRY CUSTOMER SURVEY, annual
Coverage	Results of about 3700 interviews with customers of the major cash and carry groups providing data on who is buying, what for, how much they are spending etc.
Availability	On application
Cost	£2,950 + VAT
Comments	Other services include Nielsen Retail Indexes, Compumark, CMIS, Nielsen Consumer Research, Dataquest and Clearing House.
Address	Nielsen House, Headington, Oxford OX3 9RX
Telephone	0865 64851; Telex: 83136; Fax: 0865 67029

735

Originator	NIELSEN MARKETING RESEARCH
Title	CASH AND CARRY TRADE REPORT, annual
Coverage	Information and statistics with details of shop numbers and turnover trends by store type, Nielsen region and county. Based on Nielsen's own survey.
Availability	General
Cost	£225 + VAT, £30 for extra copies
Comments	Other services include Nielsen Retail Indexes, Compumark, CMIS, Nielsen Consumer Research, Dataquest and Clearing House.
Address	Nielsen House, Headington, Oxford OX3 9RX
Telephone	0865 64851; Telex: 83136; Fax: 0865 67029

736

Originator	NIELSEN MARKETING RESEARCH
Title	CTN TRADE REPORT, annual
Coverage	Information and statistics with details of shop numbers and turnover trends by store type, Nielsen region and county. Based on Nielsen's own survey.
Availability	General
Cost	£225 + VAT, £30 for extra copies
Comments	Other services include Nielsen Retail Indexes, Compumark, CMIS, Nielsen Consumer Research, Dataquest and Clearing House.
Address	Nielsen House, Headington, Oxford OX3 9RX
Telephone	0865 64851; Telex: 83136; Fax: 0865 67029

737

Originator	NIELSEN MARKETING RESEARCH
Title	FOOD TRADE REPORT, annual
Coverage	Information and statistics on the grocery trade structure with details of shop numbers and turnover trends by type, Nielsen region and county. Based on Nielsen's own research.
Availability	General
Cost	£225 + VAT, £30 for extra copies
Comments	Other services include Nielsen Retail Indexes, Compumark, CMIS, Nielsen Consumer Research, Dataquest and Clearing House.
Address	Nielsen House, Headington, Oxford OX3 9RX
Telephone	0865 64851; Telex: 83136; Fax: 0865 67029

738

Originator	NIELSEN MARKETING RESEARCH
Title	NIELSEN MARKET INFORMATION MANUAL, annual
Coverage	Data on the annual value of over 250 markets with geographical and store type breakdowns. Sectors covered include grocery, health, confectionery, beauty aids, liquor and home improvements. Also contains general economic, demographic and advertising data. Based largely on Nielsen data (95%).
Availability	On application
Cost	£700, £100 for extra copies. Discount for previous purchasers
Comments	Other services include Nielsen Retail Indexes, Compumark, CMIS, Nielsen Consumer Research, Dataquest and Clearing House.
Address	Nielsen House, Headington, Oxford OX3 9RX
Telephone	0865 64851; Telex: 83136; Fax: 0865 67029

739

Originator	NIELSEN MARKETING RESEARCH
Title	NIELSEN RESEARCHER, regular
Coverage	Journal highlights specific Nielsen research findings and has regular reviews with statistics of grocery and retail trading.
Availability	General
Cost	Free
Address	Nielsen House, Headington, Oxford OX3 9RX
Telephone	0865 64851; Telex: 83136; Fax: 0865 67029

740

Originator	NIELSEN MARKETING RESEARCH
Title	PHARMACY AND DRUG STORE TRADE REPORT, annual
Coverage	Data on trade structure with details of shop numbers and turnover trends by store type, Nielsen region and county. Based on Nielsen's own research.
Availability	General
Cost	£225 +VAT, £30 for extra copies
Comments	Other services include Nielsen Retail Indexes, Compumark, CMIS, Nielsen Consumer Research, Dataquest and Clearing House.
Address	Nielsen House, Headington, Oxford OX3 9RX
Telephone	0865 64851; Telex: 83136; Fax: 0865 67029

741

Originator	NOP MARKET RESEARCH LTD
Title	ALCOHOLIC DRINKS SURVEY, annual
Coverage	The drinking habits of a sample of approximately 2,000 adults analysed by social class, TV area, sex and age. Covers wine, spirits and cocktails giving awareness of brands, source of purchase, frequency of drinks etc. Based on a systematic probability sample of all adults in Great Britain using pre-selected names and addresses from electoral registers.
Availability	General
Cost	£1,650, single section £700
Comments	Exclusive questions and analysis available by negotiation. Omnibus surveys also carried out on a weekly basis.
Address	Tower House, Southampton Street, London WC2E 7HN
Telephone	01 836 1511; Telex: 8953744; Fax: 01 836 2052

742

Originator	NOP MARKET RESEARCH LTD
Title	FINANCIAL RESEARCH SURVEY, quarterly
Coverage	Trend data on the personal financial and saving markets based on a sample of about 15,000 people. Monitors movements and trends in bank account holdings, usage of various savings media and credit methods. Based on a systematic probability sample of all adults in Great Britain using preselected names and addresses from electoral registers.
Availability	General
Cost	On request
Comments	Confidential questions can be added to the survey by negotiation. Omnibus surveys also carried out a weekly basis.
Address	Tower House, Southampton Street, London WC2E 7HN
Telephone	01 836 1511; Telex: 8953744; Fax: 01 836 2052

743

Originator	NOP MARKET RESEARCH LTD
Title	POLITICAL SOCIAL AND ECONOMIC REVIEW, quarterly
Coverage	Summary data and commentary from the various opinion polls carried out by NOP.
Availability	General
Cost	On application
Address	Tower House, Southampton Street, London WC2E 7HN
Telephone	01 836 1511; Telex: 8953744; Fax: 01 836 2052

744

Originator	NOP MARKET RESEARCH LTD
Title	PUBS IN GREAT BRITAIN SURVEY, regular
Coverage	Data on customers' eating habits and visiting and drinking habits Also covers attitudes to pub facilities, features and atmosphere. A survey based on a sample of 1,200 adults using a systematic prob ability sample of all adults in Great Britain with preselected names and addresses from electoral registers.
Availability	General
Cost	£1,250
Comments	Special analysis available and omnibus surveys also carried out on a weekly basis.
Address	Tower House, Southampton Street, London WC2E 7HN
Telephone	01 836 1511; Telex: 8953744; Fax: 01 836 2052

745

Originator	NOP MARKET RESEARCH LTD
Title	WINE MONITOR, quarterly. 1986–
Coverage	A regular survey on the awareness and purchasing of wine including data on the country of origin, colour preference and drinking occasions. Based on a systematic probability sample of all adults in Great Britain using preselected names and addresses from electoral registers.
Availability	General
Cost	£8,800
Comments	Special analysis available and omnibus surveys carried out on a weekly basis.
Address	Tower House, Southampton Street, London WC2E 7HN
Telephone	01 836 1511; Telex: 8953744; Fax: 01 836 2052

746

Originator	NORTH CORNWALL DISTRICT COUNCIL
Title	PLANNING AND DEVELOPMENT IN NORTH CORN WALL: REVIEW OF 19.., annual
Coverage	Statistics on land availability, developments, planning decisions initiatives and developments undertaken by the District Council and priority areas for the future. Figures are based on a survey by the Council's Planning and Development Office and 75% of the report is made up of commentary. Maps are included.
Availability	General
Cost	£1.50
Address	3-5 Barn Lane, Bodmin, Cornwall PL31 1LZ
Telephone	0208 4121,x217; Fax: 0208 4121

747

Originator   NORTH OF SCOTLAND MILK MARKETING BOARD

Title   ANNUAL REPORT, annual. 1935–
Coverage   Producer and market trends over a 10-year period. The remainder of the report is made up of financial and general information. Based on the Board's own data.

Availability   General
Cost   Free
Address   Claymore House, 29 Ardconnel Terrace, Inverness IV2 3AF
Telephone   0463 232611; Telex: 75254

748

Originator   NORTH OF SCOTLAND MILK MARKETING BOARD

Title   MILK TOPICS, monthly. 1957–
Coverage   Includes data on current prices paid to milk producers, milk supplies and utilization. Based on the Board's own data with a large amount of supporting text (60%). The statistics are usually 2 weeks old on publication.

Availability   General
Cost   Free
Address   Claymore House, 29 Ardconnel Terrace, Inverness IV2 3AF
Telephone   0463 232611; Telex: 75254

749

Originator   NORTH TYNESIDE METROPOLITAN BOROUGH COUNCIL

Title   HOUSING LAND AVAILABILITY, quarterly
Coverage   Statistics on housing starts, completions and houses under construction with additional data on the size of sites, total dwellings and their ownership and planning applications. Based on the local authority's survey with a small amount of text (10%).

Availability   General
Cost   £10
Comments   Produced as a computer printout.
Address   Stephenson House, Stephenson Street, North Shields NE30 1QA
Telephone   091 258 2043

750

Originator	NORTH TYNESIDE METROPOLITAN BOROUGH COUNCIL
Title	MONTHLY UNEMPLOYMENT STATISTICS, monthly
Coverage	General data on levels and trends in the district. Based on unemployment rates published by Central Government.
Availability	General
Cost	Free
Address	Stephenson House, Stephenson Street, North Shields NE30 1QA
Telephone	091 258 2043

751

Originator	NORTH TYNESIDE METROPOLITAN BOROUGH COUNCIL
Title	WARD PROFILE, regular
Coverage	Statistics on the trends in population, housing, social characteristics, unemployment and the socio-economic structure in various wards. Based on Central Government data with some supporting text (30%).
Availability	General
Cost	£10
Comments	First published in 1981 with the first update in 1986. Similar data available for specific housing estates in the district.
Address	Stephenson House, Stephenson Street, North Shields NE30 1QA
Telephone	091 258 2043

752

Originator	NORTH WEST WATER
Title	SUMMARY OF FISHERIES STATISTICS, annual. 1974–
Coverage	Catch data, fish culture and hatchery operations, restocking with trout and freshwater fish, fish movement recorded at authority fish counters, counts of salmon, fish mortalities and the number of fishing licences issued. Based on the authority's own surveys. Usually published 6 months after the year to which it relates.
Availability	General
Cost	£2.40
Comments	ISSN 0144 9141
Address	Box 30, New Town House, Buttermarket Street, Warrington WA 2QG
Telephone	0925 53999; Telex: 628425; Fax: 0925 415961

753

Originator	NORTHAMPTONSHIRE COUNTY COUNCIL
Title	POPULATION BULLETIN, annual
Coverage	Consists of 4 sections covering estimates of population, births and deaths, population migration and population projections to 1996. Based on a combination of the Council's own research (60%) and Central Government data (40%).
Availability	General
Cost	Free
Address	County Hall, Northampton NN1 1DN
Telephone	0604 236032; Fax: 0604 236223

754

Originator	NORTHERN IRELAND TOURIST BOARD
Title	HOTEL OCCUPANCY SURVEY, monthly. 1972–
Coverage	Room and bedspace occupancy by hotel grade and by Northern Ireland region. The statistics are based on the Board's own research and a commentary is included (25%). Data usually refers to the previous month.
Availability	General
Cost	Free
Address	River House, 48 High Street, Belfast BT1 2DS
Telephone	0232 231221; Telex: 748087; Fax: 0232 240960

755

Originator	NORTHERN IRELAND TOURIST BOARD
Title	TOURISM FACTS, annual. 1978–
Coverage	Information card giving summary of all the major volume and expenditure figures relating to the various categories of visitors to Northern Ireland and the holidaying habits of Northern Ireland residents.
Availability	General
Cost	Free
Address	River House, 48 High Street, Belfast BT1 2DS
Telephone	0232 231221; Telex: 748087; Fax: 0232 240960

756

Originator	NORTHERN IRELAND TOURIST BOARD
Title	TOURISM IN NORTHERN IRELAND, annual. 1980–

Coverage   Covers all aspects in 3 sections: incoming tourism, an accommo dation survey and holidaying by Northern Ireland residents. Base on the Board's regular surveys with supporting text (25%).

Availability   General
Cost   Free
Address   River House, 48 High Street, Belfast BT1 2DS
Telephone   0232 231221; Telex: 748087; Fax: 0232 240960

757

Originator   NORTHUMBERLAND COUNTY COUNCIL

Title   FACTS CARD, annual
Coverage   Summary statistics on the Council's activities and the local area e.g. population, education etc. The sources of the statistics are no acknowledged.

Availability   General
Cost   Free
Address   County Hall, Morpeth NE61 2EF
Telephone   0670 514343; Telex: 537048; Fax: 0670 515615

758

Originator   NORWICH AND NORFOLK CHAMBER OF COMMERCE AND INDUSTRY

Title   QUARTERLY MANUFACTURING SURVEY, quarterly October 1981–
Coverage   A survey of members and non-members giving data on economi conditions such as orders, exports, stocks, labour, production investment and business confidence for the next quarter. Give figures from previous quarters and is published one month after a stratified sample survey of firms reflecting the area's SIC structure A commentary is also included.

Availability   Members and the Press
Cost   Free
Comments   Issued as a press release.
Address   112 Barrack Street, Norwich NR3 1UB
Telephone   0603 625977; Telex: 975247; Fax: 0603 625977

759

Originator   NORWICH AND NORFOLK CHAMBER OF COMMERCE AND INDUSTRY

Title   QUARTERLY SERVICE SECTOR SURVEY, quarterly January 1987–

Coverage	Survey of members and non-members with data on sales, stocks, exports, labour, investment and business confidence for the coming quarter. Gives figures for previous quarters and the results are published one month after the survey of service sector firms in the area. A short commentary on the figures is also included.
Availability	Members and the Press
Cost	Free
Comments	Issued as a press release.
Address	112 Barrack Street, Norwich NR3 1UB
Telephone	0603 625977; Telex: 975247; Fax: 0603 625977

760

Originator	NOTTINGHAMSHIRE CHAMBER OF COMMERCE AND INDUSTRY
Title	QUARTERLY ECONOMIC SURVEY, quarterly. 1978–
Coverage	Survey of firms in the Nottinghamshire and East Midlands area covering deliveries, orders, production, stocks, cashflow, labour, investment, confidence and business factors. Based on a survey of about 100 local businesses representing most aspects of the local economy. Usually produced 1–2 weeks after completion of the survey.
Availability	Members
Cost	Free
Comments	Summary results are issued in the form of a press release.
Address	395 Mansfield Road, Nottingham NG5 2DL
Telephone	0602 624624; Telex: 37605; Fax: 0602 605981

761

Originator	NTC PUBLICATIONS LTD
Title	DRINK POCKET BOOK, annual
Coverage	Basic data on the drinks sector including general statistics on the market followed by sections on specific drinks, e.g. soft drinks, cider, beer, wine, spirits, and drink outlets. Some international comparisons are included. Based on various sources.
Availability	General
Cost	£11.50
Comments	Published in association with Stats MR. Also publish Advertising Association surveys – see entries 9–11.
Address	22/24 Bell Street, Henley on Thames RG9 2BG
Telephone	0491 574671

762

Originator   NTC PUBLICATIONS LTD

Title   DRINKS FORECAST, quarterly
Coverage   Sales, consumer expenditure, imports, exports, brand shares, regional consumption and advertising expenditure for each of the major drinks sectors. A 10-year run of figures is given with forecasts for 5 years ahead.

Availability General
Cost   £393.75
Comments   Also publish Advertising Association surveys – see entries 9–11.
Address   22/24 Bell Street, Henley on Thames RG9 2BG
Telephone   0491 574671

763

Originator   NTC PUBLICATIONS LTD

Title   FINANCIAL POCKET BOOK, annual
Coverage   Basic data on the financial sector with sections on specific areas. Based on various sources.

Availability General
Cost   £11.50
Comments   Also publish Advertising Association surveys – see entries 9–11.
Address   22/24 Bell Street, Henley on Thames RG9 2BG
Telephone   0491 574671

764

Originator   NTC PUBLICATIONS LTD

Title   FOOD FORECAST, quarterly
Coverage   Sales, consumer expenditure, prices, imports, exports, brand shares, regional consumption and advertising expenditure for the major food sectors. A 10 year run of figures is given with forecasts for 5 years ahead.

Availability General
Cost   £393.75
Comments   Also publish Advertising Association surveys – see entries 9–11.
Address   22/24 Bell Street, Henley on Thames RG9 2BG
Telephone   0491 574671

765

Originator   NURSERY TRADER

Title   WITHIN NEWSDESK, quarterly in a quarterly journal

Coverage   Market size for the industry with a product breakdown and brand
                 share details. Based on various non-official sources.

Availability General
Cost   £16.50
Address   Turret-Wheatland, 177 Hagden Lane, Watford WD1 8LN
Telephone   0923 228577; Telex: 9419706; Fax: 0923 221346

766

Originator   OFF LICENCE NEWS

Title   TAKE HOME MARKET, annual published separately from the
                 journal
Coverage   Statistics and commentary with data on beers, wines, spirits, ciders,
                 soft drinks, confectionery and snacks. Based on a survey of
                 customers plus comments from industry sources.

Availability General
Cost   Free
Address   5 Southwark Street, London SE1 1RQ
Telephone   01 407 6981; Telex: 8812648

767

Originator   OIL AND CHEMICAL PLANT CONSTRUCTORS ASSOCI-
                 ATION

Title   SITE ACCIDENT STATISTICS, quarterly. 1982–
Coverage   A review with statistics of accidents on UK oil and chemical plants.
                 Based on a regular survey by the Association. Most of the report is
                 text with statistics included.

Availability Members
Cost   Free
Address   Suites 41/48, Kent House, 87 Regent Street, London W1R 7HF
Telephone   01 734 5246

768

Originator   OVERSEAS TRADE DATA

Title   OVERSEAS TRADE DATA, continuous
Coverage   Statistics on all UK-traded products by weight and value. Various
                 breakdowns available including country of destination, country of
                 origin, UK port or airport, vessel flag, shipping mode and inland
                 container depot. Appointed as an agent for HM Customs and
                 Excise Data.

Availability General
Cost   Varies according to the information required

Comments	Data available on disc, tape, cartridge and microfiche.
Address	66c Royal Mint Street, London E1 8LG
Telephone	01 265 1625; Telex: 946240

769

Originator	OXFORDSHIRE COUNTY COUNCIL
Title	ANNUAL POPULATION FORECASTS FOR OXFORDSHIRE, annual. 1975–
Coverage	Up to 8 years ahead in total, by district, age, households and school pupil forecasts. Some supporting text (30%).
Availability	General
Cost	Free
Comments	Appendices to the report issued as separate reports.
Address	County Hall, New Road, Oxford OX1 1ND
Telephone	0865 815268; Fax: 0865 726155

770

Originator	OXFORDSHIRE COUNTY COUNCIL/OXFORDSHIRE JOINT DISTRICT HOUSING GROUP
Title	OXFORDSHIRE HOUSING STATISTICS, annual. 1975–
Coverage	Statistics on housing provision, management, maintenance, finance, housing conditions and the private sector. Based on the Council's own survey. Usually published 9 months after the survey.
Availability	Members and Officers plus generally available locally
Address	County Hall, New Road, Oxford OX1 1ND
Telephone	0865 815268; Fax: 0865 726155

771

Originator	PACKAGING WEEK
Title	BUSINESS BULLETIN, regular in a weekly journal
Coverage	General business trends and specific trends in the packaging sector with data for a number of previous months and/or quarters.
Availability	General
Cost	£49 or £1.50 per issue
Comments	ISSN 0267 6117
Address	Benn Publications, Sovereign Way, Tonbridge TN9 1RW
Telephone	0732 364422; Telex: 95162; Fax: 0732 361534

772

Originator   PACKAGING WEEK

Title   TRADE TRENDS, quarterly in a weekly journal
Coverage   Commentary and statistics on the imports and exports of various
                 packaging materials and packaging machinery. Data by major
                 country and comparative figures for the same period in the previous
                 year. Based on Central Government data.

Availability General
Cost   £49 or £1.50 for a single issue
Comments   ISSN 0267 6117
Address   Benn Publications, Sovereign Way, Tonbridge TN9 1RW
Telephone   0732 364422; Telex: 95162; Fax: 0732 361534

773

Originator   PAINTMAKERS ASSOCIATION OF GREAT BRITAIN

Title   ANNUAL STATISTICAL REVIEW, annual
Coverage   Trends in the paint industry based on the Association's survey of its
                 members.

Availability Members
Cost   Free
Address   Alembic House, 93 Albert Embankment, London SE1 7TY
Telephone   01 582 1185

774

Originator   PAINTMAKERS ASSOCIATION OF GREAT BRITAIN

Title   ANNUAL STATISTICAL REVIEW SUMMARY, annual
Coverage   General summary data from the 'Annual Statistical Review' – see
                 above. Based on a survey of the Association's members.

Availability Selected organizations and individuals
Cost   Free
Address   Alembic House, 93 Albert Embankment, London SE1 7TY
Telephone   01 582 1185

775

Originator   PAINTMAKERS ASSOCIATION OF GREAT BRITAIN

Title   QUARTERLY SALES BULLETIN, quarterly
Coverage   Sales for the quarter compared with sales for the year. Also has
                 selling prices indices and covers the last 3 years. Based on a survey
                 of 40 member companies. Supporting text covers 60%.

Availability	General
Address	Alembic House, 93 Albert Embankment, London SE1 7TY
Telephone	01 582 1185

776

Originator	PALMER, MAURICE ASSOCIATES LTD
Title	FLEXIBLE PACKAGING PRODUCTS MARKET IN THE UK, biennial. August 1986–
Coverage	The market size and forecasts up to 5 years ahead. Gives tonnage/sq metres by 22 end use sectors and analyses trends in material usage. Estimates the size of import penetration and includes an image study of suppliers. Based mainly on the company's own research (85%) with a large amount of supporting text (75%).

Availability	General
Cost	£2,000 + VAT
Comments	Report also available on disc.
Address	Chesterton Tower, Chapel Street, Chesterton, Cambridge CB4 1DY
Telephone	0223 68705; Fax: 0223 324125

777

Originator	PALMER, MAURICE ASSOCIATES LTD
Title	RIGID PLASTICS PACKAGING MARKET IN THE UK, biennial. October 1987–
Coverage	Trends in the size and structure of the market plus data on the structure of raw material supply, purchasing criteria, food preservation methods and images of suppliers. Forecasts up to 5 years ahead for consumption, materials and technical and market innovations. Based mainly on the company's own research (85%) with a large amount of supporting text (70%).

Availability	General
Cost	£3,150 + VAT
Comments	Report also available on disc.
Address	Chesterton Tower, Chapel Street, Chesterton, Cambridge CB4 1DY
Telephone	0223 68705; Fax: 0223 324125

778

Originator	PALMER, MAURICE ASSOCIATES LTD
Title	STATIONERY MARKET IN THE UK, biennial. June 1986–

Coverage	Details on the market size, growth, UK production and imports. Data on end uses and product changes in various user sectors, the distribution structure and forecasts up to 5 years ahead. Based mainly on the company's own research (85%) with a large amount of supporting text (60%).
Availability	General
Cost	£2,750 + VAT
Address	Chesterton Tower, Chapel Street, Chesterton, Cambridge CB4 1DY
Telephone	0223 68705; Fax: 0223 324125

779

Originator	PALMER, MAURICE ASSOCIATES LTD
Title	UK MARKET FOR ELECTRONIC OFFICE SUPPLIES, biennial. November 1986–
Coverage	Trends in the market size and growth plus data on the structure of distribution and image of suppliers. Forecasts up to 5 years ahead are also included. Based mainly on the company's own research (85%) with a large amount of supporting text (60%).
Availability	General
Cost	£2,800 + VAT
Address	Chesterton Tower, Chapel Street, Chesterton, Cambridge CB4 1DY
Telephone	0223 68705; Fax: 0223 324125

780

Originator	PANNELL KERR FORSTER ASSOCIATES
Title	MONTHLY BULLETIN OF TRENDS IN LONDON HOTELS, monthly. 1973–
Coverage	Performance trends by volume and revenue based on a sample survey of about 60 hotels from AA 5-star to 2-star. Hotels are grouped according to average achieved room rate and food and beverage costs.
Availability	Hotels contributing to the survey
Cost	Free
Address	78 Hatton Garden, London EC1N 8JA
Telephone	01 831 7393; Telex: 295928; Fax: 01 405 6736

781

Originator	PANNELL KERR FORSTER ASSOCIATES
Title	OUTLOOK IN THE HOTEL AND TOURISM INDUSTRY – LONDON TRENDS, annual. 1978–

Coverage	Summary of the performance of a sample of about 60 London hotels with details of occupancy levels, achieved room rate, sales and the cost of sales of food and beverage departments. Some Central Government data also included (25%) and supporting text (50%).
Availability	General
Cost	£25
Address	78 Hatton Garden, London EC1N 8JA
Telephone	01 831 7393; Telex: 295928; Fax: 01 405 6736

782

Originator	PANNELL KERR FORSTER ASSOCIATES
Title	OUTLOOK IN THE HOTEL AND TOURISM INDUSTRY – UK TRENDS, annual. 1978–
Coverage	A review of the operating and financial characteristics of a sample of about 150 provincial hotels from AA 5-star to 2-star. Details of room occupancy rates, revenues, departmental costs and expenses, income and the ratio of departmental expenses to income. Includes some Central Government statistics (25%) and supporting text (50%).
Availability	General
Cost	£25
Address	78 Hatton Garden, London EC1N 8JA
Telephone	01 831 7393; Telex: 295928; Fax: 01 405 6736

783

Originator	PANNELL KERR FORSTER ASSOCIATES
Title	QUARTERLY BULLETIN OF TRENDS IN PROVINCIAL HOTELS, quarterly. 1984–
Coverage	Analysis of operating performance in volume and revenue terms of a sample of about 100 hotels from AA 5-star to 3-star. The hotels are grouped by English Tourist Board region and Wales and Scotland with additional data on food and beverage costs.
Availability	Hotels contributing to the survey
Cost	Free
Address	78 Hatton Garden, London EC1N 8JA
Telephone	01 831 7393; Telex: 295928; Fax: 01 405 6736

784

Originator	PAPER FACTS AND FIGURES
Title	PAPER AND BOARD INDICES, 6 times a year in a journal published 6 times a year. 1983–

| **Coverage** | Indices of prices for various types of paper based on figures collected by the journal. |

Availability	General
Cost	On application
Address	Benn Publications, PO Box 20, Sovereign Way, Tonbridge TN9 1RQ
Telephone	0732 362666; Telex: 95454

785

| **Originator** | PAPER SACK DEVELOPMENT ASSOCIATION |

| **Title** | PAPERSACKS REVIEW, annual |
| **Coverage** | Data on turnover trends in the industry plus production of paper sacks in units and applications and end-uses. Based on a survey of member companies. |

Availability	Members and bona fide users of paper sacks
Cost	Free
Address	33 Southampton Street, London WC2E 7HE
Telephone	01 836 1072; Fax: 01 836 5393

786

| **Originator** | PEDDER ASSOCIATES |

| **Title** | APPLICATION USAGE BY INDUSTRY SECTOR MARKET SECTOR REPORT, annual |
| **Coverage** | Analyses the use of computers in various work categories in the the following areas: commercial and administration, manufacturing, distributive trades, banking and finance, scientific and research, other applications. Based on the Pedder annual census of IT users. |

Availability	General
Cost	£2000
Comments	The Pedder census began in 1973 but its published output has changed recently – a general report is no longer published.
Address	Parkway House, Sheen Lane, East Sheen, London SW14 8LS
Telephone	01 878 9111; Telex: 28106

787

| **Originator** | PEDDER ASSOCIATES |

| **Title** | BOARDROOM ISSUES AND IT IN MANUFACTURING INDUSTRIES, annual |

Coverage	A survey of chief executives and other main board directors to consider current and likely future business concerns, the role of IT, IT and corporate 5-year plans, how IT cost is justified, decision making processes, current and future levels of IT investment, influence of IT suppliers etc. Based on a CBI membership sample of 1,000.
Availability	General
Cost	£1750
Address	Parkway House, Sheen Lane, East Sheen, London SW14 8LS
Telephone	01 878 9111; Telex: 28106

788

Originator	PEDDER ASSOCIATES
Title	COMPUTER SYSTEMS: £15,000 AND ABOVE CENSUS REPORT, annual
Coverage	Statistics on the market for and the UK installed population of office computer systems above £15,000. Forecasts up to 5 years ahead. Based on a Pedder survey of installations as part of its annual IT census.
Availability	General
Cost	£1250
Comments	The Pedder annual census began in 1973 but its output has changed recently – a general volume is no longer published.
Address	Parkway House, Sheen Lane, East Sheen, London SW14 8LS
Telephone	01 878 9111; Telex: 28106

789

Originator	PEDDER ASSOCIATES
Title	COMPUTER SYSTEMS: £15,000 AND BELOW CENSUS REPORT, annual
Coverage	Market information and statistics on the UK installed user population for office computer systems priced at £15,000 or below. Forecasts up to 5 years ahead. Based on a Pedder survey of installations as part of its annual census of IT users.
Availability	General
Cost	£1250
Comments	The Pedder census began in 1973 but its output has changed recently – a general volume is no longer published.
Address	Parkway House, Sheen Lane, East Sheen, London SW14 8LS
Telephone	01 878 9111; Telex: 28106

790

Originator	PEDDER ASSOCIATES
Title	DATA NETWORKS CENSUS REPORT, annual
Coverage	Market information and statistics on the UK user installed population of data networks. Based on a Pedder survey of users as part of the annual census of IT users.
Availability	General
Cost	£625
Comments	The Pedder annual census began in 1973 but it has changed its output recently – the general volume is no longer published.
Address	Parkway House, Sheen Lane, East Sheen, London SW14 8LS
Telephone	01 878 9111; Telex: 28106

791

Originator	PEDDER ASSOCIATES
Title	DP EXPENDITURE BY INDUSTRY SECTOR MARKET SECTOR REPORT, annual
Coverage	Expenditure on hardware, software and services in 20 industry sectors and forecasts up to 5 years ahead. Historic trends and comparisons with industry sector revenues. Based on the Pedder annual census of IT users.
Availability	General
Cost	£2250 with the Industry/Regional report – see below
Comments	The Pedder census began in 1973 but its published output has changed recently – a general report is no longer published.
Address	Parkway House, Sheen Lane, East Sheen, London SW14 8LS
Telephone	01 878 9111; Telex: 28106

792

Originator	PEDDER ASSOCIATES
Title	INDUSTRY/REGIONAL ANALYSIS MARKET SECTOR REPORT, annual
Coverage	Market data and forecasts for computer systems valued over £30,000. Data on 23 industry sectors and 8 geographical regions. Forecasts up to 5 years ahead and historical data. Based on the Pedder census of IT users.
Availability	General
Cost	£7250
Comments	The Pedder census began in 1973 but the published output has changed recently – a general volume is no longer published.
Address	Parkway House, Sheen Lane, East Sheen, London SW14 8LS
Telephone	01 878 9111; Telex: 28106

793

Originator	PEDDER ASSOCIATES
Title	INTEGRATED OFFICE SYSTEMS CENSUS REPORT, annual
Coverage	Data on the market for and installed population of integrated office systems with information on end users, types of equipment etc. Forecasts up to 5 years ahead. Based on an annual census of IT equipment users carried out by the company.
Availability	General
Cost	£1250
Comments	The Pedder annual census began in 1973 but its output has changed recently – a general report is no longer published.
Address	Parkway House, Sheen Lane, East Sheen, LOndon SW14 8LS
Telephone	01 878 9111; Telex: 28106

794

Originator	PERSONNEL MANAGEMENT
Title	GUARDIAN RECRUITMENT MONITOR, monthly in a monthly journal. August 1983–
Coverage	The number of columns devoted to recruitment advertising in the 'quality' newspapers for the latest month compared with the previous year's figure. The percentage share per paper for the month is also given. Statistics are taken from Media Expenditure Analysis Ltd (MEAL).
Availability	General
Cost	£30 or £3 for a single issue
Address	Personnel Publications Ltd, 1 Hills Place, London W1R 1AG
Telephone	01 734 1773; Fax: 01 735 1773

795

Originator	PET FOOD MANUFACTURERS ASSOCIATION
Title	PFMA MARKETING INFORMATION, annual
Coverage	Data on the market size and value for prepared pet food products with the percentage change on the previous year. Based on the Association's own survey with a general commentary (60%) on the figures. Published about 3 months after the end of the previous year.
Availability	Members and general, on request
Cost	£3.50
Address	6 Catherine Street, London WC2B 5JJ
Telephone	01 836 2460; Telex: 299388; Fax: 01 836 0580

796

Originator   PET FOOD MANUFACTURERS ASSOCIATION

Title   PFMA PROFILE, annual
Coverage   Data on pet ownership, the cost of pet foods and the market size and
                  value of prepared pet foods. Includes some European data and
                  information on the industry, PFMA's views and current legislation.
                  Based on the Association's own survey with a significant amount
                  (80%) of text.

Availability Members and general, on request
Cost   £23.50
Address   6 Catherine Street, London WC2B 5JJ
Telephone   01 836 2460; Telex: 299388; Fax: 01 836 0580

797

Originator   PETROL PUMP INDEPENDENT

Title   PETROL PRICE GUIDE, monthly in a monthly journal. January
                  1986–
Coverage   Trends in the price of 4 star petrol in various areas around the UK.
                  Based on the journal's own survey.

Availability General
Cost   £32.50 or £2.75 for a single issue
Address   Natfuel Gazette, Regent House, Beeton Lane, Knutsford WA16
                  9AB
Telephone   0565 53283

798

Originator   PETROLEUM ECONOMIST

Title   OIL SHARE MARKETS, monthly in a monthly journal. 1968–
Coverage   A table of oil share quotations on the London Stock Exchange and
                  Petroleum Economist's share price index.

Availability General
Cost   £86 or £7.50 for a single issue
Comments   ISSN 0306 395X. Also publishes regular statistics on world oil
                  trends.
Address   Petroleum Press Bureau, 25/31 Ironmonger Row, London EC1V
                  3PN
Telephone   01 251 3501; Telex: 27161; Fax: 01 253 1224

799

Originator	PETROLEUM ECONOMIST
Title	UK NORTH SEA SURVEY, annual in a monthly journal. 1977–
Coverage	Statistics on North Sea oil fields with data on water depth, reserves, ownership, production etc. Compiled from a variety of sources.
Availability	General
Cost	£86 or £7.50 for a single issue
Comments	ISSN 0306 395X. Published in June each year. Also contains regular statistics on world oil trends.
Address	Petroleum Press Bureau, 25/31 Ironmonger Row, London EC1V 3PN
Telephone	01 251 3501; Telex: 27161; Fax: 01 253 1224

800

Originator	PETROLEUM TIMES
Title	PETROLEUM TIMES PRICE REPORT, bi-monthly in a monthly journal
Coverage	Provides prices for a complete range of petroleum products plus information on oil market movements and the economics and politics of oil. Based on the journal's own survey with some supporting text (50%).
Availability	General
Cost	£94 or £4.75 for a single issue
Comments	Journal subscribers receive the Price Report as a separate document. Also publish quarterly Business Studies separately.
Address	27 Earl Street, Maidstone ME14 1PE
Telephone	0622 59841; Fax: 0622 675734

801

Originator	PHARMACEUTICAL JOURNAL
Title	RETAIL SALES INDEX FOR CHEMISTS, monthly in a weekly journal
Coverage	General figures on the sales trends in total and for specific products sold in chemists. Based on Central Government statistics.
Availability	General
Cost	£45, free to members of the Pharmaceutical Society
Comments	The above figures are missing in occasional months. Other statistics occasionally published.
Address	1 Lambeth High Street, London SE1 7JN
Telephone	01 735 9141; Fax: 01 735 7629

802

Originator	PHILLIPS AND DREW
Title	ECONOMIC FORECASTS, monthly
Coverage	Short term forecasts and forecasts for 2 and 5 years ahead for the major economic variables plus an assessment of economic policy, economic assumptions and a summary of UK forecasts. Own forecasts based on Central Government data.
Availability	Restricted circulation
Cost	£500 or £50 for a single issue
Comments	Also produce 'one-off' reports and international reports.
Address	120 Moorgate, London EC2M 6XP
Telephone	01 628 4444; Telex: 291163; Fax: 01 588 0252

803

Originator	PHILLIPS AND DREW
Title	EQUITY MARKET INDICATORS, 6 issues per year
Coverage	Statistics and commentary on the UK equity market based on a combination of sources.
Availability	General
Cost	£250, free to clients
Comments	Also produce 'one-off' reports and international reports.
Address	120 Moorgate, London EC2M 6XP
Telephone	01 628 4444; Telex: 291163; Fax: 01 588 0252

804

Originator	PHILLIPS AND DREW
Title	UK BOND PACK, monthly
Coverage	Statistics and commentary on the general trends for gilts and bonds based on a combination of sources.
Availability	General
Cost	£1,000, free to clients
Comments	Also produce 'one-off' reports and international reports.
Address	120 Moorgate, London EC2M 6XP
Telephone	01 628 4444; Telex: 291163; Fax: 01 588 0252

805

Originator	PIGS MARKETING BOARD (NORTHERN IRELAND)
Title	ANNUAL REPORT AND ACCOUNTS, annual

Coverage	Contains statistics on the pig population, market supplies, feed costs, bacon prices, produce grading etc. Largely taken from Central Government statistics (70%) with some figures (30%) collected by the Board. 50% of the publication contains text.
Availability	General
Cost	Free
Address	New Forge Lane, Belfast BT9 5NX
Telephone	0232 381888; Fax: 0232 683179

806

Originator	PINPOINT ANALYSIS LTD
Title	PINPOINT ANALYSIS, continuous
Coverage	Population statistics and related data for specific local areas and specific target groups.
Availability	General
Cost	Depends on the range of data required
Address	Mercury House, 117 Waterloo Road, London SE1 8UL
Telephone	01 928 1874

807

Originator	PIZZA ASSOCIATION
Title	PIZZA AND PASTA MAGAZINE, 5 issues a year
Coverage	General data and market statistics on the pizza and pasta sectors. Based on various sources.
Availability	General
Cost	£8.50
Address	29 Market Place, Wantage, Oxfordshire
Telephone	02357 66339

808

Originator	PLASTICS PACKAGING INDUSTRY MONITOR
Title	SUPPLY/CONSUMPTION PLASTIC PACKAGING, continuous and available separately from the monthly journal. January 1988–
Coverage	Maintains a computer database of plastics information. Data on the UK consumption and supply of the main plastic materials is available covering the last 15 years. Based on a combination of the journal's own research (25%), Central Government data (15%) and data from other sources (60%).
Availability	General
Cost	Varies according to the information required

Comments   Services also available covering Europe, USA and the Middle East.
Address   UXCO Ltd, PO Box 14, Dorking RH5 4BH
Telephone 0306 884473

809

Originator   PLUNKETT FOUNDATION FOR COOPERATIVE STUDIES

Title   STATISTICS OF AGRICULTURAL COOPERATIVES IN
                 THE UK, annual. 1969–
Coverage   Aggregate data on 635 cooperatives in the UK. Data on sales,
                 profits, share interest and bonus payments, balance sheet figures,
                 membership and staff numbers. Based on the Foundation's own
                 data.

Availability General
Cost   £6
Comments   Also publish a press release giving summary data from the above
                 publication.
Address   31 St Giles, Oxford OX1 3LF
Telephone   0865 53960; Telex: 83147; Fax: 0865 726753

810

Originator   POLICY STUDIES INSTITUTE (PSI)

Title   FACTS ABOUT THE ARTS, every 3 or 4 years. 1983–
Coverage   A detailed review with statistics covering finance, employment and
                 specific sectors of the arts, e.g. drama, opera, music, dance, films,
                 museums etc. Also includes sections on audiences and new
                 building. Based on various sources.

Availability General
Cost   £17.95
Comments   Compiled by John Myerscough. Latest edition – 1988.
Address   100 Park Village East, London NW1 3SR
Telephone   01 387 2171

811

Originator   POLYCELL PRODUCTS

Title   POLYCELL REPORT 198–, annual
Coverage   Commentary and some statistics on the home improvements and
                 DIY sectors covering market size, improvements carried out and
                 the short term prospects. Based on Polycell research and other
                 non-official sources. Commentary covers about 70%.

Availability General
Cost   Free

| Address | Broadwater Road, Welwyn Garden City AL7 3AZ |
| Telephone | 07073 28131; Telex: 23950 |

812

Originator	POSTER MARKETING
Title	POSTERSCENE, 3 issues per year. Autumn 1986–
Coverage	News, comment and general statistics on the UK posters sector. Based largely on the company's own research (80%) and other non-official sources (20%). A large amount of text (90%).
Availability	Organizations in the industry
Cost	Free
Address	21 Tothill Street, London SW1H 9LL
Telephone	01 222 7988; Fax: 01 222 6753

813

Originator	POTATO MARKETING BOARD
Title	FLOW CHART FOR POTATOES IN GREAT BRITAIN, annual
Coverage	Charts on supply and consumption, based equally on the Board's own survey (50%) and Central Government data.
Availability	General
Cost	Free
Address	50 Hans Crescent, London SW1X 0WB
Telephone	01 589 4874; Telex: 912193

814

Originator	POTATO MARKETING BOARD
Title	POTATO PROCESSING IN GREAT BRITAIN, annual
Coverage	Consumption figures, exports and imports of raw potatoes, raw potatoes used for processing in the UK and information on the varieties used for processing purposes. Based largely on the Board's own survey (90%) with some Central Government data (10%). Supporting text comprises 50%.
Availability	General
Cost	Free
Comments	ISSN 0140 9557
Address	50 Hans Crescent, London SW1X 0WB
Telephone	01 589 4874; Telex: 912193

815

Originator   POTATO MARKETING BOARD

Title   POTATO STATISTICS BULLETIN, annual
Coverage   Data on the monthly rate of human consumption and planting by
              variety by registered producers. Based largely on the Board's own
              survey (85%) with additional data from Central Government
              (15%).

Availability General
Cost   Free
Address   50 Hans Crescent, London SW1X 0WB
Telephone   01 589 4874; Telex: 912193

816

Originator   POTATO MARKETING BOARD

Title   POTATO STATISTICS IN GREAT BRITAIN, annual
Coverage   Detailed statistics on production, consumption, processing,
              imports, exports etc. Mainly Central Government sources.

Availability General
Cost   £6
Address   Broad Field House, 4 Between Towns, Cowley OX4 3NA
Telephone   0865 714455; Telex: 83534; Fax: 0865 716418

817

Originator   POWER RESEARCH ASSOCIATES

Title   BUSINESS FORMAT FRANCHISING IN THE UNITED
              KINGDOM, annual
Coverage   Estimates of total activity in the UK plus a sample survey of
              participants' attitudes. Based on the company's own survey with a
              large amount of supporting commentary (75%).

Availability General
Cost   £95 plus VAT
Address   17 Wigmore Street, London W1H 9LA
Telephone   01 580 5816; Telex: 24637

818

Originator   PRESS COUNCIL

Title   THE PRESS AND THE PEOPLE, annual. 1953–

Coverage	Ownership, circulation of the British press with radio and television interests. Based on the Council's own survey with a large amount of supporting text (75%). The report is usually published 6 months after the year to which it relates.
Availability	General
Cost	£8.50
Address	1 Salisbury Square, London EC4Y 8AE
Telephone	01 353 1248; Fax: 01 353 8355

819

Originator	PRINTED CIRCUIT ASSOCIATION
Title	MARKET DATA, monthly. January 1985–
Coverage	Orders and sales in value and volume terms for various types of printed circuits broken down by market application area. Based on returns from a sample of members.
Availability	Participating members
Cost	Free
Address	232 Fleet Road, Fleet, Hampshire
Telephone	0252 617630; Telex: 858593; Fax: 0252 620729

820

Originator	PRINTING INDUSTRIES
Title	ECONOMIC TRENDS, monthly in a monthly journal
Coverage	Statistics on general economic trends plus specific data on prices of particular types of paper, consumption of inks and papers and a plant replacement index. Based on a combination of Central Government data and non-official sources. Data usually given for a number of years and months.
Availability	General
Cost	£45
Comments	Free to British Printing Industries Federation members. Publishes results of the Federation's survey (see entries 132 and 133).
Address	BPIF, 11 Bedford Row, London WC1R 4DX
Telephone	01 242 6904; Fax: 01 405 7784

821

Originator	PROCUREMENT WEEKLY
Title	PRICES GUIDE, weekly in a weekly journal
Coverage	Prices of various commodities including metals, scrap, plastics, soft commodities, chemicals, paper and building materials. Based on the journal's own survey.

Availability	General
Cost	£30 or 60p for a single issue
Comments	Journal published by the Institute of Purchasing and Supply (IPS).
Address	IPS, Easton House, Easton on the Hill, Stamford PE9 1QT
Telephone	0780 56777; Telex: 32251; Fax: 0780 51610

822

Originator	PROFESSIONAL PUBLISHING LTD
Title	MOTOR INDUSTRY HANDBOOK, continuously updated. July 1984–
Coverage	Data on car numbers, patterns of ownership, consumer and business use, trade, overseas markets, energy, fuel and retailing, taxation and the law regarding the motor industry and vehicles. Based on various sources: Central Government (20%), own research (20%) and other non-official sources (60%). Some supporting text (20%).
Availability	General
Cost	£30
Comments	Also publishes the Business Cars Survey for the British Institute of Management, latest issue – 1985.
Address	7 Swallow Place, London W1R 8AB
Telephone	01 409 3322; Fax: 01 629 0373

823

Originator	PROJECTION 2000
Title	PROJECTION 2000 REPORTS, regular. 1987–
Coverage	A series of reports on growth markets with market commentary and statistics. Statistics cover the latest few years and forecasts up to the year 2000. The price includes a main report and a half-yearly update.
Availability	General
Cost	£65 per report
Address	16 Evering Road, London N16 7QJ
Telephone	01 254 1669

824

Originator	PUBLIC ATTITUDE SURVEYS RESEARCH LTD
Title	BEER MARKET, quarterly
Coverage	Syndicated sample survey of drinkers' consumption and behaviour. Based on face-to-face interviews with a sample of 20,000 adults per year.

Availability	General
Cost	£25,000
Address	Rye Park House, London Road, High Wycombe HP11 1EF
Telephone	0494 32771; Fax: 0494 21404

825

Originator	PUBLIC ATTITUDE SURVEYS RESEARCH LTD
Title	WINE MARKET, quarterly
Coverage	Syndicated sample survey of drinkers' consumption and behaviour. Based on face-to-face interviews with a sample of 20,000 adults.
Availability	General
Cost	£12,000
Address	Rye Park House, London Road, High Wycombe HP11 1EF
Telephone	0494 32771; Fax: 0494 21404

826

Originator	PUBLISHERS ASSOCIATION
Title	BOOK TRADE YEARBOOK, annual. 1985–
Coverage	A commentary followed by a statistical section covering the industry structure, markets, output, prices, turnover, imports and exports, distribution and consumer and institutional spending. Statistics usually cover the last 4 or 5 years. Text covers about 25%.
Availability	General
Cost	£40
Address	19 Bedford Square, London WC1B 3HJ
Telephone	01 580 6321; Telex: 21792; Fax: 01 636 5375

827

Originator	PUBLISHERS ASSOCIATION
Title	QUARTERLY STATISTICS, quarterly
Coverage	Covers the performance of the UK publishing industry over 1 year. Statistics on turnover by book type, exports, book prices, student buying and expenditure forecasts. Each issue contains news items on special topics. Some supporting text (40%).
Availability	General
Cost	£15, free to members
Comments	ISSN 0260 5198. Various occasional publications also produced.
Address	19 Bedford Square, London WC1B 3HJ
Telephone	01 580 6321; Telex: 21792; Fax: 01 636 5375

828

Originator   PUBLISHERS ASSOCIATION

Title   SCHOOL BOOK SPENDING SERIES, 2 or 3 issues per year
Coverage   Figures by local education authority area. Individual reports are
                 produced for each area, based on the Association's own survey with
                 some supporting text (30%).

Availability General
Comments   Various occasional publications also produced.
Address   19 Bedford Square, London WC1B 3HJ
Telephone   01 580 6321; Telex: 21792; Fax: 01 636 5375

829

Originator   QED RESEARCH LTD

Title   REQUIREMENTS AND PERCEPTIONS MONITOR (RAP), 3
                 issues per year. March 1981–
Coverage   3,000 new car buyers are interviewed regularly concerning their
                 requirements for a new car and their perceptions of available
                 models. Fieldwork is continuous and conducted at weekends at
                 central locations through a street-recruited test. Text covers 25%.

Availability General
Cost   From £3,000
Comments   Data also available on tape.
Address   Edric House, Castle Street, High Wycombe
Telephone   0494 443784; Telex: 837225; Fax: 0494 442640

830

Originator   RADIO MARKETING BUREAU

Title   SURVEY OF THE RADIO AUDIENCE (JICRAR), regular.
                 1977–
Coverage   Conducted on a network, regional and individual station basis with
                 network results quarterly, regional twice a year and station data
                 annually. The main report gives results by demographic breakdown
                 showing rate card segment reach, half-hour averages and frequency
                 analysis for standard packages.

Availability General
Cost   £125+VAT. An interpretive summary is available free of charge
Comments   Data available on discs and on-line facilities available via RSGB on
                 01 997 5555.
Address   Radio House, 46 Westbourne Grove, London W2 5SH
Telephone   01 221 2535; Telex: 24543; Fax: 01 229 0352

831

Originator	RADIO PAGING ASSOCIATION
Title	ON-SITE MARKETING ANALYSIS, quarterly. 1st quarter 1987–
Coverage	Statistics on the number of radio paging installations based on a survey of members.
Availability	Participating organizations
Address	35 Lower Camden, Chislehurst BR7 5HY
Telephone	01 467 9263

832

Originator	RATING AND VALUATION ASSOCIATION
Title	GENERAL RATE POUNDAGES AND PRODUCTS, annual. 1962–
Coverage	Local authority rate poundages in the UK. Gives total rate product, total domestic rateable value, total other rateable value, percentage increase over the previous year and number of rating assessments and the population. Based on data collected by the Association.
Availability	General
Address	115 Ebury Street, London SW1W 9QT
Telephone	01 730 7258

833

Originator	REMUNERATION ECONOMICS
Title	BIM NATIONAL MANAGEMENT SALARY SURVEY, annual. 1974–
Coverage	24,000 managers are surveyed to produce statistics on earnings, fringe benefits and bonuses. The managers are employed by about 340 companies and work at 9 levels of responsibility. A separate report is published on the small business sector. A commentary (30%) accompanies the statistics.
Availability	General
Cost	£190, or £150 main report and £90 small firms report
Comments	Published in association with the British Institute of Management. Reduced prices for participants.
Address	Survey House, 51 Portland Road, Kingston-upon-Thames KT1 2SH
Telephone	01 549 8726; Telex: 263223; Fax: 01 541 5705

834

Originator	REMUNERATION ECONOMICS
Title	SURVEY OF ENGINEERING FUNCTIONS, annual. 1981–
Coverage	Engineering salaries covering 9 levels of responsibility by company size, industry, type of work, qualifications, location etc. Based on the company's own survey with some supporting text (50%).
Availability	General
Cost	£100, £60 to participants
Comments	Published in association with the Engineering Council.
Address	Survey House, 51 Portland Road, Kingston-upon-Thames KT1 2SH
Telephone	01 549 8726; Telex: 263223; Fax: 01 541 5705

835

Originator	REMUNERATION ECONOMICS
Title	SURVEY OF FINANCIAL FUNCTIONS, annual. 1975–
Coverage	A salary survey for 9 levels of responsibility by company size, industry group, location, age, qualifications etc. Additional data on fringe benefits and recruitment. Based on the company's own survey with some supporting text (50%).
Availability	General
Cost	£80, £55 to participants
Address	Survey House, 51 Portland Road, Kingston-upon-Thames KT1 2SH
Telephone	01 549 8726; Telex: 263223; Fax: 01 541 5705

836

Originator	REMUNERATION ECONOMICS
Title	SURVEY OF PERSONNEL FUNCTIONS, annual. 1975–
Coverage	Salary survey covering 9 levels of responsibility by size of company, industry group, location, age, qualifications etc. Additional data on fringe benefits and recruitment. Based on the company's own survey with some supporting text (50%).
Availability	General
Cost	£80, £55 to participants
Comments	Published in association with the Institute of Personnel Management.
Address	Survey House, 51 Portland Road, Kingston-upon-Thames KT1 2SH
Telephone	01 549 8726; Telex: 263223; Fax: 01 541 5705

837

Originator	RESEARCH SURVEYS OF GREAT BRITAIN (RSGB)
Title	BABY OMNIBUS, several times per year
Coverage	Purchasing trends for baby products plus frequency of purchase, price paid, source of purchase and brand share. Also data on advertising awareness, awareness and attitudes to new and existing products and images of products, services and companies. Analysis by 7 age groups, social class and incidence of birth. Based on a sample of 700 mothers.
Availability	General
Cost	£160 entry fee plus fees for questions
Comments	Also 'ad-hoc' surveys.
Address	Research Centre, West Gate, London W5 1EL
Telephone	01 997 5555; Telex: 261978; Fax: 01 991 2020

838

Originator	RESEARCH SURVEYS OF GREAT BRITAIN (RSGB)
Title	CATERING OMNIBUS SURVEY, 3 issues per year. 1977–
Coverage	Usage and consumption data for all product types in catering plus data on purchasing source, brand awareness, attitudes, ownership of catering equipment, advertising recall and awareness, manufacturer images and reactions to new products. Based on personal interviews in 600 catering establishments in Great Britain.
Availability	General
Cost	£295 entry fee plus prices for questions
Comments	Also 'ad-hoc' reports.
Address	Research Centre, West Gate, London W5 1EL
Telephone	01 997 5555; Telex: 261978; Fax: 01 991 2020

839

Originator	RESEARCH SURVEYS OF GREAT BRITAIN (RSGB)
Title	GENERAL OMNIBUS SURVEY, weekly. About 1972–
Coverage	Data on product purchase, brand shares, purchase source, pre- and post-advertising awareness, attitudes towards new and existing products and images of products, services and companies. Analysis by age, social class, sex and region. Based on a random location sample of 2,000+ adults.
Availability	General
Cost	£150 entry fee plus fees for questions
Comments	Also 'ad-hoc' surveys.
Address	Research Centre, West Gate, London W5 1EL
Telephone	01 997 5555; Telex: 261978; Fax: 01 991 2020

840

Originator	RESEARCH SURVEYS OF GREAT BRITAIN (RSGB)
Title	LETTERBOX, quarterly and bi-annual. 1st quarter 1988–
Coverage	A random sample of 1,000 households in Great Britain to obtain data on the sending and receipt of mail including direct mail advertising.
Availability	General
Cost	Price on application
Comments	Also 'ad-hoc' surveys.
Address	Research Centre, West Gate, London W5 1EL
Telephone	01 997 5555; Telex: 261978; Fax: 01 991 2020

841

Originator	RESEARCH SURVEYS OF GREAT BRITAIN (RSGB)
Title	MOTORISTS OMNIBUS SURVEY, monthly
Coverage	Data on products purchased, source of purchase, brand share, frequency of purchase, price paid, advertising awareness and attitudes to new or existing products, services and companies. The survey interviews 1000 motorists per month and analysis is available by age, social class and region.
Availability	General
Cost	£160 entry fee plus fees for questions
Comments	Also 'ad-hoc' surveys.
Address	Research Centre, West Gate, London W5 1EL
Telephone	01 997 5555; Telex: 261978; Fax: 01 991 2020

842

Originator	RETAIL JEWELLER
Title	PRECIOUS METAL PRICES, weekly in a weekly journal
Coverage	Selling, scrap and market prices. The price data is usually 1 week old and based on various non-official sources.
Availability	General
Cost	£27.50, free to jewellery trade
Address	100 Avenue Road, London NW3 3TP
Telephone	01 935 6611; Telex: 299973; Fax: 01 586 4649

843

Originator	REWARD GROUP
Title	CLERICAL AND OPERATIVE REWARDS, bi-annual

Coverage	Analysis of basic pay and average earnings for all main clerical and operative positions. Analysis by company size, area and industry based on Reward's own survey.
Availability	General
Cost	£54, £28 to participants
Comments	Special reports prepared to order and a Salary Advice databank and Relocation Information Packs also available.
Address	1 Mill Street, Stone ST15 8BA
Telephone	0785 813566; Telex: 36274; Fax: 0785 817007

844

Originator	REWARD GROUP
Title	CONSULTING ENGINEERS SALARY SURVEY, annual
Coverage	Details covering over 2,500 job entries from all disciplines and based on data provided by members of the Association of Consulting Engineers.
Availability	General
Cost	£130
Comments	Special reports prepared to order and a Salary Advice databank and Relocation Information Packs also available.
Address	1 Mill Street, Stone ST15 8BA
Telephone	0785 813566; Telex: 36274; Fax: 0785 817007

845

Originator	REWARD GROUP
Title	COST OF LIVING REPORT, bi-annual
Coverage	Comparisons comparing the main regions of the UK including London, for 8 life styles and income levels. A supplement on Eire is also available. Based on Reward's own survey.
Availability	General
Cost	£55, Eire supplement £45
Comments	Reports are published in March and September. Advice on house prices in any area also available.
Address	1 Mill Street, Stone ST15 8BA
Telephone	0785 813566; Telex: 36274; Fax: 0785 817007

846

Originator	REWARD GROUP
Title	DIRECTORS' REWARDS, annual
Coverage	Total remuneration and basic salary analysis overall, by appointment and by industry. Fees, bonuses and other cash benefits are also included. Based on Reward's own survey.

Availability	General
Cost	£130, £65 to participants
Comments	Produced in association with the Institute of Directors. Salary Advice databank and Relocation Information packs also available.
Address	1 Mill Street, Stone ST15 8BA
Telephone	0785 813566; Telex: 36274; Fax: 0785 817007

847

Originator	REWARD GROUP
Title	EMPLOYEE BENEFITS, annual
Coverage	A report combining all Reward's ongoing research into employee benefits and work conditions with additional regional analysis taken from 19 local surveys.
Availability	General
Cost	£50, £25 to participants
Comments	Special reports prepared to order and a Salary Advice databank and Relocation Information Packs also aviable.
Address	1 Mill Street, Stone ST15 8BA
Telephone	0785 813566; Telex: 36274; Fax: 0785 817007

848

Originator	REWARD GROUP
Title	FINANCIAL AND ACCOUNTING REWARDS, annual
Coverage	A pay report covering staff of all grades by rank, job, industry, company size, sex, age, qualifications, Institute membership, bonus payments and county. Based on Reward's own survey.
Availability	General
Cost	£80
Comments	Special reports prepared to order and a Salary Advice databank and Relocation Information packs also available.
Address	1 Mill Street, Stone ST15 8BA
Telephone	0785 813566; Telex: 36274; Fax: 0785 817007

849

Originator	REWARD GROUP
Title	LONDON WEIGHTING, annual
Coverage	Payment trends for the private sector in London and other large towns based on a Reward survey of over 160 organizations.
Availability	General
Cost	£40, £20 to participants
Comments	Special reports prepared to order and a Salary Advice databank and Relocation Information Packs also available.

| Address | 1 Mill Street, Stone ST15 8BA |
| Telephone | 0785 813566; Telex: 36274; Fax: 0785 817007 |

850

| Originator | REWARD GROUP |

| Title | PERFORMANCE REWARDS, annual |
| Coverage | Trends in the provision of additional pay and benefits as a reward for performance. Based on Reward's own surveys and containing a large amount of text (85%). |

Availability	General
Cost	£50
Comments	Special reports prepared to order and a Salary Advice databank and Relocation Information Packs also available.
Address	1 Mill Street, Stone ST15 8BA
Telephone	0785 813566; Telex: 36274; Fax: 0785 817007

851

| Originator | REWARD GROUP |

| Title | RESEARCH AND DEVELOPMENT SALARIES, annual |
| Coverage | Data on basic salaries and total renumeration in the R & D field, based on Reward's own survey. |

Availability	General
Cost	£100, £50 to participants
Comments	Special reports prepared to order and a Salary Advice databank and Relocation Information Packs also available.
Address	1 Mill Street, Stone ST15 8BA
Telephone	0785 813566; Telex: 36274; Fax: 0785 817007

852

| Originator | REWARD GROUP |

| Title | REWARD, bi-annual |
| Coverage | Management salary report covering over 175 job occupations and including advice, forecasts and comment on salary movements. Analysis by job for basic salary and total renumeration, by size of company, industry, location, qualifications and age. Based on Reward's own survey. |

Availability	General
Cost	£160, or £100 for a single issue
Comments	Special reports prepared to order and a Salary Advice databank and Relocation Information Packs also available.
Address	1 Mill Street, Stone ST15 8BA
Telephone	0785 813566; Telex: 36274; Fax: 0785 817007

853

Originator	REWARD GROUP
Title	SALARY, WAGE AND CONDITIONS OF SERVICE REPORTS, bi-annual
Coverage	Data on actual payments and analysis in 19 regional and county areas of England and Scotland. Based on Reward's own survey.
Availability	General
Cost	£100, £50 to participants
Comments	Special reports prepared to order and a Salary Advice databank and Relocation Information Packs also available.
Address	1 Mill Street, Stone ST15 8BA
Telephone	0785 813566; Telex: 36274; Fax: 0785 817007

854

Originator	REWARD GROUP
Title	SALES AND MARKETING REWARDS, annual
Coverage	Survey of salaries and benefits giving basic salary, bonus and commission, company cars and other benefits analysed by job. Based on Reward's own survey and produced in association with the Institute of Marketing.
Availability	General
Cost	£95, £80 to participants
Comments	Special reports prepared to order and a Salary Advice databank and Relocation Information packs also available.
Address	1 Mill Street, Stone ST15 8BA
Telephone	0785 813566; Telex: 36274; Fax: 0785 817007

855

Originator	REWARD GROUP
Title	SOFTWARE AND ELECTRONICS SPECIALISTS SALARY SURVEY, bi-annual
Coverage	Summary analysis by rank, region, age, size of company etc. and for a range of salaries. Based on Reward's own survey.
Availability	Participants
Cost	£120
Comments	Special reports prepared to order and a Salary Advice databank and Relocation Information Packs also available.
Address	1 Mill Street, Stone ST15 8BA
Telephone	0785 813566; Telex: 36274; Fax: 0785 817007

856

Originator   ROCHDALE METROPOLITAN BOROUGH COUNCIL

Title   INDUSTRY AND EMPLOYMENT MONITOR, about 6 issue:
per year
Coverage   Commentary, tables and maps on employment and unemploymen
trends in the area, based largely on Central Government statistics

Availability   General
Cost   Free
Address   Planning, Telegraph House, Baillie Street, Rochdale OL16 1JH
Telephone   0706 47474

857

Originator   ROMTEC PLC

Title   ANNUAL MARKET REVIEW, annual
Coverage   An overview of the UK business micro marketplace over th
previous year with data on microcomputers, software and printer
and plotters. Data on individual product and vendor sales, marke
shares and growth rates over the previous year's figures. Based o
ROMTEC's own research.

Availability   General
Cost   £695
Address   Hattori House, Vanwall Road, Maidenhead SL6 4UW
Telephone   0628 770077; Fax: 0628 785433

858

Originator   ROMTEC PLC

Title   MONTHLY SALES MONITOR, monthly
Coverage   Various monthly monitors covering specific micro and minicom
puter products with data on sales figures and market shares b
product and vendor. Based on panels comprising approximatel
10% of the computer resellers in the UK. The reports are publishe
4 weeks after the close of each reported month.

Availability   General
Cost   £450 per month, annual prices on request
Comments   The monitors are part of the Market Monitoring Service which als
includes 'Quarterly Reviews' – see below.
Address   Hattori House, Vanwall Road, Maidenhead SL6 4UW
Telephone   0628 770077; Fax: 0628 785433

859

Originator   ROMTEC PLC

Title   QUARTERLY TRENDS REVIEW, quarterly
Coverage   Sales and market shares for various micro and minicomputer pro-
              ducts and vendors with data for the previous 3 months. Based on
              panels comprising approximately 10% of the computer resellers in
              the UK, all selling their products to end-users. Published 6 weeks
              after the close of each quarter with individual reports for specific
              products.

Availability General
Cost   £950 per report per quarter, annual prices on request
Comments   The reviews are part of the Market Monitoring Service which also
              includes 'Monthly Sales Monitors' – see above.
Address   Hattori House, Vanwall Road, Maidenhead SL6 4UW
Telephone   0628 770077; Fax: 0628 785433

860

Originator   ROMTEC PLC

Title   READERSHIP SURVEY, annual. 1988–
Coverage   Computer media targeted at third party computer resellers in the
              UK. Data on circulation, advertising rates, influence of publication
              on dealership/reseller policy and procurement, preferred titles etc.

Availability General
Cost   £775
Address   Hattori House, Vanwall Road, Maidenhead SL6 4UW
Telephone   0628 770077; Fax: 0628 785433

861

Originator   ROMTEC PLC

Title   UK BUSINESS MICRO MARKETPLACE, annual
Coverage   3 volumes of market forecasts covering microcomputers, printers
              and software, with analysis of the marketplace, market size and
              growth, product trends, data on vendors and distribution channels
              and relative performance. Forecasts cover the next 5 years.

Availability General
Cost   £2240, or £1690 for 2 volumes and £995 for 1 volume
Address   Hattori House, Vanwall Road, Maidenhead SL6 4UW
Telephone   0628 770077; Fax: 0628 785433

862

Originator	ROMTEC PLC
Title	UK MONITORS MARKET, annual
Coverage	A review of the UK third party monitors market with special reference to the related graphics board market. Data on the installed base, unit sales, distribution channels, user types, existing and potential markets and forecasts. Based on ROMTEC's own survey.
Availability	General
Cost	£950
Address	Hattori House, Vanwall Road, Maidenhead SL6 4UW
Telephone	0628 770077; Fax: 0628 785433

863

Originator	ROSS FOODS LTD
Title	FROZEN FOOD RETAIL MARKET REPORT, annual
Coverage	Statistics and commentary plus information on eating habits, freezer ownership, the major growth areas and the performance of Ross brands.
Availability	General
Cost	Free
Address	Ross House, Wickham Road, Grimsby DN31 3SW
Telephone	0472 59111

864

Originator	ROYAL BANK OF SCOTLAND PLC
Title	MONTHLY SUMMARY OF BUSINESS CONDITIONS IN THE UK, monthly. 1983–
Coverage	Covers production, employment, overseas transactions, prices, wages, industrial investment, banking, short-term money rates and the Stock Exchange. Central Government statistics account for about 40%, 10% from the Bank and the remainder from other non-official sources. 50% of the report is text.
Availability	General
Cost	Free
Address	PO Box 31, 42 St Andrew Square, Edinburgh EH2 2YE
Telephone	031 5568555; Telex: 72230; Fax: 031 5568555

865

Originator	ROYAL BANK OF SCOTLAND PLC
Title	ROYAL BANK/RADIO SCOTLAND OIL INDEX, monthly. January 1983–
Coverage	Data on production from North Sea oil fields and the average daily value of oil production based on a telephone survey of oil field operators. A significant amount of text is included (75%).
Availability	General
Cost	Free
Address	PO Box 31, 42 St Andrew Square, Edinburgh EH2 2YE
Telephone	031 5568555; Telex: 72230; Fax: 031 5568555

866

Originator	ROYAL INSTITUTE OF BRITISH ARCHITECTS
Title	ARCHITECTS EMPLOYMENT AND EARNINGS SURVEY, annual. 1976–
Coverage	Employment, earnings and RIBA membership figures for public and private architects. Earnings data gives a range of figures for various job categories. Based on a survey of 1 in 5 of all private practices including RIBA members and non-members. Some supporting text (60%).
Availability	General
Cost	£25, £15 to members
Address	66 Portland Place, London W1N 4AD
Telephone	01 580 5533; Fax: 01 255 1541

867

Originator	ROYAL INSTITUTE OF BRITISH ARCHITECTS
Title	CENSUS OF PRIVATE ARCHITECTURAL PRACTICES, every 4 years. 1972–
Coverage	Data on the organization of practices, geographical and size distribution and an analysis of the main areas of work. Based on a 100% sample of all private practices. A large amount of supporting text (70%).
Availability	General
Cost	£25
Address	66 Portland Place, London W1N 4AD
Telephone	01 580 5533; Fax: 01 255 1541

868

Originator	ROYAL INSTITUTE OF BRITISH ARCHITECTS
Title	LOCAL AUTHORITY ARCHITECTURAL SERVICES: TRENDS AND PROSPECTS, every 5 years, 1982–
Coverage	Analysis of the types of work being undertaken by architects in local authorities, plus the views of chief architects on likely future trends. Based on a 100% sample survey of all local authorities. A large amount of supporting text (70%).
Availability	General
Cost	£25
Address	66 Portland Place, London W1N 4AD
Telephone	01 580 5533; Fax: 01 255 1541

869

Originator	ROYAL INSTITUTE OF BRITISH ARCHITECTS
Title	RIBA CONSTRUCTION WORKLOAD BRIEF, quarterly. 1960s-
Coverage	Data on workload of private architects only. Includes value of new commissions and production drawings by building types and information by region for different building types. Also details of rehabilitation work. Based on a survey of 1 in 4 of all private practices covering RIBA members and non-members. Some supporting text (40%).
Availability	General
Cost	£65
Comments	ISSN 0953 2471
Address	66 Portland Place, London W1N 4AD
Telephone	01 580 5533; Fax: 01 255 1541

870

Originator	ROYAL INSTITUTION OF CHARTERED SURVEYORS
Title	HOUSING MARKET SURVEY, monthly
Coverage	National figures and figures for a particular region each month for various types and ages of property. Shows the trends in prices over the previous 3 months and includes comments from various estate agents. Based on a survey of estate agents with about 450 participants.
Availability	General
Cost	Free
Comments	A press release.
Address	12 Great George Street, Parliament Square, London SW1P 3AD
Telephone	01 222 7000; Telex: 915443; Fax: 01 222 9430

871

Originator	ROYAL INSTITUTION OF CHARTERED SURVEYORS
Title	OFFICE RENT SURVEYS, quarterly
Coverage	Covers the City of London, West End, Liverpool, Newcastle and Birmingham (the latter's figures are only produced bi-annually). Figures are quarterly for a 5-year period and properties are divided into prewar built refurbished, postwar centrally heated, post and prewar air conditioned and all types. Based on the Institution's survey.
Availability	General
Cost	Free
Comments	Carried out in conjunction with the Institute of Actuaries.
Address	12 Great George Street, Parliament Square, London SW1P 3AD
Telephone	01 222 7000; Telex: 915443; Fax: 01 222 9430

872

Originator	ROYAL INSTITUTION OF CHARTERED SURVEYORS, BUILDING COST INFORMATION SERVICE
Title	BCIS QUARTERLY REVIEW OF BUILDING PRICES, quarterly
Coverage	By type of building and by region based on a survey of subscribers to BCIS.
Availability	General
Cost	£100, or £30 for a single issue
Address	85/87 Clarence Street, Kingston-upon-Thames KT1 1RB
Telephone	01 546 7554

873

Originator	ROYAL INSTITUTION OF CHARTERED SURVEYORS, BUILDING COST INFORMATION SERVICE
Title	BUILDING COST INFORMATION SERVICE, monthly
Coverage	Including tenders, labour and materials and based on information supplied by members of BCIS.
Availability	Members willing to exchange information
Cost	£190, £150 to chartered surveyors
Comments	A loose-leaf publication.
Address	85/87 Clarence Street, Kingston-upon-Thames KT1 1RB
Telephone	01 546 7554

874

Originator	ROYAL INSTITUTION OF CHARTERED SURVEYORS, BUILDING COST INFORMATION SERVICE
Title	GUIDE TO HOUSE REBUILDING COSTS FOR INSURANCE VALUATION, annual
Coverage	Data on housebuilding costs by area and condition and type of building. Based on original research by BCIS.
Availability	General
Cost	£11
Comments	Updated every month by the 'House Rebuilding Cost Index'.
Address	85/87 Clarence Street, Kingston-upon-Thames KT1 1RB
Telephone	01 546 7554

875

Originator	ROYAL SOCIETY FOR THE PREVENTION OF ACCIDENTS
Title	CARE IN THE HOME, quarterly
Coverage	Includes some statistics on home and leisure safety with data by sex, age and cause of accident. Largely based on Central Government data (80%).
Availability	General
Cost	On application
Address	Cannon House, Priory Queensway, Birmingham B4 6BS
Telephone	021 200 2461; Telex: 336546; Fax: 021 236 2850

876

Originator	ROYAL SOCIETY FOR THE PREVENTION OF ACCIDENTS
Title	CARE ON THE ROAD, monthly
Coverage	Contains a statistical review in most issues with data on a particular aspect of road accidents. Based mainly on monthly data from Central Government.
Availability	General
Cost	On application
Address	Cannon House, Priory Queensway, Birmingham B4 6BS
Telephone	021 200 2461; Telex: 336546; Fax: 021 236 2850

877

Originator	ROYAL SOCIETY FOR THE PREVENTION OF ACCIDENTS
Title	ROAD ACCIDENT STATISTICS, annual

Coverage	Personal injury data for police force areas, estimates of the cost to the nation of accidents, road traffic estimates and casualty trends. Based on Central Government data with some supporting text (15%). Published data usually refers to 2 years earlier.
Availability	General
Cost	On application
Address	Cannon House, Priory Queensway, Birmingham B4 6BS
Telephone	021 200 2461; Telex: 336546; Fax: 021 236 2850

878

Originator	ROYAL SOCIETY OF CHEMISTRY
Title	ROYAL SOCIETY OF CHEMISTRY REMUNERATION SURVEY, biennial. 1913–
Coverage	Figures on the numbers of chemists employed and remuneration of professional chemists by age group for class of employment, field of employment, location, type of work and qualification. Based on a survey by the Society.
Availability	General
Cost	On application
Address	Burlington House, Piccadilly, London W1V 0BN
Telephone	01 437 8656; Telex: 268001

879

Originator	RYDEN, KENNETH AND PARTNERS
Title	SCOTTISH INDUSTRIAL AND COMMERCIAL PROPERTY REVIEW, bi-annual
Coverage	A forecast of future trends in the level of economic activity in Scotland together with a guide to the commercial property market and a survey of new industrial and warehouse accommodation. Based on a combination of the company's own data (50%) and other non-official sources (50%). Some supporting text (25%).
Availability	General
Cost	Free
Comments	A parallel publication on residential property ceased publication in 1986.
Address	71 Hanover Street, Edinburgh EH2 1EE
Telephone	031 225 6612; Telex: 72644; Fax: 031 225 5766

880

Originator	SANDWELL METROPOLITAN BOROUGH COUNCIL
Title	HOUSING LAND STUDY, annual. 1984–

Coverage	An assessment of the principal sites for housing development and the adequacy of land supply in relation to planned levels of housing land provision. Based on the Council's records with some text (15%).
Availability	General
Cost	Free
Address	Technical Services, Wigmore, Pennyhill Lane, West Bromwich
Telephone	021 569 4034

881

Originator	SANDWELL METROPOLITAN BOROUGH COUNCIL
Title	LAND AND PROPERTY REGISTER, monthly
Coverage	Details of vacant land and property in Sandwell with aggregate data and details of specific sites. Based on the Council's records.
Availability	General
Cost	Free
Address	Technical Services, Wigmore, Pennyhill Lane, West Bromwich
Telephone	021 569 4034

882

Originator	SAUNDERS, RICHARD AND PARTNERS
Title	CITY FLOORSPACE SURVEY, monthly. 1974–
Coverage	Trends in the office letting market in the City of London and its fringes. Concentrates on the amount of floorspace let and the amount available for occupation. Breakdown by size, number, age, classification and postal districts. Based on the company's own survey.
Availability	General
Cost	On application
Address	27/32 Old Jewry, London EC2R 8DQ
Telephone	01 606 7461; Telex: 886042; Fax: 01 726 2578

883

Originator	SAVILLS
Title	CITY OF LONDON OFFICE DEMAND SURVEY, annual. 1980–
Coverage	Trends in City office floorspace, take-up, rents and occupiers with data by size band, rent band and business category. Based on Savill's own records with some supporting text (30%).
Availability	General
Cost	£25

Address	20 Grosvenor Hill, Berkeley Square, London W1X 0HQ
Telephone	01 499 8644; Telex: 263796; Fax: 01 493 0449

884

Originator   SAVILLS

Title   WEST END OFFICE DEMAND SURVEY, annual. 1987–
Coverage   Trends in office floorspace in the West End with data on take-ups, rents and occupiers analysed by size band, rent band and business category. Based on Savill's own records with some supporting text (30%).

Availability   General
Cost   £25
Address   20 Grosvenor Hill, Berkeley Square, London W1X 0HQ
Telephone   01 499 8644; Telex: 263796; Fax: 01 493 0449

885

Originator   SAVILLS AGRICULTURAL RESEARCH

Title   SAVILLS AGRICULTURAL LAND PRICE SURVEY, annual. March 1988–
Coverage   Information and statistics on the UK land market including prices by farm type, location and land grade. Data on the demand for and supply of land, types of sale, purchaser and vendor types and factors affecting prices. Data based on about 100,000 acres of land sold by Savills. A commentary accompanies the statistics (35%).

Availability   General
Cost   Free
Address   47 High Street, Cambridge CB2 2HZ
Telephone   0223 844371; Fax: 0223 845337

886

Originator   SAVILLS/INVESTMENT PROPERTY DATABANK

Title   SAVILLS/IPD AGRICULTURAL PERFORMANCE ANALYSIS, annual. May 1980–
Coverage   Data on institutional investment in farmland including rental growth, capital growth, total returns and the future. A number of tables and graphs give historical trends from the early 1970s. Data by land grade and type of tenancy and some regional figures. Based on IPDs records of investments with a supporting text (50%).

Availability   General
Cost   Free
Comments   See also separate entries for Investment Property Databank and Savills.

Address	47 High Street, Cambridge CB2 2HZ
Telephone	0223 844371; Fax: 0223 845337

887

Originator	SAVINGS MARKET
Title	SAVINGS MARKET REVIEW AND COMPARATIVE INTEREST RATES, quarterly in a quarterly journal
Coverage	Mainly statistics on particular funds, bonds, unit trusts etc but includes a general summary of trends in the savings market during the previous quarter and interest rate statistics.
Availability	General
Cost	£48 or £14 per issue
Address	United Trade Press, 33/35 Bowling Green Lane, London EC1R 0DA
Telephone	01 837 1212; Telex: 299049; Fax: 01 278 4003

888

Originator	SCOTCH WHISKY ASSOCIATION
Title	STATISTICAL REPORT, annual
Coverage	Figures on the activities of the industry including production, exports, stocks and duty paid. Figures for previous years also given. Based mainly on Central Government statistics (90%) with some original data (10%).
Availability	General
Cost	Free
Address	17 Half Moon Street, London W1Y 7RB
Telephone	01 629 4384; Telex: 28162; Fax: 01 493 1398

889

Originator	SCOTTISH COUNCIL DEVELOPMENT AND INDUSTRY
Title	SCOTTISH ECONOMIC NEWSLETTER, monthly
Coverage	A general resumé of the major economic indicators, predictions and surveys with a specific slant towards Scottish interests. Topics include employment, inflation, output, and key industrial developments in Scotland. Based on various sources.
Availability	General
Cost	£22, free to members
Address	23 Chester Street, Edinburgh EH3 7ET
Telephone	031 225 7911; Telex: 776660; Fax: 031 220 2116

890

Originator   SCOTTISH COUNCIL DEVELOPMENT AND INDUSTRY

Title   SCOTTISH MANUFACTURED EXPORTS – SUMMARY OF
             SURVEY RESULTS, annual
Coverage   Data on export trends and prospects. Surveys sent to 1600 com-
             panies with about 33% returned. A commentary (50%) is included
             with the statistics.

Availability General
Address   23 Chester Street, Edinburgh EH3 7ET
Telephone   031 225 7911; Telex: 776660; Fax: 031 220 2116

891

Originator   SCOTTISH COUNCIL DEVELOPMENT AND INDUSTRY

Title   SCOTTISH MANUFACTURED EXPORTS IN 198., annual.
             1960s-
Coverage   Estimates of the value of Scottish exports in aggregate and by
             industry and an assessment of the employment effects. Includes
             data on the destination, the use of Scottish ports, the role of
             small/large companies and export prospects. Based on a 100%
             sample of Scottish exporters with responses covering about 66% of
             Scottish employment. A commentary covers 50%.

Availability General
Cost   £10, £7 to members
Address   23 Chester Street, Edinburgh EH3 7ET
Telephone   031 225 7911; Telex: 776660; Fax: 031 220 2116

892

Originator   SCOTTISH DEVELOPMENT AGENCY

Title   SDA ANNUAL REPORT, annual
Coverage   A review of the activities of the organization with financial data and
             statistics on investments, projects, factories etc.

Availability General
Cost   On application
Comments   Various other surveys and reports published.
Address   120 Bothwell Street, Glasgow G2 7JP
Telephone   041 248 2700; Telex: 777600; Fax: 041 221 3217

893

Originator   SCOTTISH ENGINEERING EMPLOYERS ASSOCIATION

Title   LEVEL OF SETTLEMENTS, monthly. 1985–

Coverage	Wage/salary details from member companies giving average percentage rise per person, per company and lower quartile, upper quartile of rises within the member companies of the Association.
Availability	Members
Cost	Free
Comments	The Annual report also contains some summary statistics.
Address	105 West George Street, Glasgow G2 1QL
Telephone	041 221 3181

894

Originator	SCOTTISH ENGINEERING EMPLOYERS ASSOCIATION
Title	MANUAL SURVEY, bi-annual
Coverage	Average wages for various skilled, semi-skilled and unskilled job titles within the member companies of the Association.
Availability	Members
Cost	Free
Comments	The Annual report also contains summary statistics.
Address	105 West George Street, Glasgow G2 1QL
Telephone	041 221 3181

895

Originator	SCOTTISH ENGINEERING EMPLOYERS ASSOCIATION
Title	STAFF SURVEY, bi-annual
Coverage	Average salaries for various engineering job titles within the member companies of the Association.
Availability	Members
Cost	Free
Comments	The Annual Report also contains summary statistics.
Address	105 West George Street, Glasgow G2 1QL
Telephone	041 221 3181

896

Originator	SCOTTISH FARM BUILDINGS UNIT, NORTH OF SCOTLAND COLLEGE OF AGRICULTURE
Title	FARM BUILDING COST GUIDE, annual. 1975–
Coverage	Labour, plant, equipment, building cost analyses and measured rates, with historical data and predictions for the coming year. Based on a survey by the Unit. Some supporting text.
Availability	General
Cost	£12.25

Address   CRB, North of Scotland College of Agriculture, Aberdeen AB2
                9TR
Telephone   0244 713622

897

Originator   SCOTTISH MILK MARKETING BOARD

Title   ANNUAL REPORT AND ACCOUNTS, annual
Coverage   Includes a statistical section with data on production, producer
                numbers and producer distribution by regions and districts. Infor-
                mation on milk sales, utilization, haulage and prices is presented in
                various graphs and charts.

Availability General
Cost   Free
Address   Underwood Road, Paisley PA3 1TJ
Telephone   041 887 1234; Tclcx: 779012; Fax: 041 889 1225

898

Originator   SCOTTISH MILK MARKETING BOARD

Title   CATERING MARKET FOR MILK AND CREAM IN SCOT-
                LAND, triennial. 1985–
Coverage   A market review with data on sales by type, e.g. hotels, guest
                houses, restaurants, canteens, health, social services, HM Forces,
                prisons etc. Also data on prices and containers. A large scale survey
                covering the whole of Scotland carried out by the Milk Marketing
                Boards and the West of Scotland Agricultural College. Some
                supporting text (40%).

Availability General
Cost   £2
Address   Underwood Road, Paisley PA3 1TJ
Telephone   041 887 1234; Telex: 779012; Fax: 041 889 1225

899

Originator   SCOTTISH MILK MARKETING BOARD

Title   HOUSEHOLD MARKET FOR CREAM IN SCOTLAND,
                triennial. 1986–
Coverage   Types of cream purchased, frequency of purchase, purchasing
                levels, source of purchase, packaging, use of cream and prices.
                Based on a sample of 4,000 interviews throughout Scotland carried
                out by the various Milk Marketing Boards. Some supporting text
                (40%).

Availability General

Cost	£2.50
Address	Underwood Road, Paisley PA3 1TJ
Telephone	041 887 1234; Telex: 779012; Fax: 041 889 1225

900

Originator	SCOTTISH MILK MARKETING BOARD
Title	HOUSEHOLD MARKET FOR MILK IN SCOTLAND, triennial
Coverage	Liquid milk purchasing by social class, household size, region, source of purchase, shop type, packaging, milk type and price. Based on 5,000 interviews throughout Scotland carried out by the various Milk Marketing Boards. Some supporting text (20%).
Availability	General
Cost	£2.50
Address	Underwood Road, Paisley PA3 1TJ
Telephone	041 887 1234; Telex: 779012; Fax: 041 889 1225

901

Originator	SCOTTISH MILK MARKETING BOARD
Title	KEY MILK FIGURES IN SCOTLAND, annual
Coverage	Summary statistics on production, consumption etc. based on various surveys carried out by the Board.
Availability	General
Cost	£1.25
Address	Underwood Road, Paisley PA3 1TJ
Telephone	041 887 1234; Telex: 779012; Fax: 041 889 1225

902

Originator	SCOTTISH MILK MARKETING BOARD
Title	MILK BULLETIN, monthly
Coverage	Trade journal with statistics on supply, sales, prices, utilization and composition. Also statistics on bulls.
Availability	General
Cost	Free to producers
Address	Underwood Road, Paisley PA3 1TJ
Telephone	041 887 1234; Telex: 779012; Fax: 041 889 1225

903

Originator	SCOTTISH MILK MARKETING BOARD
Title	STRUCTURE OF SCOTTISH MILK PRODUCTION, triennial

Coverage	Detailed analysis based on a dairy farm census carried out by the Board.
Availability	General
Cost	£2
Address	Underwood Road, Paisley PA3 1TJ
Telephone	041 887 1234; Telex: 779012; Fax: 041 889 1225

904

Originator	SCOTTISH TELEVISION
Title	STV MARKETING HANDBOOK, regular
Coverage	General statistics on the STV area covering population, employment, industry, standard of living, consumer durables, financial services, retailing, leisure and holidays. A compilation of statistics from various sources.
Availability	General
Comments	Latest edition 1987.
Telephone	041 332 9999

905

Originator	SCOTTISH TOURIST BOARD
Title	THE CONFERENCE AND EXHIBITION MARKET IN SCOTLAND, quarterly. 1987–
Coverage	A survey of 70–80 conference and exhibition venues in Scotland giving information on expenditure, distribution, number of conferences and types of establishment. A small amount of text (10%) is included with the statistics.
Availability	General
Cost	£20
Address	23 Ravelston Terrace, Edinburgh EH4 3EU
Telephone	031 332 2433; Telex: 72272; Fax: 031 332 1513

906

Originator	SCOTTISH TOURIST BOARD
Title	RESEARCH AND PLANNING INFORMATION HANDBOOK, quarterly. 1976–
Coverage	Reports of research studies carried out by the Board, e.g. annual monitoring studies, tourism market trends and social and economic data. Based largely on the various surveys carried out by the Board with a significant amount of text (60%).
Availability	General
Cost	£40, £20 after one year

Comments	Loose-leaf format.
Address	23 Ravelston Terrace, Edinburgh EH4 3EU
Telephone	031 332 2433; Telex: 72272; Fax: 031 332 1513

907

Originator SCOTTISH TOURIST BOARD

Title SCOTTISH HOTEL OCCUPANCY SURVEY, monthly. 1974–
Coverage A sample survey of 200 hotels, weighted by region, giving room and bed occupancy rates. Data by size and status of hotel, tariff, location and group membership. Each issue usually has data 2 months old.

Availability General
Cost £25
Address 23 Ravelston Terrace, Edinburgh EH4 3EU
Telephone 031 332 2433; Telex: 72272; Fax: 031 332 1513

908

Originator SCOTTISH TOURIST BOARD

Title SCOTTISH SELF CATERING OCCUPANCY SURVEY, monthly between April and October. 1984–
Coverage A sample survey of 600 establishments weighted by region, giving information on occupancy levels by establishment size, tariff and region. A small amount of text (10%) is included with the statistics.

Availability General
Cost £25
Address 23 Ravelston Terrace, Edinburgh EH4 3EU
Telephone 031 332 2433; Telex: 72272; Fax: 031 332 1513

909

Originator SEA FISH INDUSTRY AUTHORITY

Title ANNUAL REPORT, annual
Coverage Contains a statistical section covering supplies, household consumption, the fishing fleet, international trade and grants and loans. Most of the data is taken from Central Government sources and most of the report is text.

Availability General
Cost £3.50
Comments ISBN 0903041 371. Also publishes a 'European Supplies Bulletin' covering landings and trade in 16 countries.
Address 10 Young Street, Edinburgh EH2 4JQ
Telephone 031 225 2515; Telex: 727225; Fax: 031 220 0445

910

Originator	SEA FISH INDUSTRY AUTHORITY
Title	HOUSEHOLD FISH CONSUMPTION IN GREAT BRITAIN, quarterly
Coverage	Analysis of sales by species for household consumption in Britain, split into fresh/chilled and frozen sales. The statistics are taken from a sample survey of households and comparable data for the previous year is given. Some text supports the data.
Availability	General
Cost	£55
Comments	Also publishes a 'European Supplies Bulletin' with statistics on landings and trade in 16 countries.
Address	10 Young Street, Edinburgh EH2 4JQ
Telephone	031 225 2515; Telex: 727225; Fax: 031 220 0445

911

Originator	SEA FISH INDUSTRY AUTHORITY
Title	TRADE BULLETIN, monthly
Coverage	Quantity and value of imports and exports of fish intended for human consumption. The latest month's figures with the year to date and comparative figures for the previous year. Based entirely on Central Government data.
Availability	General
Cost	Free
Comments	ISSN 0144 9303. Also publishes a 'European Supplies Bulletin' with statistics on landings and trade in 16 countries.
Address	10 Young Street, Edinburgh EH2 4JQ
Telephone	031 225 2515; Telex: 727225; Fax: 031 220 0445

912

Originator	SEFTON METROPOLITAN BOROUGH COUNCIL
Title	SEFTON FACTS AND FIGURES, annual. October 1987–
Coverage	General statistics on land, population, migration, housing, unemployment, travel to work, socio-economic groups, car ownership etc. Mainly based on Central Government data (75%) with some statistics from the local authority (20%). A small amount of supporting text (15%).
Availability	General
Cost	£5
Address	Planning Department, 375 Stanley Road, Bootle L20 3RY
Telephone	051 922 4040, x3553; Fax: 051 922 4040

913

Originator	SEWELLS INTERNATIONAL LTD
Title	FRANCHISE NETWORKS, annual
Coverage	An analysis with statistics of car, commercial vehicle and petrol retailing networks.
Availability	General
Cost	£19.50
Address	1 Queen Street, Bath BA1 2HE
Telephone	0225 318500; Telex: 444648; Fax: 0225 447239

914

Originator	SHARWOOD, J A LTD
Title	SHARWOOD'S REVIEW, annual. 1987–
Coverage	Commentary and statistics on the general trends in the Indian food and Chinese food markets. Data on the total market, brands, spending patterns etc.
Availability	General
Comments	The first issue (1987) covered Indian food and the second issue (1988) Chinese food.
Address	10 Victoria Road, London NW10 6NU
Telephone	01 965 6565; Telex: 24202

915

Originator	SHAWS PRICE GUIDES LTD
Title	SHAWS GUIDE TO FAIR RETAIL PRICES, monthly
Coverage	Fair selling prices for goods either recommended by the manufacturers or suggested by the editors. Divided into groceries, household, patent medicines, cigarettes, tobacco, cigars and soft drinks – each alphabetical by product and trade name/manufacturer. Based on regular surveys carried out by Shaws.
Availability	General
Cost	£15
Comments	ISSN 0265 2889
Address	Box 32, Abingdon, Oxfordshire OX14 3LJ
Telephone	0235 553233; Telex: 83176; Fax: 0235 553356

916

Originator	SHAWS PRICE GUIDES LTD
Title	SHAWS WINE GUIDE, monthly

Coverage   Recommended fair prices for wines, spirits, aperitifs, beers, cider
                  and soft drinks. Divided by country within type. Based on regular
                  surveys by Shaws.

Availability General
Cost   £16
Comments   ISSN 0307 1170
Address   Box 32, Abingdon, Oxfordshire OX14 3LJ
Telephone   0235 553233; Telex: 83176; Fax: 0235 553356

917

Originator   SHEARSON LEHMAN SECURITIES

Title   MONTHLY REVIEW OF THE UK ECONOMY, monthly
Coverage   Commentary and statistics covering trends in the major economic
                  indicators, based largely on Central Government sources.

Availability Primarily clients but other requests considered
Cost   On application
Comments   Also publishes a weekly Economic Monitor and reviews of specific
                  sectors, e.g. oil and gas.
Address   1 Broadgate, London EC2M 7HA
Telephone   01 601 0011; Telex: 888881

918

Originator   SHEARSON LEHMAN SECURITIES

Title   QUARTERLY UK ECONOMIC FORECAST, quarterly
Coverage   A review of trends in the major economic indicators and short term
                  forecasts for the key indicators.

Availability Primarily clients but other requests considered
Cost   On application
Comments   Also publishes a weekly Economic Monitor and reviews of specific
                  sectors, e.g. oil and gas.
Address   1 Broadgate, London EC2M 7HA
Telephone   01 601 0011; Telex: 888881

919

Originator   SHETLANDS ISLANDS COUNCIL

Title   SHETLANDS IN STATISTICS, annual. 1974–
Coverage   Statistics on the local economy, geography, industry, transport,
                  social trends and political trends. A range of sources are used.

Availability General
Cost   £1.50
Comments   More detailed data available to serious researchers.

Address	93 St Olaf Street, Lerwick, Shetland ZE1 0ES
Telephone	0595 3535; Telex: 75350; Fax: 0595 3278

920

Originator	SHOE AND LEATHER NEWS
Title	IMPORTED HIDE MARKET, weekly in a weekly journal
Coverage	Prices of imported hides with the percentage change on the previous figure. Prices for hides from various countries are given.
Availability	General
Cost	£30
Comments	ISSN 0037 4040. Other statistics are published on imports and production trends.
Address	84/88 Great Eastern Street, London EC2A 3ED
Telephone	01 739 2071; Fax: 01 729 2547

921

Originator	SHOWERINGS LTD
Title	CIDER SURVEY, annual. 1985–
Coverage	A review of the performance of the cider market with statistics by type and data on the licensed trade, take home trade and consumer trends. Includes a commentary (50%) with the statistics.
Availability	General
Address	King Street, Shepton Mallet BA4 5ND
Telephone	0749 3333; Telex: 44209; Fax: 0749 5653

922

Originator	SIEBERT/HEAD LTD
Title	SIEBERT/HEAD INDEX: MONTHLY REVIEW OF PACKAGING MATERIAL PRICES, monthly. 1977–
Coverage	Prices for raw materials and finished products. Also a quarterly report on trade, imports and exports and a quarterly graphical summary of price movements. Based on various sources including the company's own survey (30%), Central Government data (50%) and other non-official sources (20%).
Availability	Packaging Industry
Cost	£40
Address	193 Regent Street, London W1R 7WA
Telephone	01 734 4536; Telex: 261376; Fax: 01 439 7947

923

Originator	SILK ASSOCIATION OF GREAT BRITAIN
Title	SERICA, 4–6 issues per year. 1970–
Coverage	Mainly news and comment on the industry but includes statistics on imports and exports of silk. Statistics taken from Central Government sources.
Availability	General
Cost	On application
Comments	ISSN 0266 0822
Address	c/o Rheinbergs Ltd, Morley Road, Tonbridge TN9 1RN
Telephone	0732 351357; Telex: 95311; Fax: 0732 770217

924

Originator	SKINNER, THOMAS DIRECTORIES
Title	NATIONAL BUILDING PRICE BOOK, annual
Coverage	Prices of materials, work and labour in the building industry. Published in 2 volumes – the first covers major works over £250,000 and the second small works, general information, brands, trade names and company data. Prices based on the average national level with regional variations shown in map form.
Availability	General
Cost	£47.50
Address	Windsor Court, East Grinstead House, East Grinstead RH19 1XE
Telephone	0342 26972; Telex: 95127

925

Originator	SMALL BUSINESS RESEARCH TRUST
Title	QUARTERLY SURVEY OF SMALL BUSINESS IN BRITAIN, quarterly. May 1985–
Coverage	A survey of small businesses throughout the UK, 95% of which employ less than 50 people, giving information on turnover, employment, sales, exports and business problems and looking at general trends in the sector.
Availability	General
Cost	£45 or £15 for a single issue
Address	Francis House, Francis Street, London SW1P 1DE
Telephone	01 828 5327

926

Originator	SNACK NUT AND CRISP MANUFACTURERS ASSOCIATION
Title	SALES DATA: CRISPS/SAVOURY SNACKS/NUTS, monthly. January 1984–
Coverage	Statistics collected from Association members.
Availability	Members
Cost	Free
Address	Swiss Centre, 10 Wardour Street, London W1U 3HG
Telephone	01 439 2567; Telex: 297939

927

Originator	SOAP AND DETERGENT INDUSTRY ASSOCIATION
Title	SDIA PRODUCTION AND MARKET STATISTICS, annual
Coverage	Market trends and production statistics in tonnes, based on returns from Association members and issued every September.
Availability	General
Cost	£20, free to members
Address	PO Box 9, Hayes Gate House, Hayes UB4 0JD
Telephone	01 573 7992; Telex: 936310

928

Originator	SOCIAL AND COMMUNITY PLANNING RESEARCH
Title	BRITISH SOCIAL ATTITUDES: THE 198– REPORT, annual. 1984–
Coverage	Statistics and commentary on a range of current social attitudes based on the results of about 3000 interviews carried out by SCPR. The latest issue (1988) looks at regional differences in attitudes, politics and class, British institutions, right and wrong, sex and gender issues, moral issues, aids, health care, education and the countryside. Text covers about 55%.
Availability	General
Cost	£28.50 hardback, £12.50 paperback
Comments	Published by Gower Publishing Co. Ltd. Database for the surveys held at the ESRC Data Archive, University of Essex.
Address	35 Northampton Square, London EC1V 0AX
Telephone	01 250 1866; Fax: 01 250 1524

929

Originator	SOCIETY OF BRITISH PRINTING INK MANUFACTURERS
Title	PRINTING INK STATISTICS, annual. 1971–
Coverage	Home, export and total sales of member companies plus imports into the UK, UK earnings and some comparative European data. Based mainly on a survey of members (75%) with some data from Central Government (10%) and other sources (15%).
Availability	Members
Cost	Free
Address	PIRA House, Randalls Road, Leatherhead KT22 7RU
Telephone	0372 378628; Telex: 929810

930

Originator	SOCIETY OF BUSINESS ECONOMISTS
Title	BUSINESS ECONOMISTS SALARY SURVEY, annual. 1986–
Coverage	Basic salaries and fringe benefits by employment type, age and sex, with median, maximum and minimum figures in each category. Based on a self-selected sample of Society members. A significant amount of supporting text (50%).
Availability	General
Cost	£7
Comments	Published in the Spring issue of the Society's journal 'The Business Economist'.
Address	11 Baytree Walk, Watford WD1 3RX
Telephone	0923 37287

931

Originator	SOCIETY OF BUSINESS ECONOMISTS
Title	UK ECONOMIC FORECASTS, bi-annual
Coverage	Trends for the next 2 years by quarter. Covers the main GDP expenditure items by percentage and value, inflation, earnings and the balance of payments. Based on the Society's own forecasts with some supporting text (25%).
Availability	Members
Cost	Free
Address	11 Baytree Walk, Watford WD1 3RX
Telephone	0923 37287

932

Originator   SOCIETY OF CHIROPODISTS

Title   EVIDENCE TO THE PAY REVIEW BODY, annual. 1985–
Coverage   A review of manpower trends in the chiropody profession including staffing, training, finance and projected requirements. Based on the Society's survey.

Availability General
Cost   £2.50
Comments   Published in the Society's journal 'The Chiropodist'.
Address   53 Welbeck Street, London W1M 7HE
Telephone   01 486 3381

933

Originator   SOCIETY OF COUNTY TRADING STANDARDS OFFICERS

Title   TRADING STANDARD STATISTICS, annual
Coverage   Summary tables with a short commentary followed by statistics by local authority area on trading standards activities and finance. Based on returns from local authorities.

Availability General
Cost   On application
Comments   At the time of writing the address for copies of the publication is Shropshire CC, Shrewsbury.
Address   c/o Shire Hall, Shrewsbury SY2 6ND
Telephone   0743 25100; Telex: 35187; Fax: 0743 60315

934

Originator   SOCIETY OF MOTOR MANUFACTURERS AND TRADERS (SMMT)

Title   MOTORSTAT NR2, monthly
Coverage   Summary data on the registrations of new motor vehicles with an analysis by make and model range. Based on the Society's own survey.

Availability General
Cost   £400
Comments   Also publishes 'Motorstat Express' with similiar data on an international basis.
Address   Forbes House, Halkin Street, London SW1X 7DS
Telephone   01 235 7000; Telex: 21628; Fax: 01 235 7112

935

Originator	SOCIETY OF MOTOR MANUFACTURERS AND TRADERS (SMMT)
Title	SMMT MONTHLY STATISTICAL REVIEW, monthly
Coverage	Production and registrations of motor vehicles by manufacturer and model and imports and exports of products of the motor industry. Based on a combination of Central Government data (60%) and the Society's survey (40%). The main tables have monthly and cumulative year to date figures. Also includes summary short-term forecasts.
Availability	General
Cost	£60, £30 to members
Comments	Also publishes annual and bi-monthly statistics on the world motor vehicle industry.
Address	Forbes House, Halkin Street, London SW1X 7DS
Telephone	01 235 7000; Telex: 21628; Fax: 01 235 7112

936

Originator	SOFT DRINKS MANAGEMENT INTERNATIONAL
Title	MARKET REPORTS, monthly in a monthly journal
Coverage	Market trends and import/export data, largely based on Central Government data.
Availability	General
Cost	£20, or £2 for a single issue
Comments	Free to members of the British Soft Drinks Association.
Address	6 Catherine Street, London WC2B 5UA
Telephone	01 379 5737

937

Originator	SOLAR TRADE ASSOCIATION LTD
Title	REVIEW OF THE SOLAR WATER HEATING INDUSTRY, annual. 1978–
Coverage	Statistics on solar collector production, sales, imports and exports over a 10-year period based on the Association's own survey. Text covers about 60% of the report.
Availability	Members
Cost	Free
Address	Brackenhurst, Greenham Common South, Newbury RG15 8HH
Telephone	0635 46561

938

Originator	SOUTH EAST REGIONAL AGGREGATES WORKING PARTY (SERAWP)
Title	AGGREGATES MONITORING: PLANNING DATA, annual. 1983–
Coverage	Statistics and commentary on the level of planning applications and permissions for mineral workings in the South East with data by type of working and by county and Greater London. Data for earlier years given. Based on SERAWP's own survey with supporting text covering 50%.
Availability	General
Cost	£5
Address	8th Floor, 50/64 Broadway, London SW1H 0DB
Telephone	01 799 2191; Fax: 01 799 2075

939

Originator	SOUTH EAST REGIONAL AGGREGATES WORKING PARTY (SERAWP)
Title	REGIONAL COLLATION OF AGGREGATES MONITORING SURVEYS, biennial. 1981–
Coverage	A survey of the production, movement, sales and use of aggregates in the South East by county and for London as a whole. Concentrates on land-won aggregates such as sand and gravel, but includes marine-dredged aggregates, imports from other regions and alternatives to natural aggregates.Based on SERAWP's own survey with supporting text (30%).
Availability	General
Cost	£10
Address	8th Floor, 50/64 Broadway, London SW1H 0DB
Telephone	01 799 2191; Fax: 01 799 2075

940

Originator	SOUTH TYNESIDE METROPOLITAN BOROUGH COUNCIL
Title	QUARTERLY ECONOMIC DIGEST, quarterly
Coverage	Consists of 3 sections: articles on local issues, a review of the local and national economy and a statistical appendix on unemployment. Based entirely on Central Government data.
Availability	General
Cost	Free
Address	Planning Department, Westoe Road, South Shields NE33 2RL
Telephone	091 456 8841, x5593; Fax: 091 455 0208

941

Originator   SPACE PLANNING SERVICES PLC

Title   FITTING OUT COST INDEX, bi-annual
Coverage   Measures the cost of preparing a typical speculative office shell for occupation. It charts the price changes occurring in various building elements, provides a total cost figure, a cost per square metre and forecasts these 6 months ahead. Based on a sample survey with supporting text comprising 25%.

Availability   General
Cost   Free
Address   Western House, Uxbridge Road, Hillingdon UB10 0LY
Telephone   01 573 2271; Fax: 01 573 1104

942

Originator   SPACE PLANNING SERVICES PLC

Title   SCOPE SURVEY, annual
Coverage   A survey of the costs of providing office accommodation other than rents and rates. Includes data on building management, repairs, maintenance, energy, insurance etc. Based on a postal questionnaire survey of a national sample. Supporting text covers 50%.

Availability   General
Cost   Free
Address   Western House, Uxbridge Road, Hillingdon UB10 0LY
Telephone   01 573 2271; Fax: 01 573 1104

943

Originator   SPON, E & F N

Title   SPON'S ARCHITECTS' AND BUILDERS' PRICE BOOK, annual
Coverage   Prices of materials, prices for measured work and rates of wages. Based mainly on SPON's own surveys with additional data from other non-official sources.

Availability   General
Cost   £32
Comments   ISSN 0306 3046
Address   11 New Fetter Lane, London EC4P 4EE
Telephone   01 583 9855; Fax: 01 583 0701

944

Originator	SPON, E & F N
Title	SPON'S CIVIL ENGINEERING PRICE BOOK, annual. 1985–
Coverage	Prices and costs of building, services, engineering, external work, landscaping etc. Based on SPON's own surveys and other non-official sources.
Availability	General
Cost	£30
Comments	ISSN 0265 9855
Address	11 Fetter Lane, London EC4P 4EE
Telephone	01 583 9855; Fax: 01 583 0701

945

Originator	SPON, E & F N
Title	SPON'S LANDSCAPE AND EXTERNAL WORKS PRICE BOOK, annual
Coverage	Prices and costs covering hard and soft landscapes and external works generally. Based on SPON's own surveys and some other non-official data.
Availability	General
Cost	£29.50
Address	11 Fetter Lane, London EC4P 4EE
Telephone	01 583 9855; Fax: 01 583 0701

946

Originator	SPON, E & F N
Title	SPON'S MECHANICAL AND ELECTRICAL SERVICES PRICE BOOK, annual. 1969–
Coverage	Prices and costs of heating, lighting, ventilation, air conditioning and other service items in industrial and commercial property. The only publication covering costs of chemical plants and other large scale projects. Based on SPON's own surveys plus other non-official sources.
Availability	General
Cost	£32
Comments	ISSN 0305 4543. A quarterly update is included in the price.
Address	11 Fetter Lane, London EC4P 4EE
Telephone	01 583 9855; Fax: 01 583 0701

947

Originator   SPON, E & F N

Title   SPON'S PLANT AND EQUIPMENT PRICE GUIDE, monthly
Coverage   New and secondhand prices and specifications for nearly 5,000
                   models of construction plant. Based on SPON's own surveys.

Availability   General
Cost   £95
Address   11 Fetter Lane, London EC4P 4EE
Telephone   01 583 9855; Fax: 01 583 0701

948

Originator   SPORTS COUNCIL

Title   DIGEST OF SPORTS STATISTICS, every few years
Coverage   Compendium of statistics about organized and casual sports partici-
                   pation during a ten year period. Additional information on the
                   facilities and purchase of equipment and magazines, mainly in
                   England. General section and separate sections on specific sports.
                   Data mainly taken from the governing bodies of sport and the 4 UK
                   Sports Councils (95%).

Availability   General
Cost   £15
Comments   Latest issue published Autumn 1986. Data collected and collated by
                   the Centre for Leisure Research.
Address   16 Upper Woburn Place, London WC1H 0QP
Telephone   01 388 1277; Telex: 27830

949

Originator   SPORTS MARKETING SURVEYS

Title   GOLF RESEARCH PROGRAMME, annual
Coverage   Market reviews and statistics for various sectors including golf balls,
                   clubs, putters, shoes, apparel, gloves, trolleys, professional
                   interviews, golf holiday survey, Volvo tour, golf readership
                   surveys, attitudes and golf bags and holdhalls. The data is based on
                   personal interviews with sports participants.

Availability   General
Cost   £450-£3250 per report
Address   Cheltonian House, Portsmouth Road, Esher KT10 9AA
Telephone   0372 60155; Fax: 0372 69976

950

Originator	SPORTS MARKETING SURVEYS
Title	RACKET SPORTS PROGRAMME, annual
Coverage	Market reviews with statistics for various sectors including rackets, footwear, tracksuits, tennis/squash balls, shuttlecocks, player profiles, apparel observation study and Wimbledon Census. For all reports data is based on personal interviews with sports participants.
Availability	General
Cost	£300-£500 per report
Address	Cheltonian House, Portsmouth Road, Esher KT10 9AA
Telephone	0372 60155; Fax: 0372 69976

951

Originator	SPORTS MARKETING SURVEYS
Title	SOCCER SURVEY, annual
Coverage	A market survey and statistics covering soccer products and participation in the UK. Based on personal interviews with sports participants.
Availability	General
Cost	£675
Address	Cheltonian House, Portsmouth Road, Esher KT10 9AA
Telephone	0372 60155; Fax: 0372 69976

952

Originator	SPORTS MARKETING SURVEYS
Title	UK SKI SURVEY, annual
Coverage	Market surveys and statistics with reports on skis and bindings, boots, clothing, travel, dry ski slopes and readership and skier profiles. Data is based on personal interviews with sports participants.
Availability	General
Cost	£450-£950 per report
Address	Cheltonian House, Portsmouth Road, Esher KT10 9AA
Telephone	0372 60155; Fax: 0372 69976

953

Originator	SPORTS RETAILING
Title	IMPORT/EXPORT FIGURES, bi-annual in a fortnightly journal

Coverage   Imports of sports equipment by major countries with a commentary
                on the key trends. Based on Central Government data.

Availability   General
Cost   £30 or £1.10 for a single issue
Comments   ISSN 0267 6354
Address   Benn Publications, Sovereign Way, Tonbridge TN9 1RW
Telephone   0732 364422; Telex: 95162; Fax: 0732 361534

954

Originator   STANDING CONFERENCE OF EAST ANGLIAN LOCAL
                AUTHORITIES (SCEALA)

Title   EAST ANGLIA REGIONAL COMMENTARY, annual
Coverage   Text and statistics on population, employment, transport, finance
                and the environment with sections on Cambridgeshire, Norfolk and
                Suffolk. Statistics from various sources, mainly Central Govern-
                ment, with a supporting commentary (50%).

Availability   General
Cost   £3
Address   c/o Planning, County Hall, St Edmund House, Ipswich IP4 1LZ
Telephone   0473 55801

955

Originator   STANDING CONFERENCE OF NATIONAL AND UNI-
                VERSITY LIBRARIES (SCONUL)

Title   SCONUL STATISTICAL DATABASE PART 2: LIBRARY
                OPERATIONS, annual. 1985–
Coverage   Based on the annual returns from SCONUL libraries. A small
                amount of text (6%) is included.

Availability   General
Cost   £12.50
Address   102 Euston Street, London NW1 2HA
Telephone   01 387 0317

956

Originator   STANDING CONFERENCE OF NATIONAL AND UNI-
                VERSITY LIBRARIES (SCONUL)

Title   UNIVERSITY LIBRARY EXPENDITURE STATISTICS,
                annual. 1982–
Coverage   Based on the annual returns from SCONUL libraries. A small
                amount of text is included (6%).

Availability   General

Cost	£12.50
Address	102 Euston Street, London NW1 2HA
Telephone	01 387 0317

957

Originator	STANILAND HALL ASSOCIATES LTD
Title	CONSUMER SPENDING FORECASTS, quarterly. 1975–
Coverage	Economic environment and personal incomes and spending in individual sectors. A special topic is covered in each issue, e.g DIY, housing etc. Forecasts between 1 and 5 years ahead. A commentary supports the statistics (50%).
Availability	General
Cost	£335
Comments	ISSN 0307 8248. Includes 8 monthly supplements. Subscription with 'Economic Indicators' (see below) for £485
Address	PO Box 643, Alderbury House, Upton Park, Slough SL1 2UJ
Telephone	0753 691874

958

Originator	STANILAND HALL ASSOCIATES LTD
Title	ECONOMIC INDICATORS – FORECASTS FOR COMPANY PLANNING, quarterly. 1977–
Coverage	Indicators for UK production and demand and for costs and prices Forecasts for between 1 and 5 years ahead. Some world data is also given. A commentary supports the data (50%).
Availability	General
Cost	£235
Comments	ISSN 0263 7065. A combined subscription with 'Consumer Spending Forecasts' (see above) available for £485.
Address	PO Box 643, Alderbury House, Upton Park, Slough SL1 2UJ
Telephone	0753 691874

959

Originator	STATS MR LTD
Title	RETAIL AUDIT REPORTS, monthly or bi-monthly
Coverage	Individual reports on the markets within liquor retailers, both on trade and take-home, and within travel agents. All statistics are compiled from Stats MR surveys.
Availability	General
Cost	Varies according to the type of report required
Address	Gloucester House, Smallbrook Queensway, Birmingham B5 4HF
Telephone	021 631 3232; Fax: 021 631 3637

960

Originator   STOY HAYWARD

Title   ANNUAL GUIDE TO THE VENTURE AND DEVEL-
              OPMENT CAPITAL INDUSTRY, annual
Coverage   One chapter in the guide provides a statistical overview of the UK
              venture capital industry. Based on various sources.

Availability General
Cost   Free
Address   Marketing Department, 8 Baker Street, London W1M 1DA
Telephone   01 486 5888

961

Originator   STRATHCLYDE PASSENGER TRANSPORT EXECUTIVE

Title   ANNUAL REPORT AND ACCOUNTS, annual
Coverage   Mainly financial information on the Executive but a section at the
              end contains operational data, e.g. passenger journeys, number of
              vehicles etc. Based on the Executive's own surveys. 70% of the
              report is text.

Availability General
Cost   On request
Address   Consort House, 12 West George Street, Glasgow G2 1HN
Telephone   041 332 6811; Telex: 779746; Fax: 041 332 3076

962

Originator   STRATHCLYDE REGIONAL COUNCIL

Title   STRATHCLYDE ECONOMIC TRENDS, regular
Coverage   Commentary and statistics on the local economy in the region with
              data mainly from Central Government sources. Details of local
              initiatives also included.

Availability General
Cost   On application
Address   Strathclyde House, 20 India Street, Glasgow G2 4PF
Telephone   041 204 2900; Fax: 041 227 2870

963

Originator   SWANSEA CITY DISTRICT COUNCIL

Title   SWANSEA ENTERPRISE PARK MONITORING REPORT,
              quarterly

Coverage	Details the level of construction activity and the number of firms and employment trends, including the number of enquiries about the Park. Based on a survey by the Council's Development Department and published one month after the date of the survey.
Availability	General
Cost	£2
Address	Development Department, The Guildhall, Swansea SA1 4PH
Telephone	0792 50821

964

Originator	SYSTEM THREE SCOTLAND
Title	SCOTTISH SPIRITS REPORT – WHISKY, quarterly
Coverage	Data on the frequency of purchase, consumption, brand awareness and usage. Based on a survey by System Three.
Availability	General
Cost	£195 per quarter
Comments	Also published a regular report on the Scottish carry-out market with the last issue appearing in 1986.
Address	16 York Place, Edinburgh EH1 3EP
Telephone	031 556 9462; Fax: 031 556 7468

965

Originator	SYSTEM THREE SCOTLAND
Title	SCOTTISH SPIRITS REPORTS, annual
Coverage	Individual reports on sherry, vodka, white rum, dark rum, brandy and gin covering frequency of purchase, consumption, brand awareness and usage. Based on System Three's own research.
Availability	General
Cost	£195 per report
Comments	Previously published a regular report on the Scottish carry-out market with the last issue in 1986.
Address	16 York Place, Edinburgh EH1 3EP
Telephone	031 556 9462; Fax: 031 556 7468

966

Originator	TACK RESEARCH LTD
Title	SALESMEN'S PAY AND EXPENSES, biennial. 1968–
Coverage	The gross pay and pay breakdown plus additional incentives offered to salesmen in the following categories: repeat consumer goods, durable consumer goods, repeat industrial, capital equipment and services. Based on the company's own research.

Availability	General
Cost	£90, £40 to data providers
Address	TACK House, Longmoore Street, London SW1V 1JJ
Telephone	01 834 5001; Telex: 497367; Fax: 01 828 8434

967

| **Originator** | TAYLOR NELSON AND ASSOCIATES |

| **Title** | FAMILY FOOD PANEL, bi-annual. 1974– |
| **Coverage** | Continuous monitor of consumption and usage of all foods and drinks consumed in the home based upon a sample of 2100 households. Supporting commentary (50%). |

Availability	General
Cost	£15,000
Comments	Price represents full package but special reports are available from £395.
Address	44/46 Upper High Street, Epsom KT17 4QS
Telephone	03727 29688

968

| **Originator** | TAYLOR NELSON AND ASSOCIATES |

| **Title** | MONITOR SOCIAL CHANGE RESEARCH PROGRAMME, annual. 1972– |
| **Coverage** | Changes in British attitudes and behaviour patterns and the implications for public and commercial bodies. Particular emphasis on health, food, retailing, consumerism, work, family life, leisure and socio-political involvement. Based on a sample of 2000. A large amount of text (80%). |

Availability	General
Cost	£16,000
Comments	Price represents full subscription but cheaper packages and special reports are available.
Address	44/46 Upper High Street, Epsom KT17 4QS
Telephone	03727 29688

969

| **Originator** | TEA BROKERS ASSOCIATION OF LONDON |

| **Title** | TEA MARKET REPORT, weekly. pre-1950– |
| **Coverage** | Statistics on the prices obtained for tea in the London auctions. Based on the Association's own survey. |

| **Availability** | General |
| **Cost** | £30 |

Comments	Published every Friday.
Address	Sir John Lyon House, Upper Thames Street, London EC4V 3LA
Telephone	01 236 3368

970

Originator	TEXTILE MARKET STUDIES (TMS)
Title	CLOTHING AND FOOTWEAR SURVEY, weekly
Coverage	A weekly survey of clothing and footwear trends based on a sample of about 39,000 purchasers. Different product areas are covered and data on purchasing trends, prices, markets, end uses, payment methods etc. are covered. Based on TMS's own survey.
Availability	General
Cost	On application
Comments	Various other services and one-off reports also produced.
Address	182 Upper Richmond Road, London SW15 2SH
Telephone	01 785 2302; Telex: 24224; Fax: 01 788 2293

971

Originator	TEXTILE MARKET STUDIES (TMS)
Title	HOUSEHOLD SURVEY, quarterly
Coverage	Syndicated research survey of a sample of about 14,000 housewives per year with data on purchasing trends for various types of textiles, clothing and furniture products. Based on TMS's own survey.
Availability	General
Cost	On application
Comments	Various other services and one-off reports available.
Address	182 Upper Richmond Road, London SW15 2SH
Telephone	01 785 2302; Telex: 24224; Fax: 01 788 2293

972

Originator	TEXTILE STATISTICS BUREAU
Title	EXPORTS, quarterly
Coverage	A series of 6 reports available separately giving cumulative totals from the beginning of the year for exports of specific products. Product groups covered are: manmade staple fibre, waste and filament yarn; cotton yarn; spun manmade fibre yarn; woven cotton piecegoods; woven manmade piecegoods; knitted man-made piecegoods. Based on Central Government data.
Availability	General
Cost	On application, prices of the reports are under review
Address	Reedham House, 31 King Street West, Manchester M3 2PF
Telephone	061 834 7871; Telex: 666737

973

Originator   TEXTILE STATISTICS BUREAU

Title   EXPORTS OF MAN-MADE CONTINUOUS FILAMENT YARN, monthly
Coverage   Exports of creped, bulked, textured, crimped or stretch yarn by commodity type showing major country, weight, value and average value. Weight is also shown as a cumulative total. Based on Central Government data.

Availability General
Cost   On application, price under review
Address   Reedham House, 31 King Street West, Manchester M3 2PF
Telephone   061 834 7871; Telex: 666737

974

Originator   TEXTILE STATISTICS BUREAU

Title   IMPORTS, monthly
Coverage   7 reports giving cumulative totals from the beginning of the year for various products. Individual reports cover: manmade staple fibre, waste and filament yarn; cotton yarn; spun manmade fibre yarn; woven cotton piecegoods; woven manmade piecegoods; knitted manmade piecegoods; woven cotton and manmade household textiles. Based on Central Government data.

Availability General
Cost   On application, prices of specific reports under review
Address   Reedham House, 31 King Street West, Manchester M3 2PF
Telephone   061 834 7871; Telex: 666737

975

Originator   TEXTILE STATISTICS BUREAU

Title   IMPORTS OF MAN-MADE FIBRE, monthly
Coverage   Imports of staple fibre, waste, continuous filament yarns and selected spun yarns by commodity type showing major country, weight, value and average value. Weight is also shown as a cumulative total. Based on Central Government data.

Availability General
Cost   On application, price under review
Address   Reedham House, 31 King Street West, Manchester M3 2PF
Telephone   061 834 7871; Telex: 666737

976

Originator	TEXTILE STATISTICS BUREAU
Title	IMPORTS TIME SERIES, monthly
Coverage	Total monthly imports of cotton yarn, spun manmade fibre yarn, woven cotton piecegoods, woven cotton made-up goods and woven manmade fibre piecegoods. Based on Central Government data.
Availability	General
Cost	On application, price under review
Address	Reedham House, 31 King Street West, Manchester M3 2PF
Telephone	061 834 7871; Telex: 666737

977

Originator	TEXTILE STATISTICS BUREAU
Title	PRODUCTION/EMPLOYMENT/MACHINE ACTIVITY ..... monthly
Coverage	A series of 6 separate reports covering production, employment, deliveries and general activity in the following areas: manmade fibre production, spinning and waste spinning, doubling, deliveries of yarn, weaving and finishing. Based mainly on Central Government data.
Availability	General
Cost	On application, prices for individual reports under review
Address	Reedham House, 31 King Street West, Manchester M3 2PF
Telephone	061 834 7871; Telex: 666737

978

Originator	TEXTILE STATISTICS BUREAU
Title	QUARTERLY STATISTICAL REVIEW, quarterly
Coverage	Includes data on production, imports, exports and employment in the textile industry. Covers spinning, weaving, doubling and finishing of cotton plus data on manmade fibres, wool, woven and knitted fabrics, carpets and rugs and household textiles. Some international data on yarn and cloth. Based mainly on Central Government data (90%).
Availability	General
Cost	On application, prices under review
Address	Reedham House, 31 King Street West, Manchester M3 2PF
Telephone	061 834 7871; Telex: 666737

979

Originator	THAMES WATER AUTHORITY
Title	ANNUAL REPORT AND ACCOUNTS, annual. 1974–
Coverage	Contains a section entitled 'Facts and Figures' covering water supply, sewage treatment and disposal, river flows, rainfall, land drainage and population. Based mainly on the Authority's own data (80%) with some statistics from Central Government (20%). The report contains mostly text (85%).
Availability	General
Cost	£5
Address	Nugent House, Vastern Road, Reading RG1 8DB
Telephone	0734 593333; Telex: 848054; Fax: 0734 593203

980

Originator	THORPE, BERNARD & PARTNERS
Title	PROPERTY IN FOCUS, annual
Coverage	A review of property trends in the UK. Mainly text but regular statistics on office and industrial rents in various centres and some statistics on residential prices. Based on research by the company.
Availability	General
Cost	Free
Address	1 Hanover Square, London W1R 0PT
Telephone	01 499 6353; Telex: 8813389

981

Originator	TIMBER GROWER
Title	UK TIMBER MARKETING REPORT, quarterly in a quarterly journal
Coverage	The journal covers forests and woodlands in the UK and a statistical section gives forestry data in each region.
Availability	General
Cost	£12 or £3 for a single issue
Address	Agrimedia, 34 Cavendish Road, London NW6 7XP
Telephone	01 459 5330

982

Originator	TIMBER TRADE FEDERATION
Title	YEARBOOK OF TIMBER STATISTICS, regular

Availability	General
Cost	£38.50 (£16 for TCPA members) or £3.50 for a single issue
Comments	ISSN 0040 9960. Up to 1981 the review appeared annually. Usually appears in alternate November issues of the journal.
Address	17 Carlton House Terrace, London SW1Y 5AS
Telephone	01 930 8903

986

Originator	TOWN AND COUNTRY PLANNING
Title	STATISTICAL REVIEW OF NON-DEVELOPMENT CORPORATION NEW TOWN DEVELOPMENTS IN BRITAIN, biennial in a monthly journal. 1984–
Coverage	Data on the population, employment, housing, economy and the general development of private new towns and towns developed under the Town Expansion Act. Based on a survey of all known towns with a usual response rate of 100%. A brief commentary with the statistics.
Availability	General
Cost	£38.50 (£16 for TCPA members) or £3.50 for a single issue
Comments	ISSN 0040 9960
Address	17 Carlton House Terrace, London SW1Y 5AS
Telephone	01 930 8903

987

Originator	TRACKING ADVERTISING AND BRAND STRENGTH LTD (TABS)
Title	TRACKING ADVERTISING AND BRAND STRENGTH/HEALTH, 13 issues per year. August 1981–
Coverage	Monitors brand goodwill, advertising awareness, price image, brand awareness, claimed levels of buying/usage and brand image attributes. Based on a sample of 2,000 adults and covers all TV areas except NE Scotland, Border, Channel Islands and Ulster. Usually published 4–5 weeks after the survey.
Availability	General
Cost	£2,500–£4,000, depending on number of brands and markets covered
Address	18 Maddox Street, London W1R 9PL
Telephone	01 629 0424

988

Originator	TRADE INDEMNITY
Title	QUARTERLY ECONOMIC REVIEW, quarterly

Coverage	The UK economy and industrial performance by major sectors followed by annual and quarterly statistics on bad debtors and business failures by trade category. Based on debtors and failures notified to Trade Indemnity by its policy holders. Some Central Government statistics (30%) are included. Supporting text covers 50%.
Availability	General
Cost	Free
Comments	Also publishes a regular press release on business failures.
Address	Trade Indemnity Hse, 12/34 Great Eastern Street, London EC2A 3AX
Telephone	01 739 4311; Telex: 21227

989

Originator	TRANSMODAL INDUSTRIES RESEARCH
Title	SUPPLY PRESSURE IN CONTAINER SHIPPING, annual. September 1985–
Coverage	Slot capacity on container vessels by shipping line and by route. Data on the current position and forecasts. Based on the company's own research.
Availability	General
Cost	£450
Comments	Published in 2 volumes.
Address	66C Royal Mint Street, London E1 8LG
Telephone	01 480 6405; Telex: 94012668; Fax: 01 265 1625

990

Originator	TRANSMODAL INDUSTRIES RESEARCH
Title	UK UNITISED TRADE STATISTICS, annual. 1983–
Coverage	Detailed structure of UK containerized ro-ro trade. Statistics relate to loaded container and trailer trade between individual UK seaports and overseas trade areas. Also data on rail ferry and non-unitized trade and unitized penetration for individual commodities. Statistics derived from Central Government overseas trade statistics.
Availability	General
Cost	£75
Comments	The publication serves as an introduction to the more extensive OTD computer databank with specific packages for clients.
Address	66C Royal Mint Street, London E1 8LG
Telephone	01 480 6405; Telex: 94012668; Fax: 01 265 1625

991

Originator	TRANSPORT ENGINEER
Title	TRUCK OPERATING COSTS FOR 198., annual in a monthly journal. 1980–
Coverage	Standing and running costs of trucks for the coming year by weight, truck type and number of axles. Based on data collected by the journal.
Availability	General
Cost	£15 or £1.23 for a single issue
Comments	ISSN 0020 3122. Published by the Institute of Road Transport Engineers.
Address	1 Cromwell Place, London SW7 2JF
Telephone	01 589 3744

992

Originator	TRAVEL AND TOURISM RESEARCH LTD
Title	AIRLINE TRADE IMAGE SURVEY, annual. 1983–
Coverage	Examines travel agents' images of 65 international airlines. Based on the company's own survey.
Availability	General
Cost	£2,000
Address	39C Highbury Place, London N5 1QP
Telephone	01 354 3391; Telex: 262433; Fax: 01 359 4043

993

Originator	TRAVEL AND TOURISM RESEARCH LTD
Title	HOTEL GROUPS AND SHORT BREAK OPERATORS IMAGE SURVEY, annual. 1978–
Coverage	Examines in detail travel agents' images and recommendations for hotel groups and short holiday tour operators in the UK and abroad. Based on the company's own survey.
Availability	General
Cost	£2,000
Address	39C Highbury Place, London N5 1QP
Telephone	01 354 3391; Telex: 262433; Fax: 01 359 4043

994

Originator	TRAVEL AND TOURISM RESEARCH LTD
Title	TRAVEL AGENTS READERSHIP SURVEY, annual. 1980–

Coverage   Readership of travel trade media, using a representative sample of 400 ABTA travel agents. Results by agency, type, status, size, type of business and region.

Availability General
Cost   £850
Address   39C Highbury Place, London N5 1QP
Telephone   01 354 3391; Telex: 262433; Fax: 01 359 4043

995

Originator   TVS

Title   MARKETING HANDBOOK, biennial
Coverage   General data on the characteristics of the TVS area including population trends, employment, industry, living standards, retailing, consumers and the television audience. Based mainly on various non-official sources (90%).

Availability General
Cost   Free
Address   60 Buckingham Gate, London SW1E 6AJ
Telephone   01 828 9898; Telex: 291602

996

Originator   TYNE TEES TELEVISION

Title   TYNE TEES MARKETING YEARBOOK, regular
Coverage   General statistics on the Tyne Tees TV area including industry and employment, the area, population and a range of specific consumer markets. Based on various sources, mainly non-official.

Availability General
Comments   Also produces 'Pulsebeat', a marketing package for the area.
Address   15 Bloomsbury Square, London WC1A 2LJ
Telephone   01 405 8474; Telex: 266316

997

Originator   UK VENTURE CAPITAL JOURNAL

Title   REVIEW OF 198. INVESTMENT ACTIVITY, annual in a journal published 6 times a year
Coverage   A review of venture capital activity in aggregate and specific data by investor type, financing stage, financing size, industry sector and region. Comprises text (50%) and tables and graphs. Based on the investment activity survey by the British Venture Capital Association (see below).

Availability General

Cost	£375
Comments	Latest survey at the time of writing – June 1988.
Address	14 Barley Mow Passage, London W4 4PH
Telephone	01 994 8009; Fax: 01 995 0162

998

Originator   UK VENTURE CAPITAL JOURNAL

Title	UK VENTURE CAPITAL INDEX, 6 times a year in a journal published 6 times a year
Coverage	Graphs and commentary showing changes over a 15 year period.
Availability	General
Cost	£375
Address	14 Barley Mow Passage, London W4 4PH
Telephone	01 994 8009; Fax: 01 995 0162

999

Originator   ULSTER MARKETING SURVEYS LTD

Title	NORTHERN IRELAND CAR MARKET, annual. 1985–
Coverage	A statistical review of car sales in Northern Ireland and related markets. Based on a survey by the company with a supporting text (50%).
Availability	General
Cost	£30
Comments	Report is also available on disc.
Address	115 University Street, Belfast BT7 1HD
Telephone	0232 231060; Fax: 0232 243877

1000

Originator   ULSTER MARKETING SURVEYS LTD

Title	NORTHERN IRELAND ELECTRICAL APPLIANCES, annual. 1985–
Coverage	Data on the ownership of a wide range of electrical appliances based on a sample survey of 830 households. A commentary (50%) supports the statistics.
Availability	General
Cost	£80
Comments	Report is also available on disc.
Address	115 University Street, Belfast BT7 1HP
Telephone	0232 231060; Fax: 0232 243877

1001

Originator	ULSTER MARKETING SURVEYS LTD
Title	NORTHERN IRELAND FINANCIAL MONITOR, annual. 1984–
Coverage	Information on all aspects of Northern Ireland financial markets amongst the general public including data on bank and building society accounts, credit, mortgages, loans and insurance. Based on a survey of 4,400 people. A commentary supports the statistics (50%).
Availability	General
Cost	£8,700
Comments	Report is also available on disc.
Address	115 University Street, Belfast BT7 1HD
Telephone	02032 231060; Fax: 0232 243877

1002

Originator	ULSTER MARKETING SURVEYS LTD
Title	NORTHERN IRELAND PETROL MARKET, annual. 1988–
Coverage	Analysis by volume of petrol sales in Northern Ireland based on a survey of a sample of 500 motorists. A commentary supports the statistics (50%).
Availability	General
Cost	£850
Comments	Report is also available on disc.
Address	115 University Street, Belfast BT7 1HP
Telephone	0232 231060; Fax: 0232 243877

1003

Originator	ULSTER MARKETING SURVEYS LTD
Title	NORTHERN IRELAND READERSHIP MONITOR, bi-annual. 1988–
Coverage	Statistics on the readership of daily and Sunday papers in Northern Ireland based on a survey of a sample of 4,400 adults. A commentary (50%) supports the data.
Availability	General
Cost	£750
Comments	Report is also available on disc.
Address	115 University Street, Belfast BT7 1HP
Telephone	0232 231060; Fax: 0232 243877

1004

Originator   ULSTER MARKETING SURVEYS LTD

Title   NORTHERN IRELAND YOUTH MARKETS, biennial. 1984–
Coverage   Lifestyle and media behaviour of 12-24 year olds in Northern
              Ireland based on a survey of a sample of 1,000 people. A commen-
              tary (50%) supports the data.

Availability General
Cost   £400
Address   115 University Street, Belfast BT7 1HD
Telephone   0232 231060; Fax: 0232 243877

1005

Originator   ULSTER TELEVISION

Title   MARKETING GUIDE TO NORTHERN IRELAND, regular
Coverage   Sections on the population, television audience, economy, agricul-
              ture, consumer expenditure, motor vehicles, leisure, tourism,
              retailing, communications and research and production facilities.
              Based on a combination of official (60%) and non-official sources
              (40%). A small amount of supporting text (20%).

Availability General
Cost   £5
Address   Havelock House, Ormeau Road, Belfast BT7 1EB
Telephone   0232 328122; Telex: 74654; Fax: 0232 246695

1006

Originator   UNIT FOR RETAIL PLANNING INFORMATION (URPI)

Title   CONSUMER RETAIL EXPENDITURE ESTIMATES, conti-
              nuous
Coverage   Expenditure estimates for small areas in Great Britain by goods
              type categories.

Availability General
Cost   On application
Comments   Various other reports and packages available including shopping
              surveys, demographic profiles, floorspace data etc.
Address   26 Queen Victoria Street, Reading RG1 1TG
Telephone   0734 588181

1007

Originator   UNIT FOR RETAIL PLANNING INFORMATION (URPI)

Title   DEMOGRAPHIC PROFILES, continuous

Coverage	Demographic statistics for a population group in various specific local areas.
Availability	General
Cost	On application
Comments	Various other reports and packages available including shopping surveys, demographic profiles, floorspace figures etc.
Address	26 Queen Victoria Street, Reading RG1 1TG
Telephone	0734 588181

1008

Originator	UNIT FOR RETAIL PLANNING INFORMATION (URPI)
Title	SHOPPING CENTRE TRADE AREA DEMOGRAPHIC PROFILES, continuous
Coverage	Demographic profiles available for population groups in 350 major shopping centres.
Availability	General
Cost	On application
Comments	Various other reports and packages available covering shopping surveys, demographic profiles, floorspace figures etc.
Address	26 Queen Victoria Street, Reading RG1 1TG
Telephone	0734 588181

1009

Originator	UNIT TRUST ASSOCIATION
Title	MONTHLY UNIT TRUST SALES STATISTICS, monthly
Coverage	Sales of unit trusts and the value of the industry overall. Based on the Association's survey with some commentary (50%).
Availability	General
Cost	Free
Comments	Statistics also published in the CSO's Financial Statistics.
Address	65 Kingsway, London WC2B 6TD
Telephone	01 831 0898; Fax: 01 831 9975

1010

Originator	UNIT TRUST ASSOCIATION
Title	QUARTERLY UNIT TRUST PERFORMANCE STATISTICS, quarterly
Coverage	The performance over 5, 10 and 15 years of the median fund of the different unit trust sectors, compared with building society accounts, bank deposit accounts and National Savings. Based on the Association's own survey with a supporting text (50%).

Availability	General
Cost	Free
Comments	These quarterly figures include monthly figures for January, April, July and October.
Address	65 Kingsway, London WC2B 6TD
Telephone	01 831 0898; Fax: 01 831 9975

1011

Originator	UNITED KINGDOM AGRICULTURAL SUPPLY TRADE ASSOCIATION LTD (UKASTA)
Title	FEED FACTS, annual
Coverage	Livestock numbers, output of compounds, compound production on a regional basis, use of raw materials, expansion of UK food production, household consumption, prices etc. Also some EEC data. Based on a combination of official and non-official sources.
Availability	General
Cost	Free
Address	3 Whitehall Court, London SW1A 2EQ
Telephone	01 930 3611; Telex: 917868; Fax: 01 930 3952

1012

Originator	UNITED KINGDOM ASSOCIATION OF PROFESSIONAL ENGINEERS (UKAPE)
Title	UKAPE BENEFITS SURVEY, annual. About 1969–
Coverage	A survey of benefits received and desired based on replies from approximately 800 engineers. Statistics are given in total, by age group and for key sectors and companies, e.g. aerospace, steel, ICI, GEC and consultancies. A small amount of text summarizes the findings (10%).
Availability	General
Cost	Free
Address	Hayes Court, West Common Road, Bromley BR2 7AU
Telephone	01 462 7755; Fax: 01 462 4959

1013

Originator	UNITED KINGDOM ASSOCIATION OF PROFESSIONAL ENGINEERS (UKAPE)
Title	UKAPE SALARY SURVEY, annual. About 1969–
Coverage	Salary levels of UKAPE members and allied colleagues in engineering organizations. Based on a survey of approximately 800 engineers and salaries quoted are medians and quartiles. Aggregate data and data for key sectors and companies, e.g. aerospace, steel, ICI, GEC and consultancies.

Availability	General
Cost	Free
Address	Hayes Court, West Common Road, Bromley BR2 7AU
Telephone	01 462 7755; Fax: 01 462 4959

1014

Originator	UNITED KINGDOM IRON AND STEEL STATISTICS BUREAU
Title	UK IRON AND STEEL INDUSTRY: ANNUAL STATISTICS, annual
Coverage	Figures on production, consumption and trade of iron and steel products. Also details of raw materials consumed, cokemaking, iron foundries and manpower. Historical figures given in most tables. Based almost entirely on the Bureau's own data (95%).
Availability	General
Cost	£40
Comments	Also publishes annual and quarterly statistics on steel in specific countries with 14 countries covered.
Address	Canterbury House, 2 Sydenham Road, Croydon CR9 2LZ
Telephone	01 650 9050; Telex: 932575; Fax: 01 680 8616

1015

Originator	UNIVERSITIES CENTRAL COUNCIL ON ADMISSIONS (UCCA)
Title	ANNUAL REPORT, annual. 1964–
Coverage	Includes statistics on total university applications and acceptances within the UCCA scheme by subject category. Based on data collected by UCCA with supporting text representing 50%.
Availability	General
Cost	£2
Address	Box 28, Cheltenham GL50 1HY
Telephone	0242 222444; Telex: 43662; Fax: 0242 221622

1016

Originator	UNIVERSITIES CENTRAL COUNCIL ON ADMISSIONS (UCCA)
Title	STATISTICAL SUPPLEMENT, annual. 1966–
Coverage	Detailed figures on university applicants by age, subject, sex, type of school, A-levels, parental occupation, region, social class etc. Based on UCCA's survey.
Availability	General

Cost	£3
Address	Box 28, Cheltenham GL50 1HY
Telephone	0242 222444; Telex: 43662; Fax: 0242 221622

1017

Originator	UNIVERSITIES CENTRAL COUNCIL ON ADMISSIONS (UCCA)
Title	UNIVERSITY APPLICATIONS FOR 19- ENTRY, 5 issues per year
Coverage	The numbers of university applications by sex and UK/overseas distribution. Based on figures collected by UCCA. One table with supporting text (80%).
Availability	General
Cost	Free
Comments	Press release.
Address	Box 28, Cheltenham GL50 1HY
Telephone	0242 222444; Telex: 43662; Fax: 0242 221622

1018

Originator	UNIVERSITY COLLEGE OF WALES, DEPARTMENT OF AGRICULTURAL ECONOMICS
Title	FARM MANAGEMENT SURVEY IN WALES: STATISTICAL RESULTS, annual. 1982–
Coverage	Results of a survey of a sample of 500 farms in Wales, classified by farm type and subclassified by farm size (European size units). Based on the University's own survey with some supporting text (10%). Usually published about 6 months after the survey.
Availability	General
Cost	£4
Comments	Also publish 'Welsh Studies in Agricultural Economics' with articles and a summary of the Farm Management Survey.
Address	Penglais, Aberystwyth SY23 3DD
Telephone	0970 623111; Telex: 35181

1019

Originator	UNIVERSITY OF CAMBRIDGE, AGRICULTURAL ECONOMICS UNIT
Title	ECONOMIC RESULTS FROM HORTICULTURE, annual. 1966–

Coverage	Income and cost data for glasshouse, vegetable, dessert apple and miscellaneous fruit farms. Usually published 6 months after the survey has taken place and the results are based on a random sample of farms, excluding the smallest farms. A small amount of Central Government data and text is also included.
Availability	General
Cost	£6
Address	Department of Land Economy, 19 Silver Street, Cambridge CB3 9EP
Telephone	0223 337147; Fax: 0223 334748

1020

Originator	UNIVERSITY OF CAMBRIDGE, AGRICULTURAL ECONOMICS UNIT
Title	PIG MANAGEMENT SCHEME RESULTS, annual. 1936–
Coverage	Statistics on the income, costs and general economic performance of the pig producing sector by degree of end product. Based on a random sample of pig units recorded in the agricultural census. A small amount of text and some Central Government statistics are also included. Usually published within 3 months of the survey.
Availability	General
Cost	£2.75
Address	Department of Land Economy, 19 Silver Street, Cambridge CB3 9EP
Telephone	0223 337147; Fax: 0223 334748

1021

Originator	UNIVERSITY OF CAMBRIDGE, AGRICULTURAL ECONOMICS UNIT
Title	REPORT ON FARMING IN THE EASTERN COUNTIES OF ENGLAND, annual. 1978–
Coverage	Data on agricultural incomes, costs and investment in the eastern counties based on a random sample survey excluding the smallest farms. A general text (50%) supports the statistics and a few statistics from Central Government are also included. Usually published 6 months after the survey has taken place.
Availability	General
Cost	£7
Address	Department of Land Economy, 19 Silver Street, Cambridge CB3 9EP
Telephone	0223 337147; Fax: 0223 334748

1022

Originator   UNIVERSITY OF EXETER, AGRICULTURAL ECONOM-
ICS UNIT

Title   FARM INCOMES IN SOUTH WEST ENGLAND, annual.
1940s-

Coverage   Changes in outputs, inputs and income, net cash flows and changes
in credit use and trends in incomes, capital and borrowing.
Aggregated by type of farm. Based on a sample of over 300 farms
with data collected by the University. Some supporting text (40%).

Availability   General
Cost   £3
Comments   ISSN 0306 8277
Address   Lafrowda House, St German's Road, Exeter EX4 6TL
Telephone   0392 263839; Telex: 42894; Fax: 0392 263108

1023

Originator   UNIVERSITY OF EXETER, AGRICULTURAL ECONOM-
ICS UNIT

Title   FARM MANAGEMENT HANDBOOK, annual. 1976–

Coverage   Farm results, including financial and physical standards by type of
farming group and gross margins covering crop and livestock
enterprises, tenants' capital, assets and liabilities. Covers South
West England and is based largely on the University's survey of
about 300 farms. A small anmount of supporting text (15%).

Availability   General
Cost   £3.50
Address   Lafrowda House, St German's Road, Exeter EX4 6TL
Telephone   0392 263839; Telex: 42894; Fax: 0392 263108

1024

Originator   UNIVERSITY OF EXETER, AGRICULTURAL ECONOM-
ICS UNIT

Title   MILK PRODUCTION IN SOUTH WEST ENGLAND, annual.
1940s-

Coverage   Changes in physical resource use in milk production in aggregate
and by herd size in the South West. Analysis of changes in output,
costs and margins and of family income levels. Based on a sample of
farms with data collected by the University (70%). Some supporting text (45%).

Availability   General
Cost   £2.50
Comments   ISSN 0531 5344

Address	Lafrowda House, St Germans Road, Exeter EX4 6TL
Telephone	0392 263839; Telex: 42894; Fax: 0392 263108

1025

Originator	UNIVERSITY OF EXETER, AGRICULTURAL ECONOM-ICS UNIT
Title	PIG PRODUCTION IN SOUTH WEST ENGLAND, annual. 1940s-
Coverage	Costs of production, herds by size, performance factors, prices and financial data for pig farms in the South West. Based on the University's own survey. Some supporting text (30%).
Availability	General
Cost	£3
Comments	ISSN 0306 8900
Address	Lafrowda House, St German's Road, Exeter EX4 6TL
Telephone	0392 263839; Telex: 42894; Fax: 0392 263108

1026

Originator	UNIVERSITY OF LONDON, WYE COLLEGE
Title	FARM BUSINESS STATISTICS FOR SOUTH-EAST ENG-LAND, annual
Coverage	Financial and physical data on farms divided by size and type into 18 groups. Based on a survey of 200 farms with a small amount of supporting text (10%).
Availability	General
Cost	£3
Address	Agricultural Economics Department, Wye College, Ashford TN25 5AH
Telephone	0233 812401; Telex: 96118

1027

Originator	UNIVERSITY OF LONDON, WYE COLLEGE
Title	FARM MANAGEMENT POCKETBOOK, annual
Coverage	Gross margin data for a range of crops and livestock, labour, machinery and miscellaneous data. The sources for most of the tables are not acknowledged. Text comprises 30%.
Availability	General
Cost	£4.25
Address	Agricultural Economics Department, Wye College, Ashford TN25 5AH
Telephone	0233 812401; Telex: 96118

1028

Originator	UNIVERSITY OF LONDON, WYE COLLEGE
Title	A STATISTICAL HANDBOOK OF UK AGRICULTURE, regular
Coverage	Various statistics on agriculture and farming in the UK with data on livestock, crops, machinery, labour etc.
Availability	General
Cost	£8.50
Comments	The latest issue is the 3rd edition published in 1987.
Address	Agricultural Economics Department, Wye College, Ashford TN25 5AH
Telephone	0233 812401; Telex: 96118

1029

Originator	UNIVERSITY OF LOUGHBOROUGH, LIBRARY AND INFORMATION STATISTICS UNIT
Title	AVERAGE PRICES OF BRITISH ACADEMIC BOOKS, bi-annual. 1984–
Coverage	A survey of approximately 10,000 titles per annum bought by Blackwells of Oxford. Prices analysed by 64 subject categories with half-yearly, calender year and academic year indexing.
Availability	General
Cost	£7.50
Comments	ISSN 0261 0302. The Unit also publishes average prices of USA academic books.
Address	Loughborough University, Loughborough, Leicestershire LE11 3TU
Telephone	0509 223071; Telex: 34319; Fax: 0509 231983

1030

Originator	UNIVERSITY OF LOUGHBOROUGH, LIBRARY AND INFORMATION STATISTICS UNIT
Title	PUBLIC LIBRARY BOOKFUNDS ESTIMATES, annual. 1986–
Coverage	A survey by the Unit at Loughborough giving bookfund original estimates, current provisional actual expenditure for the past year and the current provisional estimate for the coming year for UK public library authorities.
Availability	General
Cost	£12
Comments	ISSN 0951 8991
Address	Loughborough University, Loughborough, Leicestershire LE11 3TU
Telephone	0509 223071; Telex: 34319; Fax: 0509 231983

1031

Originator	UNIVERSITY OF LOUGHBOROUGH, LIBRARY AND INFORMATION STATISTICS UNIT
Title	PUBLIC LIBRARY STATISTICS: A TREND ANALYSIS, annual. 1984–
Coverage	A ten-year trend analysis of CIPFA annual statistics of UK public libraries covering expenditure, stock and staff analysed by country, counties, boroughs and districts. Some text supports the statistics.
Availability	General
Cost	£10
Comments	ISSN 0951 8983
Address	Loughborough University, Loughborough, Leicestershire LE11 3TU
Telephone	0509 223071; Telex: 34319; Fax: 0509 231983

1032

Originator	UNIVERSITY OF MANCHESTER, DEPARTMENT OF AGRICULTURAL ECONOMICS
Title	AN ECONOMIC REVIEW OF FARMING IN THE NORTH WEST, annual
Coverage	A survey of farms in the North West with data for the last 3 years. Covers arable, lowland dairy and upland farms with data on physical characteristics, trading trends, assets and liabilities and gross margin analysis. The data is collected by the University from a sample of approximately 270 farms. A brief commentary supports the statistics.
Availability	General
Cost	£5
Address	Agricultural Economics, Manchester University, Manchester M13 9PL
Telephone	061 275 4794; Fax: 061 273 5187

1033

Originator	UNIVERSITY OF NEWCASTLE-UPON-TYNE, DEPARTMENT OF AGRICULTURAL ECONOMICS AND FOOD MARKETING
Title	FARM INCOMES IN THE NORTH OF ENGLAND, annual
Coverage	Income changes for a sample of farms in the North of England. Physical and financial data relate to farm size, type, output, input and capital structure. Based on a random sample of farms in Durham, Northumberland, Tyne and Wear and Cumbria. A small amount of supporting text (15%).

Availability	General
Cost	£4.50
Address	University of Newcastle-upon-Tyne, Newcastle-upon-Tyne NE1 7RU
Telephone	091 232 8511; Fax: 091 261 1182

1034

Originator	UNIVERSITY OF NOTTINGHAM, DEPARTMENT OF AGRICULTURE AND HORTICULTURE
Title	FARMING IN THE EAST MIDLANDS, annual
Coverage	Statistics on agriculture outputs, inputs and incomes based on the Department's survey of 240 farms in the area classified by type and by size.
Availability	General
Cost	£3
Address	School of Agriculture, Sutton Bonington, Loughborough LR12 5RD
Telephone	0602 506101; Fax: 0602 420816

1035

Originator	UNIVERSITY OF READING, DEPARTMENT OF AGRICULTURAL ECONOMICS AND MANAGEMENT
Title	FARM BUSINESS DATA, annual
Coverage	A report in 3 parts: whole-farm data based on the Farm Business Survey for the area; a summary of recently completed surveys of individual enterprises and research reports; forward planning. The Farm Business Survey is carried out by the University.
Availability	General
Cost	£3
Address	4 Earley Gate, Whiteknights Road, Reading RG6 2AR
Telephone	0734 875123; Telex: 847813

1036

Originator	UNIVERSITY OF READING, DEPARTMENT OF AGRICULTURAL ECONOMICS AND MANAGEMENT
Title	FINANCIAL RESULTS OF HORTICULTURAL HOLDINGS, annual
Coverage	Results given for 3 groups: glasshouse holdings, vegetable and mixed horticultural holdings and fruit holdings. Gives data on the level of total costs, total revenue and total income. Based largely on the University's survey (85%) supplemented by some Central Government data (15%). Some supporting text (30%).

Availability	General
Cost	£2
Comments	Part of the Farm Business Survey mentioned above.
Address	4 Earley Gate, Whiteknights Road, Reading RG6 2AR
Telephone	0734 875123; Telex: 847813

1037

Originator UNIVERSITY OF WARWICK, INSTITUTE FOR EMPLOYMENT RESEARCH

Title REVIEW OF THE ECONOMY AND EMPLOYMENT, every 1-2 years

Coverage Forecasts of employment by industry, occupation and region with a commentary on the structure of employment and a review of recent economic developments and the medium term economic outlook. Based on the Institute's own research (80%) with some Central Government data (20%). A commentary accompanies the data (65%).

Availability	General
Cost	£20
Comments	Also publish various one-off reports.
Address	Gibbett Hill Road, Coventry CV4 7AL
Telephone	0203 523503

1038

Originator VODKA TRADE ASSOCIATION

Title RETURNS FOR THE FOUR HALF YEARS ENDED 31ST DECEMBER, annual

Coverage Gives production of vodka and home trade sales and export trade sales to EEC countries and non-EEC countries for the last 4 six month periods. Based on returns from members. Published in 1 table 2 months after the end of the year.

Availability	General
Cost	Free
Address	37 Waterford House, 110 Kensington Park Road, London W11 2PJ
Telephone	01 229 9222

1039

Originator WALES TOURIST BOARD

Title ANNUAL REPORT, annual

Coverage   Mainly a review of the work of the board and financial accounts but
            includes a statistical appendix with data for a number of years on
            visitors to tourist attractions, tourism revenues, passenger journeys
            etc. Based on the Board's data (50%) and Central Government
            statistics (50%).

Availability General
Cost   On application
Address   Brunel House, 2 Fitzalan Road, Cardiff CF2 1UY
Telephone   0222 499909; Telex: 497269

1040

Originator   WALES TOURIST BOARD

Title   HOTEL OCCUPANCY IN WALES, annual
Coverage   Analysis of trends in hotel demand by county and size of hotel. Data
             for a number of years and based on the Board's own survey.

Availability General
Cost   Free
Address   Brunel House, 2 Fitzalan Road, Cardiff CF2 1UY
Telephone   0222 499909; Telex: 497269

1041

Originator   WALES TOURIST BOARD

Title   VISITORS TO TOURIST ATTRACTIONS, annual
Coverage   Factsheet showing visitors to tourist attractions in Wales over a
             number of years. Based on a survey by the Board.

Availability General
Cost   Free
Address   Brunel House, 2 Fitzalan Road, Cardiff CF2 1UY
Telephone   0222 499909; Telex: 497269

1042

Originator   WALSALL CHAMBER OF COMMERCE AND INDUSTRY

Title   WALSALL CHAMBER ECONOMIC SURVEY, quarterly.
             1978–
Coverage   A survey of 100 local manufacturing companies to determine
             industrial trends, e.g. deliveries, production, stocks, cash-flow,
             labour, investment, confidence etc.

Availability General
Cost   Free
Address   Chamber of Commerce House, Ward Street, Walsall WS1 2AG
Telephone   0922 721777; Telex: 338212; Fax: 0922 647359

1043

Originator	WARWICKSHIRE COUNTY COUNCIL
Title	INDUSTRIAL LAND AVAILABILITY STATISTICS, bi-annual. 1980–
Coverage	Data on the amount of industrial land and planning status by districts and areas within districts. One sheet for each district, prepared by the Planning and Transportation Department.
Availability	General
Cost	£5 per district
Comments	Also publish the 'Structure Plan Information Report' bi-annually with some statistics.
Address	Planning & Transportation, Box 43, Shire Hall, Warwick CV34 4SX
Telephone	0926 410410; Telex: 311419; Fax: 0926 491665

1044

Originator	WARWICKSHIRE COUNTY COUNCIL
Title	RESIDENTIAL LAND AVAILABILITY STATISTICS, bi-annual. 1975–
Coverage	Data on the amount and planning status of residential land by district and areas within each district. Individual sheets are produced for each district by the Planning and Transportation Department.
Availability	General
Cost	£5 per district
Comments	Also publish a 'Structure Plan Information Report' bi-annually with some statistics.
Address	Planning & Transportation, Box 43, Shire Hall, Warwick CV34 4SX
Telephone	0926 410410; Telex: 311419; Fax: 0926 491665

1045

Originator	WATER AUTHORITIES ASSOCIATION
Title	WATER POLLUTION FROM FARM WASTE, annual. 1985–
Coverage	Results of the Association's annual survey into the causes of pollution incidents traced to farm sources. A commentary accompanies the statistics (50%).
Availability	General
Cost	£5
Comments	Graphs available on 35mm slides or overheads for a small charge.
Address	1 Queen Anne's Gate, London SW1H 9BT
Telephone	01 222 8111; Telex: 918518; Fax: 01 222 1811

1046

Originator   WATER AUTHORITIES ASSOCIATION

Title   WATERFACTS, annual. 1984–
Coverage   Statistics on all aspects of the water industry including income,
                 expenditure, charges, demand, supply, sewage, river quality, fish
                 catches and manpower. Largely based on the Association's own
                 survey (80%) supported by data from other sources (20%). A
                 limited amount of supporting text (10%).

Availability General
Cost   £4
Comments   Graphs are available on 35mm slides or overheads for a small
                  charge.
Address   1 Queen Anne's Gate, London SW1H 9BT
Telephone   01 222 8111; Telex: 918518

1047

Originator   WATER COMPANIES ASSOCIATION

Title   WATER COMPANIES: THE FACTS AND FIGURES, every 2
                 or 3 years
Coverage   Mainly information on the organization and structure of the water
                 companies but includes comparative statistics on the 28 companies
                 and their areas covering population, area, connections, water
                 supply, capital expenditure, average bill per household etc. Text
                 covers 75%.

Availability General
Cost   Free
Address   14 Great College Street, London SW1P 3RX
Telephone   01 222 0644; Fax: 01 222 3366

1048

Originator   WELSH DEVELOPMENT AGENCY

Title   WDA ANNUAL REPORT, annual. 1977–
Coverage   General information and financial data on the agency plus statistics
                 on advance factory projects, land reclamation and investments for
                 Wales in total and by county. Also key economic statistics.

Availability General
Cost   Free
Comments   ISSN 0264 9284
Address   Pearl Assurance House, Greyfriars Road, Cardiff CF1 3XX
Telephone   0222 222666; Telex: 497513; Fax: 0222 223243

1049

Originator	WESSEX ELECTRONIC PUBLISHING LTD
Title	WESSEX DATABASE FOR BUILDING, annual. February 1983–
Coverage	Encyclopedia of prices and costs for building materials, plant and labour, including labour and plant time allowances. Also information on estimate pricing, dayworks, fees and technical data. Over 500,000 price elements are included. Largely based on the company's own survey (90%). Published in 2 volumes.
Availability	General
Cost	£45
Comments	ISSN 0269 8935. All the data is available on various Wessex software packages.
Address	Park Place, North Road, Poole BH14 0LE
Telephone	0202 735332; Fax: 0202 742043

1050

Originator	WESSEX ELECTRONIC PUBLISHING LTD
Title	WESSEX DATABASE FOR CIVIL ENGINEERING, annual. November 1985–
Coverage	Civil engineering cost data for material prices, labour, plant, estimate pricing and fees. Based largely on the company's own survey (90%).
Availability	General
Cost	£49
Comments	ISSN 0268 7690. All the data is available in various Wessex software packages.
Address	Park Place, North Road, Poole BH14 0LE
Telephone	0202 735332; Fax: 0202 742043

1051

Originator	WEST MIDLANDS ENTERPRISE BOARD
Title	ECONOMIC BRIEFING, monthly
Coverage	Text and statistics on unemployment and vacancies in the West Midlands and the effects of Central Government policies. Based largely on Central Government data.
Availability	General
Cost	Free
Address	Wellington House, 31/34 Waterloo Street, Birmingham B2 5TJ
Telephone	021 236 2706; Fax: 021 233 3942

1052

Originator	WEST MIDLANDS ENTERPRISE BOARD
Title	SECTOR REVIEWS, annual
Coverage	Individual reviews with statistics on the sectors important to the West Midlands. Includes mechanical and electrical engineering, machine tools, CADCAM, consumer goods, rubber and plastics, motor vehicles and components and productive services. Includes data on national markets as well as local trends. Based on various sources.
Availability	General
Cost	On application
Address	Wellington House, 31/34 Waterloo Street, Birmingham B2 5TJ
Telephone	021 236 2706; Fax: 021 233 3942

1053

Originator	WEST MIDLANDS REGIONAL FORUM
Title	INDUSTRIAL LAND AVAILABILITY IN THE WEST MID-LANDS REGION, annual
Coverage	Data for a number of years on industrial land stocks, land ownership, land availability and planning permissions. Based on local authority data. A supporting text covers 50%.
Availability	General
Cost	£2
Address	1 Duchess Place, Hagley Road, Birmingham B16 8ND
Telephone	021 235 4198; Fax: 021 236 4767

1054

Originator	WEST MIDLANDS REGIONAL FORUM
Title	RESIDENTIAL LAND AVAILABILTY IN THE WEST MID-LANDS REGION, annual
Coverage	Data for a number of years on stocks of land, housing completions and progress towards structure plan targets by county. Based on local authority data. A supporting text covers 50%.
Availability	General
Cost	£2
Address	1 Duchess Place, Hagley Road, Birmingham B16 8ND
Telephone	021 2354198; Fax: 021 2364767

1055

Originator	WEST SUSSEX COUNTY COUNCIL
Title	COMMERCIAL AND INDUSTRIAL DEVELOPMENT SURVEY, annual. 1975–
Coverage	A survey of land and floorspace available for industry, offices, shops and storage with an examination of changes to commitment. Based on a Council survey with a small amount of supporting text (10%).
Availability	General
Cost	£12
Address	Planning Department, County Hall, Chichester PO19 1RL
Telephone	0243 777100; Telex: 86279; Fax: 0243 777952

1056

Originator	WEST SUSSEX COUNTY COUNCIL
Title	HOUSING LAND SUPPLY IN WEST SUSSEX, annual. 1980–
Coverage	Results of a regular Council survey of housing land in the county with a comparison with the Structure Plan housing provision. A small amount of supporting text (10%).
Availability	General
Cost	£10
Address	Planning Department, County Hall, Chichester PO19 1RL
Telephone	0243 777100; Telex: 86279; Fax: 0243 777952

1057

Originator	WEST SUSSEX COUNTY COUNCIL
Title	POPULATION TRENDS AND FORECASTS, annual. August 1987–
Coverage	Reviews recent demographic trends in the county and presents revised population forecasts. Based on Central Government data (70%) and County Council surveys (30%). Some supporting text (35%).
Availability	General
Cost	£3
Comments	The second in a proposed series of reports on relevant topics.
Address	Planning Department, County Hall, Chichester PO19 1RL
Telephone	0243 777100; Telex: 86279; Fax: 0243 777952

1058

Originator	WHARTON INFORMATION SYSTEMS
Title	BOSS – BRITISH OFFICE SYSTEMS SURVEY, annual

Coverage A review of the automated office equipment market with data on sales and use by type of equipment. Data for the last 5 years and forecasts 5 years ahead. Based on Wharton's survey of sales.

Availability General
Cost £500
Comments Dealer surveys and specialist analysis also available. Data available on disc.
Address Regal House, London Road, Twickenham TW1 3QS
Telephone 01 891 6197

1059

Originator WHARTON INFORMATION SYSTEMS

Title UK PERSONAL COMPUTER MARKET, annual
Coverage Market data on personal computers with figures for a number of earlier years and forecasts up to 5 years ahead. Includes data on the performance of vendors and the aspirations of users. Largely based on the company's own research.

Availability General
Cost £650
Comments Dealer surveys and specialist analysis also available. Data available on disc.
Address Regal House, London Road, Twickenham TW1 3QS
Telephone 01 891 6197

1060

Originator WHARTON INFORMATION SYSTEMS

Title USER OMNIBUS, quarterly
Coverage An omnibus survey covering the purchases, anticipated purchases and forward plans of users of personal computers. Participants are able to add their own questions to the survey.

Availability Participants
Cost On application
Comments Dealer surveys and specialist analysis also available. Data available on disc.
Address Regal House, London Road, Twickenham TW1 3QS
Telephone 01 891 6197

1061

Originator WHITE OILS ASSOCIATION

Title QUANTITY RETURNS, monthly
Coverage Sales of white oils, petroleum jellies and transformer oils in the domestic market and abroad. Based on members' returns.

Availability	Members
Address	1 Puddle Dock Road, Blackfriars, London EC4V 3PD
Telephone	01 236 8000; Fax: 01 583 1938

1062

Originator	WIGAN RICHARDSON INTERNATIONAL

Title	HOP REPORT, annual. 1952–
Coverage	Feature articles and statistics on the production, growing areas, prices, market demand and trade for hops and hop products. Based on Central Government data (70%) and the company's own surveys (30%). Text accounts for 50% of the report.

Availability	Trade and other selected organizations
Cost	Free
Address	3 Church Road, Paddock Wood, Tonbridge TN12 6ES
Telephone	089 2832235; Telex: 957022; Fax: 089 2836008

1063

Originator	WINE AND SPIRIT ASSOCIATION OF GREAT BRITAIN AND NORTHERN IRELAND

Title	SURVEY OF COUNTRIES OF ORIGIN OF WINES CLEARED TO HOME USE, monthly
Coverage	A survey of the countries of origin of wines imported for home use based entirely on trade statistics produced by Central Government.

Availability	General
Cost	£120, minimum 2-year subscription
Address	Five Kings House, Kennet Wharf Lane, London EC4V 3BH
Telephone	01 248 5377

1064

Originator	WIRRAL METROPOLITAN DISTRICT COUNCIL

Title	QUARTERLY ECONOMIC REPORT, quarterly. 1986–
Coverage	A review of national and local economic trends based on Central Government (25%) and other sources (75%). A large amount of commentary is included in the report (80%).

Availability	General
Cost	Free
Address	Wirral Business Centre, Dock Road, Birkenhead
Telephone	051 630 6060

1065

Originator   WIRRAL METROPOLITAN DISTRICT COUNCIL

Title   REVIEW OF DEMAND/SUPPLY OF INDUSTRIAL PREM-
                 ISES, regular. 1987–
Coverage   Commentary and statistics on industrial premises in the Wirral
                 area. Based on the Council's own survey. Text covers 85%.

Availability General
Cost   Free
Address   Wirral Business Centre, Dock Road, Birkenhead
Telephone   051 630 6060

1066

Originator   WOLVERHAMPTON BUSINESS SCHOOL, MARKETING
                 RESEARCH CENTRE

Title   WEST MIDLANDS BUSINESS SURVEY, regular
Coverage   The results of a survey of about 1,300 companies in the West
                 Midlands looking at business conditions and business confidence.

Availability General
Cost   £25
Address   Compton Road West, Wolverhampton WV3 9DX
Telephone   0902 24286

1067

Originator   WOLVERHAMPTON   METROPOLITAN   BOROUGH
                 COUNCIL

Title   HOUSING LAND AVAILABILITY SCHEDULE, bi-annual
Coverage   Summary statistics on the land available for housing in the district
                 with details of individual sites. Based on the Council's own records.

Availability General
Cost   £5 per issue
Address   OCEPC, Civic Centre, St Peter's Square, Wolverhampton WV1
                 1SH
Telephone   0902 27811; Telex: 335060; Fax: 0902 26644

1068

Originator   WOLVERHAMPTON   METROPOLITAN   BOROUGH
                 COUNCIL

Title   INDUSTRIAL LAND AVAILABILITY SCHEDULE, annual.
                 1987–

Coverage	Summary statistics on the availability of industrial land in the district with details on the specific sites. Based on the Council's records.
Availability	General
Cost	£5
Address	OCEPC, Civic Centre, St Peter's Square, Wolverhampton WV1 1SH
Telephone	0902 27811; Telex: 335060; Fax: 0902 26644

1069

Originator	WOOL INDUSTRY BUREAU OF STATISTICS
Title	MONTHLY BULLETIN OF STATISTICS, monthly
Coverage	UK wool textile production, deliveries, consumption and stocks. Additional data on machinery and personnel. Based on various sources and the data in most tables refers to the previous month.
Availability	General
Cost	£36, free to members
Address	60 Toller Lane, Bradford BD8 9BZ
Telephone	0274 491241

1070

Originator	WOOL INDUSTRY BUREAU OF STATISTICS
Title	QUARTERLY REVIEW OF UK TRADE STATISTICS, quarterly
Coverage	UK wool textile imports and exports by country and by region. Figures for the latest quarter and year to date figures. Based on HM Customs and Excise statistics.
Availability	General
Cost	£22, free to members
Address	60 Toller Lane, Bradford BD8 9BZ
Telephone	0274 491241

1071

Originator	WOOLWICH BUILDING SOCIETY
Title	WOOLWICH COST OF MOVING SURVEY, annual. 1983–
Coverage	The costs of buying and selling property of different values including specific data on solicitors, estate agents, surveyors and removal fees.
Availability	General
Cost	Free
Address	Equitable House, Woolwich, London SE18 6AB
Telephone	01 854 2400; Fax: 01 855 5892

1072

Originator   WOOLWICH BUILDING SOCIETY

Title   WOOLWICH IN FOCUS, 6 issues per year. December 1986–
Coverage   General data on the housing market including prices, financial
trends etc.

Availability   General
Cost   Free
Address   Equitable House, Woolwich, London SE18 6AB
Telephone   01 854 2400; Fax: 01 855 5892

1073

Originator   WOOLWICH BUILDING SOCIETY

Title   WOOLWICH SURVEY, quarterly. 1987–
Coverage   Statistics on the costs of buying and selling property of different
values plus data on house prices, home improvements and delays in
local authority searches. Based largely on the Society's own data.

Availability   General
Cost   Free
Address   Equitable House, Woolwich, London SE18 6AB
Telephone   01 854 2400; Fax: 01 855 5892

1074

Originator   WREN, JONATHAN AND CO. LTD

Title   GUIDE TO CURRENT SALARIES IN BANKING, bi-annual.
1978–
Coverage   Average figures, based on London salaries, for about 140 job titles
in banking at all levels. For each job title, 3 types of information are
given: applicants' salaries, vacancy salaries registered by companies
and salaries on appointment. Over a 140 tables based on a questionnaire sent to all the banks and published about 6 months after
the survey.

Availability   Financial Institutions
Cost   £120
Comments   Also publishes an annual Guide to Fringe Benefits in Banking.
Address   1 New Street, London EC2M 4PT
Telephone   01 623 1266; Telex: 8954673; Fax: 01 626 5258

1075

Originator   YORKSHIRE TELEVISION

Title   MARKETING HANDBOOK, regular

Coverage	General statistics on the Yorkshire TV area including sections on economic activity, retailing, finance, consumer spending, leisure, the media, advertising and television viewing. Based on various sources.
Availability	General
Comments	Latest edition at the time of writing 1987.
Address	Television House, 32 Bedford Row, London WC1R 4HE
Telephone	01 242 1666; Telex: 295386

1076

Originator	ZINC DEVELOPMENT ASSOCIATION
Title	MARKETS FOR ZINC DIE CASTINGS IN THE UNITED KINGDOM IN 19––, annual. 1973–
Coverage	Data on the end-uses of die castings and prices plus a commentary on the industry structure and the general consumption of die castings. Historical figures are given for a number of years. Based on the Association's survey which they estimate covers 90% of all consumption of die castings.
Availability	Primarily members but older reports generally available
Cost	Free
Address	34 Berkeley Square, London W1X 6AJ
Telephone	01 499 6636; Telex: 261286; Fax: 01 493 1555

1077

Originator	ZINC DEVELOPMENT ASSOCIATION
Title	TRENDS IN GENERAL GALVANISED PRODUCTS IN THE UNITED KINGDOM 19–– TO 19––, annual. 1974–
Coverage	Figures on the production of galvanized steel and end-use markets for galvanized steel products. Data for the last few years given in most tables. Based on the Association's own survey with some supporting text.
Availability	Primarily members but older reports generally available
Cost	Free
Address	34 Berkeley Square, London W1X 6AJ
Telephone	01 499 6636; Telex: 261286; Fax: 01 493 1555

Part II
Title index

Coverage	Production, consumption, imports, exports and stocks of various types of timber and wood products. Most tables give figures for the latest 2 years available, i.e. year of publication is usually 2 years after the years covered. Based on Central Government data (100%).
Availability	General
Cost	On application
Comments	Although titled 'Yearbook' it has not been published on a yearly basis. Latest issue published 1987 with data for 1985/1984.
Address	26/27 Oxendon Street, London SW1Y 4EL
Telephone	01 839 1891; Fax: 01 930 0094

983

Originator	TIMBER TRADES JOURNAL AND WOOD PROCESSING
Title	MARKET STATISTICS, weekly in a weekly journal
Coverage	Various statistics on timber and wood consumption, trade, prices etc. Different statistics appear each week.
Availability	General
Address	Benn Publications, Sovereign Way, Tonbridge TN9 1RW
Telephone	0732 364422; Telex: 95162; Fax: 0732 361534

984

Originator	TIN INTERNATIONAL
Title	LME PRICES/STOCKS/TURNOVER, monthly in a monthly journal. 1928–
Coverage	Prices, stocks and turnover of tin on the London Metal Exchange plus a general market report.
Availability	General
Cost	£66 or £6 for a single issue
Comments	Various other statistics produced including trends in international markets, futures and prices of metals.
Address	60 Worship Street, London EC2A 2DJ
Telephone	01 377 9134; Telex: 25254; Fax: 01 377 2654

985

Originator	TOWN AND COUNTRY PLANNING
Title	STATISTICAL REVIEW OF BRITAIN'S NEW TOWNS, biennial in a monthly journal. 1955–
Coverage	Data on the population, employment, housing stock, economy and general development of each new town. Based on a survey of all new towns with a usual response rate of 100%.

ANNUAL REPORT
UNIVERSITIES CENTRAL
COUNCIL ON ADMISSIONS
(UCCA)

ANNUAL REPORT
WALES TOURIST BOARD

ANNUAL REPORT AND
ACCOUNTS
BRITISH RAILWAYS BOARD

ANNUAL REPORT AND
ACCOUNTS
BRITISH WATERWAYS
BOARD

ANNUAL REPORT AND
ACCOUNTS
BRITISH WOOL MARKETING
BOARD

ANNUAL REPORT AND
ACCOUNTS
LONDON REGIONAL
TRANSPORT

ANNUAL REPORT AND
ACCOUNTS
MANMADE FIBRES
INDUSTRY TRAINING
ADVISORY BOARD

ANNUAL REPORT AND
ACCOUNTS
NATIONAL DOCK LABOUR
BOARD

ANNUAL REPORT AND
ACCOUNTS
PIGS MARKETING BOARD
(NORTHERN IRELAND)

ANNUAL REPORT AND
ACCOUNTS
SCOTTISH MILK
MARKETING BOARD

ANNUAL REPORT AND
ACCOUNTS
STRATHCLYDE PASSENGER
TRANSPORT EXECUTIVE

ANNUAL REPORT AND
ACCOUNTS
THAMES WATER
AUTHORITY

ANNUAL REPORT AND
FINANCIAL STATEMENTS
NATIONAL SULPHURIC
ACID ASSOCIATION LTD

ANNUAL REPORT AND
REVIEW
BRITISH TEXTILE
CONFEDERATION

ANNUAL REPORT ON
EMPLOYMENT AND
UNEMPLOYMENT
GRAMPIAN REGIONAL
COUNCIL

ANNUAL REVIEW
BUSINESS EQUIPMENT AND
INFORMATION
TECHNOLOGY
ASSOCIATION

ANNUAL REVIEW OF THE
RETAIL MARKET
CIL SYSTEMS LTD

ANNUAL STATISTICAL
REVIEW
PAINTMAKERS
ASSOCIATION OF GREAT
BRITAIN

ANNUAL STATISTICAL
REVIEW SUMMARY
PAINTMAKERS
ASSOCIATION OF GREAT
BRITAIN LTD

ANNUAL STATISTICAL
SUMMARY
INVESTORS CHRONICLE

ANNUAL STATISTICS
BRITISH WOOL MARKETING
BOARD

ANNUAL STATISTICS
NATIONAL CAVITY
INSULATION ASSOCIATION

ANNUAL STUDY OF
EMPLOYEE RELOCATION
POLICIES AMONG MAJOR
UK COMPANIES
MERRILL LYNCH

ANNUAL SUMMARY OF
CLEARING STATISTICS
ASSOCIATION FOR
PAYMENT CLEARING
SERVICES (APACS)

ANNUAL SUMMARY OF
MONTHLY RETURNS
NATIONAL SULPHURIC
ACID ASSOCIATION LTD

ANNUAL SURVEY OF DATA
PROCESSING USERS
COMPUTER WEEKLY

ANNUAL SURVEY OF
OCCUPATIONAL PENSION
SCHEMES
NATIONAL ASSOCIATION
OF PENSION FUNDS LTD

APPLICATION USAGE BY
INDUSTRY SECTOR
MARKET SECTOR REPORT
PEDDER ASSOCIATES

ARCHITECTS EMPLOYMENT
AND EARNINGS SURVEY
ROYAL INSTITUTE OF
BRITISH ARCHITECTS

ARCHIVES ESTIMATES
CHARTERED INSTITUTE OF
PUBLIC FINANCE AND
ACCOUNTANCY (CIPFA)

ASA ANNUAL REPORT
ADVERTISING STANDARDS
AUTHORITY

AUDIENCE PROFILE REPORTS
EXHIBITION SURVEYS LTD

AVERAGE BOOK PRICES
BOOKSELLER

AVERAGE PRICES OF BRITISH
ACADEMIC BOOKS
UNIVERSITY OF
LOUGHBOROUGH

A-Z OF UK MARKETING DATA
EUROMONITOR
PUBLICATIONS LTD

BAA ANNUAL REPORT
BRITISH AGROCHEMICALS
ASSOCIATION

BABY OMNIBUS
RESEARCH SURVEYS OF
GREAT BRITAIN (RSGB)

BACMI STATISTICAL
YEARBOOK
BRITISH AGGREGATE
CONSTRUCTION
MATERIALS INDUSTRIES
(BACMI)

BALANCES OF THE CLSB
GROUPS
COMMITTEE OF LONDON
AND SCOTTISH BANKERS
(CLSB)

BAMA ANNUAL REPORT
BRITISH AEROSOL
MANUFACTURERS
ASSOCIATION

BANK OF ENGLAND
QUARTERLY BULLETIN
BANK OF ENGLAND

BARCLAYS REVIEW
BARCLAYS BANK

BARGAINING REPORT
SPECIAL ISSUE
LABOUR RESEARCH

BARNSLEY ECONOMIC
REVIEW
BARNSLEY METROPOLITAN
BOROUGH COUNCIL

BASIC DATA
BRITISH WOOL MARKETING
BOARD

BASIC FACTS
MACHINE TOOL TRADES
ASSOCIATION

BASIC PLANNING STATISTICS
CORNWALL COUNTY
COUNCIL

BASIC ROAD STATISTICS
BRITISH ROAD
FEDERATION

MARKETPLACE BULLETIN
  HEATING AND
  VENTILATING
  CONTRACTORS
  ASSOCIATION

MARKETS FOR ZINC DIE
  CASTINGS IN THE UNITED
  KINGDOM IN 19--
  ZINC DEVELOPMENT
  ASSOCIATION

MARKETS INFORMATION
  MEAT TRADES JOURNAL

MASTER LIST OF CINEMAS
  CINEMA ADVERTISING
  ASSOCIATION LTD

MCA ANNUAL REPORT AND
  CHAIRMAN'S STATEMENT
  MANAGEMENT
  CONSULTANCIES
  ASSOCIATION

MEASURED RATES SUPPLIES
  BUILDING

MEASURES OF HEALTH
  HENLEY CENTRE

MEAT RETAILER
  LIVESTOCK MARKETING
  COMMISSION FOR
  NORTHERN IRELAND

MEMBERS' SALES OF
  CERAMIC TILES
  GLAZED AND FLOOR TILE
  HOME TRADE
  ASSOCIATION

MERCHANDISING AND
  PROMOTIONAL
  INTELLIGENCE
  MS SURVEYS AND
  PROMOTIONAL SERVICES
  LTD

MERSEYSIDE ECONOMIC
  PROSPECT
  LIVERPOOL
  MACROECONOMIC
  RESEARCH LTD

METAL ORE MARKETS
  MINING JOURNAL

MGN MARKETING MANUAL
  OF THE UK
  MIRROR GROUP
  NEWSPAPERS 86 LTD

MID-GLAMORGAN IN
  FIGURES
  MID-GLAMORGAN COUNTY
  COUNCIL

MID-YEAR POPULATION
  ESTIMATES
  ESSEX COUNTY COUNCIL

MILK BULLETIN
  SCOTTISH MILK
  MARKETING BOARD

MILK PRODUCER
  MILK MARKETING BOARD

MILK PRODUCTION IN SOUTH
  WEST ENGLAND
  UNIVERSITY OF EXETER

MILK TOPICS
  NORTH OF SCOTLAND MILK
  MARKETING BOARD

MINTEL MONTHLY DIGESTS
  MINTEL

MOBILE RIG FLEET DRILLING
  ABERDEEN PETROLEUM
  REPORT

MONETARY BULLETIN
  GREENWELL, MONTAGU &
  CO.

MONEY INTO PROPERTY
  DEBENHAM, TEWSON AND
  CHINNOCKS

MONITOR SOCIAL CHANGE
  RESEARCH PROGRAMME
  TAYLOR NELSON AND
  ASSOCIATES

MONITORING THE LOCAL
  ECONOMY
  HULL CITY COUNCIL

MONTHLY BULLETIN OF
  STATISTICS
  WOOL INDUSTRY BUREAU
  OF STATISTICS

Part III

Subject index

Note

Indexing terms such as 'Agriculture – Specific crops', 'Wages and Salaries – Specific sectors', 'Motor Vehicles – Specific types', 'Marketing – Local areas', etc, bring together all the sources that relate to specific products, sectors, areas, etc. To trace sources on a particular product, sector or local area, however, please look for that product, sector or local area by name in the index.